Jane Austen's Men

I0593122

Jane Austen rewrites masculinity through the courtship romance genre in the socially, politically and culturally turbulent Romantic era. Austen pioneers and celebrates a new vision of masculinity that could complement the Romantic desire for agency, individualism and selfhood embodied in her heroines. Rewriting masculinity as an internalised, psychologically complex and authentic gender identity — a model of manhood that drives the ongoing appeal and cultural power of her men in the twenty-first century — Austen explores both challenges and opportunities for male selfhood, romantic love and feminine agency.

Jane Austen's Men is among the first full-length works to explore Jane Austen's male protagonists as textual constructions of masculinity. Sarah Ailwood reveals the depth of Austen's engagement with her predecessors and contemporaries, including Mary Wollstonecraft, Jane West, Maria Edgeworth and Jane Porter, on critical questions of masculinity and its relationship to femininity and narrative form. This book illuminates in new ways Jane Austen's ambitions for the novel and the political power of the courtship romance genre in the Romantic era, and beyond.

Sarah Ailwood is an assistant professor at the University of Canberra. She completed her PhD on Jane Austen and masculinity at the University of Wollongong, and has published essays and articles on Austen's men. She co-edited *Katherine Mansfield and Literary Influence* (EUP, 2015) and has wide research interests in women's writing, life narrative and legal experience.

Routledge Studies in Romanticism

For more information about this series, please visit: https://www.routledge.com

Jane Austen's Men

Rewriting Masculinity in
the Romantic Era

Sarah Ailwood

Routledge
Taylor & Francis Group

NEW YORK AND LONDON

First published 2020
by Routledge
605 Third Avenue, New York, NY 10017

and by Routledge
2 Park Square, Milton Park, Abingdon, Oxon, OX14 4RN

First issued in paperback 2021

Routledge is an imprint of the Taylor & Francis Group, an informa business

Library of Congress Cataloging-in-Publication Data
A catalog record for this title has been requested

ISBN 13: 978-1-03-224058-9 (pbk)
ISBN 13: 978-0-367-32134-5 (hbk)

Typeset in Sabon
by codeMantra

To Tim, Peter, Max and James

Contents

Acknowledgments

I owe debts of gratitude to the many people who have contributed in different ways to the completion of this book, over so many years.

First, I would like to acknowledge the love and support of my husband, Tim Lear, who has lived with my obsession with Jane Austen since our first date in 1998. Tim supported me in leaving my job as a budding commercial lawyer to pursue a PhD on Jane Austen's men instead. He has ceaselessly encouraged me in pursuing an academic career, and especially in the researching and writing of this book. His support has become even stronger with the birth of our sons Peter, Max and James. This book is dedicated to all my gorgeous boys.

This book began as my PhD thesis, which I completed at the University of Wollongong in 2008 under the supervision of Associate Professor Anne Collett. Since I met Anne in my first year as an undergraduate English student, she has been a teacher, supervisor, mentor, colleague and friend. In supervising my PhD, Anne was both caring and determined to push me to produce the best work and the best writing that I could. Her confidence in me was instrumental throughout the PhD process, and to my decision to pursue an academic career. I would also like to acknowledge the support of past and present academics in Literary Studies at the University of Wollongong. Professor Louise D'Arcens (now at Macquarie University) was a terrific co-supervisor of my PhD. Dr Anne Lear opened my eyes to eighteenth-century literature and culture, and first suggested to me the idea of undertaking a PhD and pursuing an academic career. I will always remember Carmel Pass whispering, 'You could always do your PhD on Jane Austen'. I thank Anne and Carmel for their ongoing support, their humour, and their feedback on the draft chapters of this book.

In 2006, I was awarded a Menzies Australia Institute Bicentennial Scholarship, which enabled me to travel to Cardiff University, where I worked with Dr Anthony Mandal and accessed the Corvey Collection of early nineteenth-century novels. This experience illuminated Austen's many dialogues with her contemporaries and changed the direction of my research into Austen and masculinity.

My PhD was examined by Professor Devoney Looser and Professor Emerita Jocelyn Harris, who have since given me advice, mentoring, practical assistance and moral support in publishing this book.

Devoney's advice on my proposals and drafts, and her intellectual engagement with my work, has been invaluable in making this book possible. Jocelyn has supported me since we first met at a Jane Austen Society of Australia conference in the first year of my PhD, and her advice on my writing has been particularly priceless.

After completing my PhD, I joined the Canberra Law School in the Faculty of Business, Government & Law at the University of Canberra in 2009. I acknowledge the support of colleagues past and present for me to continue my literary studies research, particularly Lawrence Pratchett, Maree Sainsbury, Susan Priest, Murray Raff, Don Fleming, Wendy Bonython and Bruce Arnold. I also acknowledge the moral support and advice I have received on various parts of the book from academic friends and colleagues, including Megan Brown, Melinda Harvey, Julieanne Lamond, Will Christie, and the Romantic Studies Association of Australasia colleagues I met at the Immortal Austen Conference in Adelaide in 2017. It has also been a pleasure to be part of the lively conversation and rigorous debate of the Canberra chapter of the Jane Austen Society of Australia over the years, particularly when completing my PhD.

In 2014, I moved to Hong Kong with a toddler, a newborn and a determination to publish my PhD. I began the process of rewriting this book during my three-year residence there, and I particularly acknowledge the care and dedication of Emely Lazarte for me and my family, which made it possible for me to continue my work. I also thank Tanya Berry for her friendship and support during this time, and beyond.

Tim and I are blessed with loving and generous families who have supported us in our education, in our professional lives and as parents. I thank my parents David and Louise Ailwood, my brother and sister-in-law Joshua and Alison Ailwood, Grandma and Pa, Grannie and Pebs, and my aunts and uncles as well as Tim's parents David and Lynne Lear and the extended Lear family for sustaining me in so many ways. My thanks will never be enough.

Texts and Sources

References to Jane Austen's works are to the following editions

Emma, ed. Fiona Stafford (London: Penguin, 2015).

Jane Austen's Letters, ed. Deirdre Le Faye (Oxford: Oxford University Press, 1995) (abbreviated in the text as *Letters*).

Lady Susan, The Watsons, Sanditon, ed. Margaret Drabble (London: Penguin, 2015).

Mansfield Park, ed. Kathryn Sutherland (London: Penguin, 2014).

Northanger Abbey, ed. Marilyn Butler (London: Penguin, 2003).

Persuasion, ed. Gillian Beer (London: Penguin, 2015).

Pride and Prejudice, ed. Vivien Jones (London: Penguin, 2014).

Sense and Sensibility, ed. Ros Ballaster (London: Penguin, 2014).

Introduction

Rewriting Masculinity in the Romantic Era

In August 2014, a three-metre tall fibreglass statue of Fitzwilliam Darcy, as played by Colin Firth in the 1995 television adaptation of *Pride and Prejudice*, was installed in an ornamental lake at Ripponlea Estate in suburban Melbourne. Making his Australian appearance more than two hundred years after the novel was published — and 173 years since its pages were first opened in 1841 by the eager patrons of a circulating library in the newly-founded colony of Port Phillip[1] — the Darcy sculpture symbolises the iconic cultural status of Jane Austen's men. Jane Austen's male protagonists uniquely resonate across time, place, form and genre. Their influence on literary masculinity and the form of the novel throughout the Victorian era may be traced in Charlotte Brontë's Rochester, Emily Brontë's Heathcliff, George Eliot's Lydgate and Elizabeth Gaskell's Thornton. Dramatisations of Austen's men in theatre and screen adaptations drove her popularity throughout the twentieth century.[2] Their star has risen still further since the mid-1990s through screen adaptations that explore their depth and complexity in scenes that extend beyond the narrative scope of Austen's novels.[3] Indeed, the Darcy sculpture, who made his debut in London in 2013, was commissioned not to celebrate the bicentenary of the publication of *Pride and Prejudice*, but instead to launch a new 'Drama' channel on British television. Such visualisations of Austen's men now form a discreet genre of their own, which is referenced in literary and fan fiction and videos, biopics, cross-cultural reimaginings, mash-ups with genre fiction, and in the online role-playing game *Ever Jane* — over and above their textual origins in Austen's Romantic-era novels.[4] In the twenty-first century, Jane Austen's men have a cultural valence of their own.

The spectacular cultural power not only of Mr Darcy, but also of Mr Knightley and Captain Wentworth, and in different though no less significant ways of Edward Ferrars, Henry Tilney and Edmund Bertram, is the modern legacy of Jane Austen's creation of a new vision of literary masculinity in the Romantic era. Through the courtship romance genre, Austen celebrates an emerging feminine agency and subjectivity in her heroines: young women whose sense of self is rational and autonomous yet intimately relational, embedded within strong familial, social and communal bonds.[5] Austen also creates a pioneering vision of masculinity to complement her heroines' modern feminine selfhood. Austen places a dialogue between masculine gender identities and evolving forms of Romantic feminine individualism and agency as the central drama of her courtship romance novels, rewriting and redefining masculinity itself.

Through her male protagonists, Austen celebrates a masculine ideal that is introspective, authentic and defined by a strong sense of individual selfhood. She distinguishes her male protagonists from culturally-dominant models of masculinity defined by a social performance of masculine status and reputation among male peers and the subordination of women within a sexual hierarchy. In her courtship romance plots, Austen reveals the reliance of performative masculinities on ideologies of sexual difference, precluding such men from forming romantic relationships with her heroines. Austen's male protagonists, by contrast, seek and achieve liberation from the demands of social display and its emphasis on prescriptive gender roles. Defined instead by an internalised, authentic subjectivity, they are empowered to forge relationships with her heroines that offer space for the realisation and expression of feminine individualism and agency. Austen's rewriting of masculinity celebrates the transformative effects of romantic love on male selfhood and the possibilities it offers men and women. Austen also charts the social and economic barriers men face in developing and expressing such a masculine identity, and explores the complexity and conflict in dialogic relationships between masculine authenticity and feminine agency.

Austen interrogates masculine gender identities through the lens of men's relationships with women dramatised by the courtship romance genre. Indeed, her male protagonists are central not only to the courtship plot that forms the crux of each of her novels, but also to her vision of romantic love itself. Recreating masculinity as an authentic, internalised mode of male selfhood, Austen's 'romance-centred happy endings'[6] signify more than the heroine's narrative resolution through marriage. If, as Ashley Tauchert argues, Austen 'narrates the daydream of the heroine's persistent desire to be *somehow* saved by an ideal gentleman: a common desire to be rescued from "all this", and to live "happily ever after"',[7] how that 'ideal gentleman' understands himself and the relationship he shares with the heroine are central to Austen's conception of romance. Mary Poovey argues that 'if a woman could legitimately express herself *only* by choosing to marry and then sustaining her marriage, Austen suggests, she *could*, through her marriage, not only satisfy her own needs but also influence society'[8]; such fulfilment and influence would depend, however, on how a male partner understood not only her identity, but his own in relation to her. To Austen, not only marriage but romance itself requires a man who can offer her heroines scope for individual self-fulfilment and agency. The marriages that conclude her novels defy an equation in which matrimony signifies an endorsement of established patriarchal structures or the curtailing of feminine selfhood as the heroine assumes the role of 'wife'. Austen offers an alternative vision of masculinity within romantic love, courtship and marriage, dramatising both its challenges and its liberating possibilities for women and for men.

*****

Two decades ago, Devoney Looser asked 'isn't it possible that Austen, who has been so influential in our histories of women, is also an important voice in histories of men, masculinities and the novel?' While Looser did 'not have an authoritative answer to this question', she suggested: '"All signs point to yes"'.[9] It is now clear that Jane Austen is, indeed, a critical voice in the history of masculinities and their textual representation. Although early scholarly investigations explored links between her male relatives, neighbours and friends and the men of her novels,[10] this research did not treat masculine gender as a category of inquiry in its own right. Scholarship by Looser, Joseph Kestner, Claudia L. Johnson and E. J. Clery pioneered the investigation of Austen's men as textual constructions of masculinity.[11] Austen's men have since been historicised in relation to the several varied and often conflicting masculine ideals that circulated in print culture of the late eighteenth century and Romantic period. By the time Austen was writing her juvenilia in the 1780s, masculinity was already a matter of fervent public debate; it would be even further politicised throughout her writing career, as socially-approved models of the desirable man were projected into narratives of civilisation, social upheaval and national survival in response to the French Revolution, the Napoleonic Wars and the Regency.[12]

The depth of Austen's engagement with masculine ideals associated with politeness and refinement, professionalism, domesticity, chivalry and nationalism is now beyond dispute.[13] In *Disciplining Love: Austen and the Modern Man*, Michael Kramp explores Austen's negotiation of diverse models of 'proper' masculinity in post-Revolutionary English society and argues that in the face of conflict and uncertainty, her men relinquish the pursuit of individual sexual desires to fulfil the greater demands that the modernising nation places upon them.[14] Kramp's edited collection *Jane Austen and Masculinity* similarly emphasises the 'diversity of men who engage with complicated historical events such as the political debates of the 1790s, the Regency crisis, and the post-Revolutionary Wars'.[15] Megan A. Woodworth and Jason D. Solinger further argue that Austen, among other writers, reinvents gentlemanly masculinity from its association with birth and inheritance to a new definition grounded in merit and substance.[16]

Jane Austen's rewriting of masculinity through the male protagonist's central relationship with the heroine in the context of the courtship romance genre remains unaddressed.[17] Austen privileges the romantic relationships of her male protagonists above all other aspects of their characterisation, including their place within their political, social and economic matrix. Her rewriting of masculinity through romance is not an accidental result of her choice of genre and nor does the courtship plot merely function as scaffolding to support an exploration of men as social, political and economic agents whose value is stamped by their acceptance or rejection by the heroine. The trend in current literary and screen adaptations to privilege the courtship romance plot over other elements of Austen's novels, including her social and political critique and her satiric comedy, reveals that the relationships Austen's men form with her heroines are critical to her enduring relevance and appeal. Indeed, Austen's men and the ideas about masculinity they represent have not fundamentally changed as they have been repeatedly reinterpreted and creatively reimagined across the last two centuries. They remain essentially static while other aspects of her work — including her minor characters and occasionally also her heroines — are reworked to reach new audiences.

Austen's men clearly possess certain qualities publicly endorsed in Romantic-era debates over the desirable man, including a value for merit and professional work, a strong sense of domestic responsibility, and an ethic of social and national service. These qualities, however, are not the reason why Henry Tilney, Fitzwilliam Darcy and George Knightley are suitable husbands for Catherine Morland, Elizabeth Bennet and Emma Woodhouse; they are not what make Austen's men desirable. Mr Darcy was not recreated as an arresting fibreglass sculpture because he combines a conservative gentry ideal with a modern socially- and economically-responsible outlook. Jane Austen's men are desirable because of how they see themselves as men and what this offers her heroines that is different to their counterparts. She redefines masculinity through male protagonists who are capable of complementing — and indeed enabling — her heroines and their desire for an independent and individual selfhood. Austen rewrites masculinity as a mode of identity — a way of understanding the individual male self — through its relationship to feminine agency.

*****

In creating a new vision of literary masculinity, Austen responds to an anxiety over masculinity that was debated by her more explicitly philosophical and polemical counterparts throughout the post-Revolutionary era. From the 1790s, women writers across the political spectrum examine the status of women and, with varying degrees of candour, attribute their marginalised social, economic and political positions to men. Writers including Catharine Macaulay, Mary Woll-stonecraft, Mary Hays, Priscilla Wakefield, Mary Robinson and Lucy Aikin criticise established modes of male privilege and behaviour. They particularly target stylised images of the desirable man associated with refinement, chivalry and other 'ideals', and challenge definitions of adult male identity underpinned by aggressive sexuality and the repression of women.[18]

In *Letters on Education* (1790), Catharine Macaulay attributes what she identifies as deficiencies in women's character and behaviour to their lack of education, and asserts that 'in the same proportion as the male sex have consulted the interests of their own happiness, they have relaxed in their tyranny over women'.[19] Mary Wollstonecraft pursues this argument in *A Vindication of the Rights of Woman* (1792),[20] in which she expands Macaulay's ideas to assert that the enforced ignorance of women was a socially-damaging consequence of male tyranny and a product of men's insistence on female intellectual and moral inferiority.[21] For Wollstonecraft, the realisation of a new woman — educated, rational, and equipped for a life of domestic, social and national service — depended on a fundamental shift in male attitudes and behaviour. Consequently, she directly addresses *Rights of Woman* to men:

> I then would fain convince reasonable men of the importance of some of my remarks; and prevail on them to weigh dispassionately the whole tenor of my observations. — I appeal to their understandings; and, as a fellow-creature, claim, in the name of my sex, some interest in their hearts. I entreat them to assist to emancipate their companion, to make her a *help meet* for them![22]

In 1798, Wollstonecraft's intellectual protégée Mary Hays titled her own treatise *An Appeal to the Men of Great Britain in Behalf of Women* (1798), suggesting that she was perhaps the most strident of these writers in asserting that women's advancement demanded a fundamental transformation of masculinity itself. Hays draws on rhetoric associated with the British love of liberty and justice to implore men 'to restore female character to its dignity and independence; though I trust, neither at the expence of the peace, the happiness, or the self-importance of MAN'.[23]

Although they devote pages to the scrutiny of women's status, its probable causes, its pernicious effects, and plans for its future improvement, these writers limit their investigation to extrapolating *why* men need to change; they do not explore the question of *how* men could change to complement the progressive feminine agency they champion.[24] They acknowledge a complementarity to masculine and feminine genders — according to Macaulay, 'the happiness and perfection of the two sexes are so reciprocally dependent on one another that, till both are reformed, there is no expecting excellence in either'[25] — but do not offer a vision of how masculinity could be transformed to achieve the liberation they desire for women. Hays dedicates entire sections of her *Appeal* to questions of 'what women are' and 'what women ought to be' but leaves unaddressed the question of 'what men ought to be'.

Established definitions of masculine gender identities presented a seemingly insurmountable conundrum because in the eighteenth century, as John Tosh argues, masculinity was primarily a social identity that was 'constructed in three arenas — home, work and all-male association'.[26] Each of these public and private spaces was inscribed by ideologies of sexual difference and the marginalisation of women, meaning that adult male identity itself was dependent on sexual hierarchies incompatible with feminine agency. The establishment and protection of a household and the control of the women within it had 'long been a crucial stage in winning social recognition as an adult, fully masculine person' and was 'necessary' to a man's 'masculine self-respect'.[27] The systemic exclusion of women from educational, professional, commercial, and public settings ensured that men also dominated and controlled the workplace, the second arena in which adult male identity was forged. The externalised nature of this identity and its proof through social display was reflected in the importance of a man's relationships and associations with other men, confirming the 'central role of peer approval in confirming masculine status'.[28] Leonore Davidoff and Catherine Hall's account of gentry masculinity as 'based on sport and codes of honor derived from military prowess, finding expression in hunting, riding, drinking and "wenching"', similarly locates masculine status in peer group approval.[29] This feature of masculine identity endured despite the ascendancy of male refinement in the eighteenth century: as Philip Carter argues, 'gender identity was conferred, or denied, by men's capacity for social performance'.[30] Masculinity was, according to Tosh, 'a set of values by which men judged other men' and 'a social attainment in the gift of one's peers'.[31]

As a status that was socially conferred, masculinity was defined through a range of externalised forms and practices that shifted with prevailing political, religious, social and economic trends throughout the period. Despite these distinctions, however, each conception of 'manliness' was premised on an ideology of sexual difference that prescribed a marginalised and often passive mode of femininity tailored to complement and promote the public expression of masculinity. The polite, refined man valued the accomplished, modest woman for her gently civilising influence and demure compliance in the context of polite sociability. Attempts to trace Austen's men to literary 'romantic heroes' who embody this 'ideal', such as Samuel Richardson's Sir Charles Grandison and Fanny Burney's Lord Orville,[32] overlook Austen's interrogation of the thinness of this masculine identity in *Sense and*

Sensibility, Northanger Abbey and *Pride and Prejudice*. At its best, such a masculine standard remains tied to a sexualised treatment of women; at its worst, it conceals male tyranny, predation and violence. Although new models of masculinity emerged to correct the risks associated with male politeness, they persisted with a sexual hierarchy oppressive to feminine gender identities. Evangelical masculinity was premised on a personal relationship to faith rather than performance to male peers, yet naturalised the male as inherently superior and prescribed a supporting role for women, a heterosexual dynamic Austen rejects in *Mansfield Park*. The hard-working, domesticated *pater familias* achieved social recognition by uniting professional competence with a domestic orientation that confined women to domesticity, in the manner of John Knightley in *Emma*. The revival of chivalry in the post-Revolutionary era promoted a new model of patriotic English masculinity, in which masculine status was achieved by artificially elevating women's status and denying them an active role in fostering the national wellbeing — a mode of manliness in which Captain Wentworth takes refuge in *Persuasion*. Regardless of his affiliation with polite, religious, economic or patriotic worth, a man who adhered to a socially-prescribed male ideal was participating in the sexualised, hierarchical treatment of women.

Jane Austen places this conundrum – the question of what men ought to be – at the centre of her novels. Austen interrogates the inherent conflict between established models of masculinity defined by social performance and recognition, and the feminine agency championed by progressive women writers and embodied in her heroines. She realised that pitching one masculine ideal against another was insufficient to effect real change because *all* prevailing models of 'manliness' were dependent on achieving social acknowledgment of masculine status through the performance of a sexual hierarchy. Austen does not merely scrutinise and critique socially-approved models of the desirable man, she challenges the very foundation of masculinity as a status created by social prescription and achieved through public display.[33] In their place, Austen reconstructs masculinity as an internalised, individual way of understanding the self that is measured by personal authenticity rather than social recognition. Indeed, her male protagonists reflect Tosh's argument that 'the period 1750–1850 marked a significant stage in the shift from masculinity as a social reputation to masculinity as an interiorised sense of personal identity'[34]:

> Modern notions of masculinity (and femininity also) emphasise the inner consciousness of the individual. Masculinity may be culturally determined, in the sense of featuring only a limited repertoire of traits, but it is also understood to be an expression of the self, and up to a point can be a matter of individual choice, tormenting and liberating as the case may be.[35]

Authenticity rather than social recognition became 'the exacting standard by which contemporary gender identities are judged'.[36]

Through the courtship romance genre, Jane Austen reframes the terms on which a masculine identity could be defined. Rewriting masculinity as an internalised male subjectivity, Austen is deeply engaged with the Romantic-era turn towards an individual sense of self and its realisation through the novel.[37] As Dror Wahrman argues, the Romantic era witnessed the emergence of an understanding of identity as 'personal, interiorized, essential, even innate' and claims that the novel both reflected and fostered the internalisation of identity, making it 'synonymous with self'.[38] Although Deidre Lynch links the novel's focus on an 'ordinary-looking heroine, possessing an extraordinary, indescribable soul' to a new psychological depth that was 'understood in feminine terms',[39] Austen exploits the new technologies of reading and writing to construct textual masculinity as a representation of introspective, psychologically-complex male selfhood. Austen's exposition of the psychological depth of her male protagonists — most striking in Fitzwilliam Darcy and Frederick Wentworth — inscribes into the courtship romance Romanticism's 'traditional identification with the lone poet, withdrawn into productive introspection, with individualism rather than collective activity, and with the cultivation of the authentic rather than the performative self'.[40] The courtship romance genre is not readily associated with Romanticism, either in the way definitions of the Romantic canon have been limited to the work of a narrow group of male poets, or in revisions to the canon that have tended to focus on women poets or fictional genres that flourished in the post-Revolutionary era. Austen's courtship romances, however, present as alternative vision of an authentic, independent male self that is neither solitary nor socially-detached, but achieves fulfilment through the transformative power of romantic love.[41]

*****

Austen's choice of the courtship romance genre to rewrite masculinity reveals in new ways her shrewd and strategic engagement with the Romantic literary marketplace.[42] Austen's scrutiny of the literary masculinities of her predecessors and contemporaries drives her creativity as a developing and professional writer; as Olivia Murphy argues, 'it is through critical reading that Austen produced her creative contributions to the novel'.[43] From her debut novel *Sense and Sensibility* to the unfinished fragment *Sanditon*, Austen revises stylised modes of literary heroism and villainy inherited from her predecessors, pioneers new narrative techniques for representing an alternative, psychologically-complex Romantic male self, and responds to emerging literary masculinities in Evangelical fiction, the national tale, and the historical novel. Exploring Austen's male protagonists as literary constructions of masculinity illuminates in new ways her commitment to advancing the novel as a literary form.

Writing men is an inherently risky literary act for women, and to write masculinity is to claim a form of political power. The literary men that women create are framed in response to myriad political, social and cultural ideologies, and provide an avenue for public commentary and the representation of alternative social and individual desires.[44] With its emphasis on psychological depth and individual selfhood, the Romantic-era novel endowed Austen and other women writers with new textual capabilities to interrogate, critique and ultimately rewrite the male. Unlike Austen, whose investigation of masculinity takes place wholly through the courtship romance genre, contemporaries including Jane West, Maria Edgeworth and Jane Porter experimented with critiquing masculinity through a range of literary modes, including didactic conduct literature, and pioneering fictional genres associated with Evangelicalism, the national tale and the historical novel. Although Austen's men are often analysed in terms of their eighteenth-century literary forbears and, in Romantic terms, the Byronic hero,[45] the textual practices and generic innovations of women writers in the early decades of the nineteenth century illuminate her choice to rewrite masculinity through courtship romance.

Through their experimentation with genre and literary form, West, Edgeworth and Porter embark on a more politically-explicit and polemical interrogation of masculinity than Austen. They actively cultivate a feminine authority to overtly critique and rewrite masculinity through ideologies of domesticity and civilisation and the connections they establish between women and social and national well-being.[46] In the introduction to her 1803 conduct book *Letters to a Young Man*, the prolific writer Jane West at once reveals a fear that she may be straying into subject matter beyond the scope of her authority as a woman writer, and the source of her authority to offer such direct advice to men:

> Should the author ... seem to trespass on a province wisely withheld from her sex, let it be remembered, ... that the original idea of this work is, that of a mother speaking to a child on whose improvement she had bestowed considerable attention from his earliest years. In this light, observations may be admitted which, if introduced in the character of a public instructor, might be thought too masculine.[47]

Emphasising her 'very retired domestic life, and the care of a young family', West uses her role as a wife, mother and homemaker to beg the reader's patience as to the form of the work: 'the little leisure which she can borrow from her domestic duties will not allow her to bestow much time on the cultivation of logical correctness, or the graces of perspicuous polished composition'.[48] Austen's correspondence reveals that she had read *Letters to a Young Man* and the stress that West lays on her laborious domesticity made an impression, as Austen wrote to Cassandra in 1816:

> how good Mrs West c^d have written such Books & collected so many hard words, with all her family cares, is still more a matter of astonishment! Composition seems to me Impossible, with a head full of Joints of Mutton & doses of rhubarb.[49]

West's protestations, however, are strategically deceptive, as Austen, who read West and expressed ambivalent feelings about her, would have known. West's publication of no less than nine works of fiction, two conduct books, and six volumes of poetry between 1786 and 1827 indicates that her range of activities was anything but domestically confined, and her self-deprecating tone belies a firm moral and intellectual sanction for her attempt at reforming masculinity: 'this apology, however, is not designed to extend to the *tendency* of her observations. If the principles on which they are founded are estimable, the sex of the writer will not authorise the reader to reject them'.[50] West's introduction to *Letters to a Young Man* reveals that despite the cultural authority of domesticity, women who directly addressed masculinity as a subject had cause to fear breaching gendered literary boundaries.

Maria Edgeworth and Jane Porter each discovered the scope and the strength of those boundaries in their literary experiments with critiquing masculinity through the politicised genres of the national tale and the historical novel. Both genres were linked to national politics: the national tale by interrogating England's relationships with Ireland and Scotland and their national cultures, and the historical novel by 'the generic interpretation of the past' which 'had become a matter of national importance, used to consider the desirability and mode of (political and economic) progress in the present'.[51] The reception of Edgeworth and Porter's work reveals that the invocation of domestic and nationalist ideologies and the adoption — or eschewing — of a domestic focus to interrogate masculinity could be a two-edged sword. Edgeworth and Porter devise innovative narrative strategies in their attempts to strike a balance between adhering to domestic authority and influencing public debate, including by adopting a male rather than a female narrative perspective, which placed a feminine critique of masculinity at the centre of their writing. Yet the reception of their work reveals a public that was divided, at best, about the authority of women to scrutinise and critique men in public and professional settings.

Jane Porter's pioneering establishment of the historical novel genre provided new opportunities to critique masculinity through fiction. In *Thaddeus of Warsaw* (1803) and *The Scottish Chiefs* (1810), Porter develops a deliberate strategy of choosing 'to feature actual and fictional "great men" as the central nexus of her innovative historical fiction',[52] whose masculine exemplarity she reveals through their professional and private lives, balancing public greatness and military conflict with romantic love, companionate marriage, and domestic family life.[53] Yet, neither Porter's cultural authority nor the critical acclaim and commercial success of her novels could protect her from a public backlash that specifically targeted her vision of the desirable man.[54] Despite invoking domestic and patriotic ideologies in her dedication of *Thaddeus of Warsaw* to the military hero Sir Sidney Smith, the real 'Great Man' at its centre, Porter became a target of 'ridicule and gossip' and rumours emerged of her engagement to Smith.[55] Porter also drew criticism for rewriting William Wallace in *The Scottish Chiefs* as a blend of the patriotic warrior and the sensitive romantic hero.[56] In idealising a model of masculine gender that combined military strength and national heroism with romantic love and affective domesticity, Jane Porter breached the boundaries of women's literary authority.

Maria Edgeworth similarly discovered the perils of turning a critical eye on masculinity in domains of male prerogative when she published *Patronage* in 1814. Her Irish national tales, *Castle Rackrent* (1800), *Ennui* (1809) and *The Absentee* (1812), were well reviewed despite their clear interrogation of male patriarchal power and, through it, masculinity itself.[57] When she deployed the same strategy to expose corruption and vice at the heart of English political and professional life in *Patronage*, however, Edgeworth drew a critical response of a different kind. The first edition of her novel, exploring the social advancement of two families through young men drawn from the medical, legal, military, clerical and political professions, was declared inferior to her previous works and damned by some reviewers who explicitly targeted Edgeworth as a woman writer straying into an exclusively male domain.[58] The *Quarterly Review*, which had heaped glowing praise on *Ennui* and *The Absentee*, took umbrage with Edgeworth's characterisation of English politicians — 'we utterly deny that the want of social affections, still less cruelty, has been characteristic of those who have enjoyed great power in this country ... this we maintain to be a gross misconception, and consequent misrepresentation, of the character of an important class of men'[59] — as well as her descriptions of the substance and process of the law and the idleness of the aristocracy. The *British Critic* specifically linked what it viewed as Edgeworth's misleading representation of 'men and manners' in public life to her gender — 'Miss Edgeworth, in the person of herself, not of her hero, penetrates into the very sources of intrigue; she sees what with common eyes she never could have seen; she knows what it is impossible she could ever have known' — and ridiculed her account of professional men:

Very few of our readers can observe without a smile the palpable absurdities in which our authoress is involved, when she attempts to describe the process of legal investigation, or the practice of the courts. We fear also that she will be convicted of having passed the bounds of all probability in her views of the medical profession.[60]

Edgeworth's portrayals of women and domestic life, by contrast, were condescendingly praised: 'in her acquaintance with all the secret springs of the female heart, Miss Edgeworth appears quite at home'.[61] Although Marilyn Butler and Connor Carville describe such reviews of *Patronage* as a back-handed compliment signifying Edgeworth's literary standing — 'she of all writers was expected to get her facts right'[62] — they expose a deep anxiety with women writers embarking on such an overt critique of masculinity in political and professional life.

The experiences of Porter and Edgeworth and the chauvinistic literary culture they expose illuminate Jane Austen's own commentary on writing men in professional and public settings in her correspondence with James Stanier Clarke while negotiating the dedication of *Emma* to the Prince Regent in 1815. Clarke unctuously advised Austen to 'delineate in some future Work the Habits of Life and Character and enthusiasm of a Clergyman — who should pass his time between the metropolis & the Country ... Fond of, & entirely engaged in Literature' and expanded his vision of literary self-acclaim to include professional duties within a country parish, at sea with the navy and at court.[63] Austen's decline of Clarke's suggestions reveals her awareness of the gendered limits of literary authority:

> I am quite honoured by your thinking me capable of drawing such a Clergyman ... But I assure you I am *not*. The comic part of the Character I might be equal to, but not the Good, the Enthusiastic, the Literary. Such a Man's Conversation must at times be on subjects of Science & Philosophy of which I know nothing — or at least be occasionally abundant in quotations & allusions which a Woman, who like me, knows only her Mother-tongue & has read very little in that, would be totally without the power of giving.[64]

Austen's denial of her abilities is clearly a subterfuge to appease Clarke, and her biting satire of his suggestions in her 'Plan of a Novel' demands that it should, like West's introduction to *Letters to a Young Man*, be interpreted as rather tongue-in-cheek.[65] As E. J. Clery notes, Austen 'had in fact a remarkably wide experience of men's lives and men's work', having six brothers, five undertaking a range of professional endeavours, and being raised 'in a household centered on the formation of men'.[66] Indeed, Austen's scrutiny of masculinity through men's professional lives in *Mansfield Park* defeats the argument that writing men in such contexts was beyond her capabilities. Yet in a cultural climate that could so damn and ridicule such accomplished novelists as Jane Porter and

Maria Edgeworth for taking precisely the approach to writing masculinity Clarke advises, it is little wonder that Austen declined his suggestions, even should they have been of interest to her. In critical terms, Austen's 'practice of adhering in her fiction to what was "knowable" from the perspective of a gentlewoman'[67] was highly successful: the reception of Austen's novels, both at the time of their publication and in the decade after her death, particularly praised her men,[68] in direct contrast to the critical reception of Porter and Edgeworth.

*****

Austen's declaration to Clarke — 'I must keep to my own style & go on in my own Way' — is much more than a thinly-veiled, self-deprecating resistance to his perverse suggestions for her literary advancement (and his own).[69] The Romantic literary marketplace presented Austen with a wealth of textual and generic possibilities to rewrite masculinity through the novel. Her selection of the courtship romance genre could be interpreted as rather a safe, risk-averse decision given the repercussions experienced by contemporaries who strayed beyond women's perceived literary authority. Austen's professional dedication to courtship romance should, however, be recognised as a deliberate literary strategy that offered her scope to rewrite masculinity where its positive influence for women would be greatest: in the context of heterosexual love, companionate marriage, and social and community relationships. The courtship romance genre — focused on domestic and sociable settings, privileging heterosexuality, and overtly concerned with dramatising dynamic relationships between men and women — was the ideal form for Austen to rewrite masculinity through the lens of modern feminine subjectivity.[70] As Ashley Tauchert puts it, Austen 'does not attempt to represent objective history, perhaps, because she had already noticed there were bigger fish to fry'.[71]

Austen's debut novel *Sense and Sensibility* (1811) is a literary manifesto for the future of the courtship romance genre. I begin my discussion of Austen's professional career with *Sense and Sensibility* in Chapter 1 because there are compelling reasons to give it precedence over *Northanger Abbey*, with which accounts of Austen's work often commence. Austen sold the copyright of *Northanger Abbey* under its original title of *Susan* to Crosby & Co in 1803, but of the works she commenced in the 1790s that she completed, *Sense and Sensibility*'s epistolary original *Elinor and Marianne* was the earliest, begun in around 1795. When Austen returned to the manuscript in the latter half of 1809, she would almost certainly have expected it to be her debut novel, having unsuccessfully attempted to urge Crosby to publish *Susan* earlier that year.[72] In her first published work, Austen rejects the masculine stereotypes that dominated mass fictional genres of the period, beloved by her

sentimental heroine Marianne Dashwood, and their inscription of performative masculine identities. Austen's portrayal of John Willoughby
raises and rejects no less than three generic masculine modes — the
dashing hero, the rake and the villain — as she manipulates her readers' expectations of literary masculinity. Her marriage of Marianne and
Elinor Dashwood to Colonel Brandon and Edward Ferrars demands
that her readers overthrow assumptions about desirable literary heroism
and embrace the men of 'real Life' instead. Discarding such stylised approaches to writing men was necessary because, although they comple-
mented externalised, performative definitions of masculinity, they did
not possess the scope for interiority and psychological depth she needed
to rewrite masculinity as an individual, internal and authentic identity.
Austen pioneers such a masculine vision in Edward Ferrars, as she exposes the harm inflicted by patriarchal systems of social and economic
power that control young men, and forces her readers to imagine a very
different man as a romantic hero.

In *Northanger Abbey* (1818), my focus in Chapter 2, Austen dramatises a psychological change in Henry Tilney that fundamentally
alters his understanding of masculine selfhood. In *Sense and Sensibility*, Austen gradually reveals Edward's internalised, introspective sense
of self as his position becomes increasingly untenable; in *Northanger
Abbey*, by contrast, she charts Henry's development of a new conception
of masculinity that is triggered by his love for Catherine Morland. When
Henry quips '"I will prove myself a man"' (108), he not only comically
exaggerates proof of manhood, but also prefaces the transformation of
his gender identity throughout the novel. In *Northanger Abbey*, Austen
both champions the courtship romance genre and satirises its conventions to launch a sustained critique of masculinity within sociable and
domestic contexts. She exploits the generic courtship heroine, her male
partner and conventional courtship rituals extolled by conduct literature
such as John Gregory's *Legacy to his Daughters* (1774) to comically
invert the prescribed sexual politics of romantic love and desire. Austen critiques masculinities defined by display, reputation and brinkmanship through her portrayal of John Thorpe, Captain Tilney and General
Tilney, men who prove their masculine status through the public expression of sexual hierarchies. Finally recognising the deception and danger
of the masculine identities embodied in his father and brother, Henry
not only proves himself as 'a man', but also redefines masculinity itself.
Breaking with his father and embracing masculinity as an individual,
internalised and authentic identity, Henry can enter a companionate
marriage with Catherine that complements her strong feminine agency.

In Chapter 3, I explore Austen's rewriting of masculinity through an
explicitly dialectical relationship between the male protagonist and the
heroine in *Pride and Prejudice* (1813). In her correspondence, Austen describes Fitzwilliam Darcy as 'that mixture of Love, Pride & Delicacy',[73]

a remark that synthesises his psychological complexity with his consuming love for Elizabeth Bennet. This combination made Darcy a remarkable literary creation in 1813, has left an indelible stamp on the courtship romance genre, and ensured his enduring popularity into the twenty-first century. Darcy is, for virtually the entire novel, 'a man violently in love' (346), and the depth of his love for Elizabeth is the defining characteristic that has secured his timeless appeal. *Pride and Prejudice* is Austen's first interrogation of the male self as a subject in its own right, who she reveals through innovative narrative techniques that endow Darcy with his own narrative perspective. Projecting the courtship romance into Romantic ideology, Austen constructs Darcy's self-fulfilment not through emotions excited by the natural sublime, or through social detachment or inclusion, but through the powerful and transformative effects of romantic love. The internalised male self is not only a thematic concern of the novel, but also a critical component of its narrative structure, as Austen invests Darcy with an introspective psychological depth that is unmatched by his predecessors. Austen exploits this complexity to dramatise Darcy's inner conflict between external and internalised masculine identities, a torment that is ultimately resolved by his fundamental need to be desirable to Elizabeth. Although Darcy's eroticism has been the focus of recent debate, I argue that Austen's more radical statement on masculinity lies in the dialogic process of gender formation that takes place between a male protagonist who is a bastion of gentry masculinity and a heroine who embodies the determined, disruptive, and rational feminine agency emerging in the Romantic era.

In the early decades of the nineteenth century, Jane Austen revolutionised the courtship romance genre and the construction of masculinity in text by interrogating relationships between male selfhood, romantic love and feminine agency. Simultaneously, new fictional genres emerged in response to the social, economic and political upheaval of the post-Revolutionary era. Austen's response to this heightened political climate in *Mansfield Park*, *Emma* and *Persuasion* encompasses not only national and international events, including the Regency and the Napoleonic Wars, but also popular fictional genres including the Evangelical novel, the national tale, and the historical novel, that emerged with them. In *Mansfield Park* and *Emma*, it is evident that Austen perceived Evangelical fiction and the national tale — genres that reinscribed a conservative sexual hierarchy into the novel — as threatening the courtship romance genre and its unique capacity to celebrate the relationship between authentic masculinity and feminine agency that she brought to a stunning climax in *Pride and Prejudice*. Olivia Murphy argues that in Austen's 'Plan of a Novel', composed after the publication of *Emma* at Christmas 1815, she 'was demonstrably and deliberately writing against the established tastes of her conservative contemporaries'[74]; similarly, *Mansfield Park* and *Emma* reveal that Austen's rewriting of masculinity was driven, at least in part, by disapproval, antagonism, and at times outright hostility to representations of gender in the work of contemporary novelists. In *Emma*, however, Austen identifies the historical novel, and particularly Jane Porter's *The Scottish Chiefs*, as offering a dialogic rewriting of masculinity and feminine agency that complements her own vision for the courtship romance.

Mansfield Park (1814), my focus in Chapter 4, is Jane Austen's rejoinder to the Evangelical fiction that emerged to critical and popular acclaim in the years she was establishing her place as a professional novelist. In 1809, Austen responded to the publication of Hannah More's *Coelebs in Search of a Wife* (1808), a novel that explores a central male character's critique of various models of femininity in his quest for a conservative feminine exemplar, with the blunt declaration, "'I do not like the Evangelicals'".[75] In *Mansfield Park*, Austen resists the model of male subjectivity and conservative gender ideologies endorsed by Evangelicalism and its associated fictions, against which she had written in her first three novels. Although Austen exploits men's roles as political, social and economic agents to critique a variety of contemporary issues in *Mansfield Park*, the greatest test of masculinity lies in the courtship narrative of Austen's own model of conservative femininity, the heroine Fanny Price.

Through Fanny's courtship narratives with both Henry Crawford and Edmund Bertram, superintended by the patriarch Sir Thomas Bertram, Austen rejects an Evangelical gender dynamic in which male superiority is naturalised within a sexual hierarchy but paradoxically dependent on the feminine for moral and spiritual sustenance. Each of these men is determined to reinstate a model of modest, passive womanhood, revealing their conception of the male self to be indivisible from ideologies of sexual difference. Despite his best efforts, Henry Crawford is unable to develop the internalised masculine identity Austen celebrates; even if he did, its stability would be secured by Fanny rather than his own self-belief. Austen constructs Edmund Bertram as a mouthpiece of conservative ideology, first encouraging Fanny to accept Henry out of gratitude and a conviction that she will improve him, and then lacking the self-awareness required to identify his own failures and commit to self-improvement. Sir Thomas is an overbearing *pater familias*; in his appalling behaviour to Fanny, Austen reveals the worst of conservative gender ideologies. She illuminates the extent to which masculine subjectivities associated with Evangelicalism were essentially self-serving, as each man seeks redemption through Fanny at the precise moment that he realises the inadequacy of his own gender identity. Fanny's resistance lies in her steadfast refusal to provide a salve for masculine weakness, as Austen unequivocally condemns men who are willing to participate in such a sexual exchange.

In Chapter 5, I explore Austen's most radical and explicit celebration of an authentic, internalised masculine identity and its enabling power for feminine agency in *Emma* (1815). Austen's unsubtle portrayal of George Knightley as a beacon of conservative English masculinity masks the revolution in sexual politics taking place in this novel. Although Mr Knightley is often read as a wartime hero who can save the nation, his real power lies not in what he can offer England, but in what he can offer Emma Woodhouse, who refuses to compromise her individualism, influence or agency. Emma is the Austen heroine who is least compatible with a conventional marriage, and Austen is quite clear that it is Mr Knightley's internalised and authentic gender identity — which resists the value placed on social performance and is ultimately resilient enough to enable him to leave his own home in preference for hers — that makes their relationship possible. Austen contrasts Mr Knightley's refusal to participate in ideologies of sexual difference with the attitudes and behaviour of every other man in the novel, particularly Frank Churchill.

Austen illuminates the contrast between these men and their relationships with the women they love through her interrogation of two fictional genres, the national tale and the historical novel. The relationship Austen draws between Frank Churchill and Jane Fairfax mirrors the heterosexual dynamic governing romantic relationships in the national tale, particularly in Sydney Owenson's *The Wild Irish Girl* (1801) and Maria Edgeworth's *Ennui* and *The Absentee*, in which the accomplished, sexualised heroine acts as both a salve for the jaded English protagonist and a reward for his labour. Such a vision of heterosexuality is repugnant to both Mr Knightley and Emma, as Austen exposes the failure of the national tale to offer a new vision of masculine gender that can enable feminine agency. I argue that the historical novel, however, may have offered Austen a prototype, and explore parallels between Mr Knightley and William Wallace in Jane Porter's *The Scottish Chiefs*, including their rejection of chivalric discourse, their refusal to participate in ideologies of sexual difference, and their value for feminine individualism and agency. In *Emma*, Austen domesticates the relationship Porter envisaged between Wallace and Lady Helen Mar, relocating it to rural England and celebrating again the power of the courtship romance genre to rewrite masculinity as enabling feminine agency.

In Chapter 6, I argue that in *Persuasion* (1818), Austen confounds a teleological trajectory in her reinventing of masculinity, which reaches its zenith in *Emma*, by radically rewriting the conventional courtship romance plot and, in the process, constructing Captain Frederick Wentworth as her most complex male protagonist. Austen recasts the terms on which an authentic masculine subjectivity could be expressed by removing her male protagonist from the security of the landowning classes and associated professions, locating him in an uncertain post-war context and projecting him into contemporary cults of masculine celebrity associated with Lords Nelson and Byron. Austen's post-war sensibility in *Persuasion* drives a renewed focus on the emotional volatility of the male self that, particularly in the context of romantic love, recalls Darcy in *Pride and Prejudice*. Racked by an inner doubt resulting from his stymied love for Anne Elliot and his uncertain social status in relation to her, Wentworth reflects the darker side of Austen's construction of a modern male subjectivity, a man for whom the open expression of an authentic identity and romantic love has produced rejection, disappointment and resentment. Wentworth's involuntary return to England and renewed association with the Elliot family force him to confront a past he has buried through exile and estrangement. Unable to manage the emotional and psychological turmoil triggered by his reunion with Anne, Wentworth retreats into scripted modes of social performance grounded in ideologies of chivalry and polite sociability; the authentic expression of his inner self is hampered by uncertainty over who he is and his relationship to the woman he loves. Austen's upended courtship plot empowers Anne to effectively choose him through her conversation with Captain Harville at the White Hart Inn in Bath, writing feminine agency into the courtship romance. Even so, in *Persuasion* Austen interrogates the reality that masculine authenticity and feminine agency will not always be complementary, even between two people passionately committed to each other.

In my Conclusion, I draw on Walter Scott's distinction between Austen's novels of modern realism, the sentimental novel and stock popular fiction in his review of *Emma*, as a lens through which to interpret Austen's rewriting of masculinity in her incomplete novel *Sanditon*, or, as Austen referred to it, 'The Brothers'. I also outline possible future directions in research on Austen and masculinity beyond the courtship romance genre.

The feminine selfhood that Jane Austen identified, explored and celebrated in the Romantic era has crystallised and flourished in the two centuries since her novels were published. Austen's rewriting of masculinity to match this modern feminine subjectivity through the courtship romance genre was a highly successful strategy that has secured her literary legacy and the enduring relevance of her novels. The towering wet shirt-clad sculpture of Colin Firth as Darcy that graced Hyde Park in London, Lyme Park in Cheshire and Ripponlea Estate in Melbourne is a powerful image of a masculine ideal with which, in the twenty-first century, Jane Austen has become readily associated. Given Austen's determination to reveal the psychological depth, complexity and instability of masculinity as a contested gender identity, it is ironic that her male protagonists are now equated with a particularly stylised model of romantic literary heroism. The extraordinary range of Austen's male protagonists, from *Sense and Sensibility* to *Persuasion*, confounds any interpretation of her work as focused on the creation of a singular masculine ideal. Rather, it is the individual and dynamic relationships between her heroines and her male protagonists and the model of authentic male selfhood they embody that sustains their resonance and relevance for contemporary readers.

1 The Men of 'real Life'

Educating the Reader in *Sense and Sensibility*

Between July and October 1814, Jane Austen and her niece Anna shared a lively correspondence regarding Anna's manuscript novel. Austen's letters to Anna are among the few sources in which she writes as a literary artist and critic. Austen was then the successfully published and well-reviewed author of *Sense and Sensibility, Pride and Prejudice* and *Mansfield Park*, who was hard at work on *Emma*, and she writes with a voice of confidence and authority. Her letters reveal her literary method, her commitment to realism, and her professional acumen. Among her meticulous and exhaustive observations on Anna's characters and plot, Austen identifies one young man for particular criticism: 'Henry Mellish I am afraid will be too much in the common Novel style – a handsome, amiable, unexceptionable Young Man (such as do not much abound in real Life) desperately in Love, & all in vain'.[1] Alluding to a generic style of idealised masculinity that, in her view, dominated the 'common Novel', Austen cautions her niece against hackneyed, stylised male characterisation that flouted realism and hampered the development of the novel.

Austen's reference to the 'common Novel' targets works of fiction produced and distributed by the major London publishing houses Minerva Press and Longman, which filled the shelves of booksellers and circulating libraries throughout Britain and the empire. As a commercial enterprise, the production, distribution and consumption of fiction in the Romantic era depended on the deployment of familiar, predictable and what J. M. S. Tompkins describes as 'stock' characters, incidents and themes in the contemporary novel.[2] The Minerva Press produced nearly one-third of all fiction published in England between 1790 and 1815; as Peter Garside argues, it 'stood in need of reliable suppliers, capable of sustaining their readers' attention through recognizable kinds of material'.[3] In the courtship romance novel that developed throughout the eighteenth century, such 'stock' male characters include the heroine's father or guardian and potential suitors, who feature to the extent that they affect the courtship plot.[4] Male characterisation in courtship romance novels was influenced by changing literary fashions and, increasingly, the political persuasions and didactic purposes of authors.[5] Fathers are figures of kind benevolence or oppressive tyranny; suitors are honest and worthy gentlemen, deceptively flirtatious rakes, or seductive libertines. In their social behaviour, men are cultivated members of a civilised society; conceited, servile and self-serving; fops; and boors. In Tompkins' account, the 'New Hero' of women's courtship romance novels bears a remarkable resemblance to Anna Austen's Henry Mellish:

> that devastating blend of the susceptibility of Saint-Preux with the morals of Sir Charles Grandison and the devotion of the Grand Cyrus, who corrects the perspective of the heroine's sketches, defers implicitly to her notions of right and wrong, and receives the promise of her hand with a bosom thrilling with the most delicate sensations of felicity.[6]

The romantic hero, or as Tompkins describes him, 'dream-figure', is a paragon of virtue, feeling and competence.[7] Austen's correspondence with Anna reveals her opposition to such 'common Novel' styles of literary masculinity: not only to the male paragon represented in Henry Mellish, but to the generic reliance on stereotyped male characterisation.

Austen's rejection of male typecasting — in her correspondence with Anna, and in her fiction — brings realism to the courtship romance novel and establishes a platform from which she rewrites masculinity itself. Austen revises and rejects the stereotyped men who dominated the 'common Novel style' of her contemporaries and, argues Deidre Lynch, the works of her eighteenth-century predecessors, and redefines masculinity as a complex, internalised gender identity.[8] Polite, urbane, refined romantic heroes reproduced in fiction a vision of masculinity as an externalised identity defined by social performance and recognition among male peers. Stock literary characters were well adapted to this performative stylisation of masculinity because they lacked interiority, introspection and a capacity for psychological depth. To rewrite masculinity as an individual, internalised and authentic subjectivity, Austen would need to overthrow established, predictable formulas for writing the male.

In *Sense and Sensibility* (1811), Austen exposes, rejects and replaces the stock literary men that dominated the 'common Novel' of her predecessors and contemporaries. Her debut novel is a manifesto for the radical overhaul of conventional literary masculinities and for the future of the courtship romance genre. Austen targets clichéd literary figures, including the idealised romantic hero, the male coquet or rake and the seductive libertine, in her characterisation of John Willoughby, Colonel Brandon and Edward Ferrars. Contemporary readers who took up *Sense and Sensibility* did not find within its pages the comfortable predictability of the typical male characters that populated the 'common Novel'. They must, like Anna Austen on receiving her aunt Jane's letters of advice, steel themselves for a forceful literary education. Any ideas about desirable and undesirable male stereotypes that readers bring to the novel are about to be challenged, ridiculed, and ultimately replaced with a much more complex vision of masculinity in fiction.

Austen's strategy of forcing upon her readers so drastic a change in the literary representation of masculinity was received with mixed success. The *Critical Review* overtly commended *Sense and Sensibility* as standing apart from the superfluity of novels 'which are continually presenting themselves to our notice' that were 'in substance, style, and size, so much alike'.[9] As E. J. Clery notes, the *Critical Review* praised Austen's 'knowledge of character' and linked it to her depictions of men,[10] though it did not remark upon the striking differences in male characterisation, particularly the romantic hero, between Austen and her fashionable contemporaries. Anna preferred *Sense and Sensibility* to Austen's other works, even though her aunt's fresh approach to writing the male does not appear to have influenced her own manuscript composition: Austen recorded in 'Opinions of *Mansfield Park*' that Anna liked *Mansfield Park* better than *Pride and Prejudice* 'but not so well as S. & S.', and her 'Opinions of *Emma*' reveals that Anna 'rank'd *Emma* as a composition with S & S'.[11] Anna's preference is singular among Austen's early readers. Of all the opinions Austen collected, Anna alone refers to Austen's first published work; the others compare *Mansfield Park* and *Emma* with *Pride and Prejudice*. Beyond Austen's family and social circle, early responses to *Sense and Sensibility* register unease with the novel, and particularly its narrative conclusion. Lady Bessborough, now famously, thought it a 'clever Novel' that ended 'stupidly', and in its first French translation in 1815, Isabelle de Montolieu changed the ending so that Willoughby married Eliza Williams.[12]

Dissatisfaction with the narrative conclusion of *Sense and Sensibility* is a constant theme in the novel's reception among generations of readers and scholars.[13] Austen's characterisation of Willoughby, Colonel Brandon, and Edward frustrates readers because of its implications for the narrative resolution of her heroines Marianne and Elinor Dashwood. Disappointing her readers about the men Elinor and Marianne marry do and do not marry is among Austen's primary objectives. Austen methodically dissects the stereotyped masculinities that dominated the courtship novel and demands that her readers confront the assumptions about desirable literary masculinity they have brought to her text. Exposing their susceptibility to authorial manipulation, she repeatedly and purposefully deceives her readers about these men before revealing their 'true' identities and forcing her readers to accept two very unusual and fundamentally flawed men as romantic heroes. Indeed, recurring criticism of Colonel Brandon and Edward Ferrars as imperfect and unattractive illuminates the extent to which the idealised romantic hero has become culturally embedded, despite Austen's challenge to its literary dominance in 1811.

Austen's overhaul of literary masculinity in *Sense and Sensibility* targets not only the 'common Novel' she described to Anna, but also works with higher literary ambitions. Jane West's *A Gossip's Story; and A Legendary Tale* (1796), often cited as a probable source for *Sense and Sensibility*, is a crucial point of reference for Austen's reconstruction of literary masculinity. West was a prolific, politically-engaged writer in a variety of genres, who, though often labelled a conservative and Anti-Jacobin novelist, recognised the flaws in established institutions of power and sought to improve them. Although critical appraisals of *A Gossip's Story* and *Sense and Sensibility* tend to focus on points of convergence and departure between West's Marianne and Louisa Dudley and Austen's Marianne and Elinor Dashwood and their narrative resolutions,[14] exploring the male protagonists of these works illuminates the extent of Austen's reform of masculine stereotypes in the courtship romance genre. West clearly embarked on her own critique of masculinity in *A Gossip's Story*, castigating men who fail to fulfil their responsibilities to women and children and challenging the conventional sentimental romantic hero, who proves a tyrannical and faithless husband. In *Sense and Sensibility*, Austen advances West's critique by exploding the myth not only of the idealised romantic hero, but of the stereotyping of literary masculinity itself.

A Gossip's Story, like *Sense and Sensibility*, features three male characters as potential suitors to the heroines: Sir William Milton, a wealthy and conceited young man whose courtship of Louisa Dudley is terminated by the revelation that he has abandoned his mistress and children; Clermont, a sentimental romantic hero whose superficial adoration of the passionate and naive Marianne Dudley dissipates soon after their marriage; and Henry Pelham, an idealised paragon of virtue, amiability and professional competence who, after being initially dismissed as a suitor by Marianne, eventually marries Louisa. In *Sense and Sensibility*, Austen collapses Sir William Milton and Clermont into Willoughby, whose characterisation she deftly manipulates to deconstruct the stereotypes not only of the sentimental romantic hero, but also the male coquet and the libertine. Austen reveals the fallacy of such clichés, exposing Willoughby to be an ordinary young gentry man doing precisely what his society expects of him. Whereas West uncritically endorses Henry Pelham as a male paragon, Austen resists even this form of generic male characterisation; through Colonel Brandon and Edward Ferrars, she disrupts such idealised visions of masculine perfection by forcing her reader to accept that flawed but realistic men can be romantic heroes.

In *Sense and Sensibility*, Austen discredits multiple literary masculinities inherited from her eighteenth-century predecessors by spreading her narrative focus across three men rather than focusing on one identifiable romantic hero, a strategy for which she has been criticised as leaving the men of this novel undeveloped. Through her split narrative focus,

Austen both discredits stylised literary masculinity and tackles broader social, economic and political issues, a pattern of male characterisation she repeats in *Mansfield Park* and *Sanditon*. In *Sense and Sensibility*, Austen's critical focus is on men's positions within the patriarchal social and economic order, as she dwells on the accumulation and disposition of money, analyses the management of capital and scrutinises the ramifications of economic power. She informs the reader of the monetary worth of virtually every character and the terms on which it is held. Conversations about wealth recur: Elinor, Marianne and Edward discuss wealth as a relative concept; Mrs Dashwood fantasises about what she can achieve on her income; and John Dashwood is incapable of conversing about anything else. Although the opening chapters powerfully dramatise the impact of the established system of property inheritance and income distribution on women, Austen is equally concerned with its effects on men. She complicates her endorsement of masculinity as an internalised, individual gender identity by illuminating the social and economic pressures that come with a man's status as an elder or younger son within a patrilineal and primogenital system for the disposition of property.[15] Much of the drama surrounding Willoughby, Colonel Brandon and Edward is focused on each man's relationship to his social world and economic status, as Austen exposes the invidious position of men who develop an authentic male identity in an environment that recognises and values only performative masculinities.

Austen's socio-economic commentary is intertwined with her critique of conventional literary heroism. Austen presents Willoughby, Colonel Brandon and Edward as lacking the independence, agency and competence typically associated both with the 'common Novel style' of desirable masculinity and performative masculine identities. Each man lacks agency because he is subject to external control, at different times and in different ways; none of these men possesses the 'personal freedom' that Matthew McCormack argues formed 'a prominent aspects of a Georgian man's sense of his gender – as well as his social and political being ... commonly articulated in terms of "manly independence"'.[16] The want of masculine agency thwarts the fulfilment of romantic love, as each man is incapable of pursuing the woman he loves because of an economic dependence Austen explicitly links to the system of property inheritance: Willoughby is unable to propose to Marianne because he is disinherited by an older female relative, who later changes her mind; Colonel Brandon's attempt to elope with his cousin Eliza fails and he is later unable to protect her daughter, his consolation being that Marianne eventually decides to love him; and Edward is manipulated by his mother and family first into economic dependence and then into indigence, and is ultimately only able to marry Elinor because Lucy Steele decides to marry his brother instead. The powerlessness of these men is underscored by their lack of personal growth. Unlike the male protagonists who succeed them — Henry Tilney and Mr Darcy — none of the men of *Sense and Sensibility* develops in the course of the novel; their circumstances change through forces beyond their control but the men themselves remain essentially static. Neither Willoughby nor Colonel Brandon nor Edward emerges as a masculine ideal who can heroically transcend life's harsh realities. Austen's men of 'real Life' prove to be essentially powerless, subject to the whim of a cruel and callous world.

Austen introduces the reader to each man through the eyes of Marianne Dashwood, a 'self-conscious heroine of sensibility with a special relationship to books'.[17] Lifting Marianne from the pages of a sentimental courtship romance novel, Austen frames the reader's perception of each man through the lens of the literary stereotypes she later discredits. Marianne's index of masculine worth emphasises not only sentimental literary heroism but also, uniquely within Austen's works, the desirability of the male body, reflecting Austen's challenge to externalised masculinities associated with public display. Marianne's value for physical beauty echoes sentimental ideology's alignment of male refinement with the experience of feeling and the cultivation of artistic genius. Austen draws this correlation through Marianne's love of William Cowper, who, argues Philip Carter, regarded the refined male body as reflecting 'the benefits of a delicate nervous system ... profound intellect, moral standing and/or creative genius'.[18]

Edward Ferrars is the first man to fall under Marianne's critical eye. Edward is lacking in both mind and body in comparison with her idealised man of taste, possessed of refined feeling as well as artistic, literary and musical discernment: his '"eyes want all that spirit, that fire, which at once announce virtue and intelligence"', his figure is not '"striking"', and he is deficient in '"real taste"' (19). His praise of Elinor's painting is wanting:

> He admires as a lover, not as a connoisseur. To satisfy me, those characters must be united. I could not be happy with a man whose taste did not in every point coincide with my own. He must enter into all my feelings; the same books, the same music must charm us both (19).

Marianne despairs of finding a man who can satisfy her considerable demands:

> the more I know of the world, the more am I convinced that I shall never see a man whom I can really love. I require so much! He must have all Edward's virtues, and his person and manners must ornament his goodness with every possible charm (20).

Such a measure of male value automatically disqualifies Colonel Brandon, the next man Marianne evaluates, from either experiencing or exciting feeling. To Marianne, the Colonel's perceived rheumatic complaints and his use of a 'flannel waistcoat' are each associated with '"the old and the feeble"' (40).

In contrast to Edward Ferrars and Colonel Brandon, John Willoughby materialises as Marianne's vision of masculine perfection. Willoughby is an ingenious literary creation through whom Austen dissects and denounces three literary masculinities that dominated the 'common Novel style': the romantic hero, the male coquet and the seductive libertine. By characterising Willoughby as Marianne's man of taste come to life, Austen draws her readers into expecting that he will play the role of romantic hero, establishing a platform from which she later refutes the assumptions about desirable literary masculinities they have brought to the novel. Austen draws on a range of rhetorical strategies to present each incarnation of Willoughby as the 'true' or 'real' Willoughby before removing the mask and, with it, the reader's intellectual anchoring in stock conventions and comfortable reliance on narrative authority. Not content with exploding the fallacy of such clichés, however, Austen ultimately uses Willoughby to challenge her society's valorisation of an adult male identity constituted wholly by the public performance of fashionable sociability, with no capacity for psychological depth whatsoever. 'Willoughby' ultimately possesses no subjectivity or sense of selfhood beyond the performance dictated by gentry society.

From his appearance as Marianne's rescuer on the Devonshire Downs, Austen casts Willoughby in the image of a romantic hero derived from sentimental print culture: 'His person and air were equal to what her fancy had ever drawn for the hero of a favourite story' (44–45). She dwells on his body: his 'manly beauty' immediately captivates the Dashwood women, who 'fix' their eyes on him 'with an evident wonder and a secret admiration which equally sprung from his appearance' (44). To Marianne, 'his person, which was uncommonly handsome, received additional charms from his voice and expression' (44). Marianne's inquiry of Sir John Middleton — '"what are his manners on more intimate acquaintance? What his pursuits, his talents and genius?"' (45) — frames his characterisation as a man of taste, which appears to be validated in their subsequent meetings: 'They speedily discovered that their enjoyment of dancing and music was mutual, and that it arose from a general conformity of judgment in all that related to either' (49). Austen emphasises the extent to which their relationship is driven by Marianne:

> her favourite authors were brought forward with so rapturous a delight, that any young man of five and twenty must have been insensible indeed, not to become an immediate convert to the excellence of such works, however disregarded before. Their taste was strikingly alike (49).

Willoughby joins '"not only a captivating person, but a natural ardour of mind which was now roused and increased by the example of her own, and which recommended him to her affection beyond every thing else"' (50). Willoughby-as-romantic-hero is 'exactly formed to engage Marianne's heart' and seems to be 'all that her fancy had delineated' because he has consciously set out to become Marianne's masculine ideal, quite literally a projection — and nothing more — of her vision of male perfection (51).

With his abrupt departure, Austen shifts Willoughby's characterisation from sentimental hero of taste and feeling to male coquet who has won Marianne's heart with no intention of returning her love. Refusing to believe that he has toyed with Marianne's affections, Mrs Dashwood asks: '"Is he not a man of honour and feeling? Has there been any inconsistency on his side to create alarm? can he be deceitful?"' (81). Elinor, by contrast, immediately fears 'that no serious design had ever been formed on his side' (78). His failure to call or write during their stay in London increases her suspicions, which are eventually validated by their public meeting and his subsequent letter:

> if I have been so unfortunate as to give rise to a belief of more than I felt, or meant to express, I shall reproach myself for not having been more guarded in my professions of that esteem. That I should ever have meant more you will allow to be impossible, when you understand that my affections have been long engaged elsewhere (174).

Through Willoughby's letter, Austen convinces Marianne, Elinor and the reader that he has never loved and had no intention of marrying Marianne. Elinor reflects on it as:

> a letter which, instead of bringing with his desire of a release any professions of regret, acknowledged no breach of faith, denied all peculiar affection whatever – a letter of which every line was an insult, and which proclaimed its writer to be deep in hardened villainy (174).

Austen endows Willoughby with a third layer of characterisation through Colonel Brandon's revelation to Elinor of his seduction and abandonment of Eliza Williams:

> He had left the girl whose youth and innocence he had seduced, in a situation of the utmost distress, with no creditable home, no help, no friends, ignorant of his address! He had left her promising to return; he neither returned, nor wrote, nor relieved her (197–98).

Colonel Brandon's comment that '"he had already done that, which no man who *can* feel for another, would do"' (197) wholly destroys the image of Willoughby as a man of strong feeling and principled morality that both the Dashwood women and the reader have believed him. To Colonel Brandon, he is '"expensive, dissipated, and worse than both"' (198), linking his treatment of Eliza to a broader pursuit of pleasure that now resonates as an immoral lack of self-control rather than the aesthetic experience of artistic beauty. Through the testimony of Colonel Brandon, whose veracity seems assured, Austen convinces the characters in the novel and the reader that Willoughby is neither a sentimental hero nor a male coquet, but instead a libertine who preys on unprotected young women. Marianne is forced to reflect on her own vulnerability:

> his seduction and desertion of Miss Williams, the misery of that poor girl, and the doubt of what his designs might *once* have been on herself, preyed altogether so much on her spirits, that she could not bring herself to speak of what she felt even to Elinor (200).

Uniquely within her novels, in *Sense and Sensibility* Austen permits her 'villain' to speak for his 'crimes'. Willoughby's confession to Elinor exposes the fallacy of each of the literary masks he has worn, and with them the stylisation of literary masculinity itself. He discloses that his courtship of Marianne was, at least initially, a way of amusing himself during his stay in Devonshire; he so closely resembled her ideal of masculine perfection because that is what he consciously set out to become. The sentimental romantic hero is not a man of 'real Life', but neither is the male coquet, for Willoughby-as-coquet ultimately fell in love: '"I found myself, by insensible degrees, sincerely fond of her; and the happiest hours of my life were what I spent with her, when I felt my intentions were strictly honourable, and my feelings blameless"' (299–300). His resolution to propose despite his financial straits and Marianne's poverty is destroyed by Mrs Smith's decision to disinherit him over his treatment of Eliza Williams. Willoughby-as-libertine, however, is further revealed as a sham. Austen allows Willoughby to contest the view that he preyed on and seduced Eliza — '"because she was injured she was irreproachable, and because *I* was a libertine *she* must be a saint"' (300) — redrawing the relationship as the result of mutual desire.

In a single character, Jane Austen explodes three myths reproduced by stereotyped male characterisation. Her reader, co-opted into assuming Willoughby is a romantic hero, deceived into believing him a male coquet through a letter dictated by his fiancée, and convinced by the partial account of Colonel Brandon that he is a libertine, has been thoroughly duped. Having exposed the fallacy of Willoughby's masks and the ease with which she has applied and removed them, Austen demands that her reader contemplate a more complex vision of literary masculinity. Through Willoughby's confession, Austen holds out to the reader the possibility that beneath the masks he has worn there is a 'true' or 'real'

Willoughby, but he is revealed as nothing more than an incarnation of gentry society's value for wealth and display. He is an idle, expensive male heir who attributes his decision to leave Marianne and marry Miss Grey to wholly mercenary motives:

> My affection for Marianne, my thorough conviction of her attach-ment to me – it was all insufficient to outweigh that dread of pov-erty, or get the better of those false ideas of the necessity of riches, which I was naturally inclined to feel, and expensive society had increased (301–02).

Elinor contemplates the corrupting influence of Willoughby's socio-economic position:

> the irreparable injury which too early an independence and its con-sequent habits of idleness, dissipation, and luxury, had made in the mind, the character, the happiness, of a man who, to every advan-tage of person and talents, united a disposition naturally open and honest, and a feeling, affectionate temper (308).

Willoughby is not merely 'ordinary', as some critics have suggested,[19] in the sense that he is gripped by the trappings and performance of gen-try masculinity; he possesses no real sense of individual selfhood at all. Willoughby's lack of identity is ultimately his most damning quality, as Austen reinforces in her concluding sardonic remark: 'in his breed of horses and dogs, and in sporting of every kind, he found no inconsider-able degree of domestic felicity' (353).

Austen offers Marianne and the reader an alternate vision of senti-mental masculinity, and its links to male subjectivity and sociability, through Colonel Brandon, who is narratively linked to Willoughby by their shared connections with Marianne and Eliza. Willoughby, mir-roring Marianne, reflects the experience and expression of feeling as solitary, isolating and, taken to its logical conclusion, risking the an-nihilation of the self; Marianne declares after her illness that had she died, '"it would have been self-destruction"' (322). As Peter Knox-Shaw argues, for Willoughby and Marianne the experience of feeling 'be-gins and ends – such is their boast – with themselves', meaning that 'Marianne, after Willoughby's desertion, finds herself in a social con-text which she has emptied of all meaning'.[20] Colonel Brandon offers Marianne an alternative, authentic approach to feeling that is grounded in Adam Smith's *Theory of Moral Sentiments* (1759) with its emphasis on sympathy as a vehicle for interpersonal exchange and improvement. Smith, argues Philip Carter, deplored outlandishly physical displays of emotion and favoured 'practical assistance' enabled by self-command and an 'overt show of forbearance and dignity'.[21] Colonel Brandon's repeated acts of social sympathy — offering the Delaford living to the penniless Edward Ferrars, riding to Barton to bring Mrs Dashwood to an afflicted Marianne — embodies Smith's celebration of 'a peculiarly male synthesis of moderation, self-discipline, benevolence and sincere sympathy'.[22] Austen valorises the power of such qualities through Colonel Brandon's response to Marianne's illness:

> *He*, meanwhile, whatever he might feel, acted with all the firmness of a collected mind, made every necessary arrangement with the utmost dispatch, and calculated with exactness the time in which she might look for his return. Not a moment was lost in a delay of any kind (291).

His self-command and exertion to bring comfort to the Dashwood women contrasts sharply with the intoxicated, self-obsessed and almost violent demands Willoughby makes of Elinor during Marianne's illness. As Clara Tuite argues, Austen 'attempts to transform a discredited sensibility into a respectable sympathy ... a synthesizing, stabilizing third term that lies between "sense" and "sensibility"'.[23]

Austen's characterisation of Colonel Brandon through the moral philosophy of Adam Smith has been insufficient, however, to appease readers appalled by the narrative resolution she inflicts on Marianne Dashwood. Austen's assertion that 'Marianne could never love by halves; and her whole heart became, in time, as much devoted to her husband, as it had once been to Willoughby' (352) has left readers unconvinced, to say the least.[24] The relationship between Marianne and Colonel Brandon, no less than the relationship between Marianne and Willoughby, bears the marks of a novelist determined to disabuse her readers' expectations of what they ought to find in the pages of a courtship romance novel. In the same way that Austen draws her readers into assuming Willoughby will be the novel's romantic hero, she deceives them into denying the possibility that Colonel Brandon could marry Marianne by raising, rejecting and even ridiculing the idea. When Sir John Middleton and Mrs Jennings hint that the Colonel could be in love with her, Marianne interprets their jests as 'an unfeeling reflection on the colonel's advanced years, and on his forlorn condition as an old bachelor', and declares '"you cannot deny the absurdity of the accusation ... Colonel Brandon is certainly younger than Mrs Jennings, but he is old enough to be *my* father"' (39). Elinor, usually considered the voice of wisdom and prudence, concedes '"thirty-five and seventeen had better not have any thing to do with matrimony together"' (39); her later observation of the Colonel's increasing love for Marianne leads her to reflect that 'as she could not even wish him successful, she heartily wished him indifferent' (51). Marianne's marriage to Colonel Brandon at the novels' conclusion is an affront to the faith the reader has placed in Austen's narrator and in Elinor's judgment.

Unsatisfied with marrying her heroine to a man of 'real Life' who flouts the 'common Novel style', Austen underlines her rejection of conventional literary heroism by constructing Colonel Brandon as a failed romantic hero whose own romance narrative took place years before the novel opens, the disastrous effects of which are ongoing. Marianne's remark that '"if he were ever animated enough to be in love, must have long outlived every sensation of the kind"' (39) evokes a younger, passionate and energetic Colonel Brandon in clear contrast to the broken man whose wellbeing has been destroyed by traumatic life events beyond his control and from which he has not recovered. Physically present but emotionally and mentally absent, he is silent, grave and reserved in the Dashwoods' circle in Devonshire. Sir John Middleton's hint to Elinor of 'past injuries and disappointments' implies that he suffers from a kind of melancholia:

> She liked him – in spite of his gravity and reserve, she beheld in him an object of interest. His manners, though serious, were mild; and his reserve appeared rather the result of some oppression of spirits, than of any natural gloominess of temper (51).

It is not until Willoughby deserts Marianne in London that Elinor, Marianne, and the reader learn that Colonel Brandon's 'oppression of spirits' results from his tragic personal history: he is a younger son whose happiness has been thwarted by the primogenital disposition of property. Passionately in love with his cousin Eliza, he witnessed his father force her marriage to his brother, another profligate male heir, only to find her years later divorced, with an illegitimate child, and dying of consumption in a spunging-house. His emotional scars are evident from his struggle to relate his personal history to Elinor; his silence and gravity in company arise from an emotional and mental turmoil that has no acceptable public face. Austen emphasises his physically damaged body, which saw the trials of military service during his self-imposed exile from Eliza, a tangible symbol of the emotional wreckage within. Retraumatised by the disappearance of his ward Eliza Williams and the discovery that she has fallen from grace in similar circumstances to her mother, he is afflicted not only by sadness, but also by guilt: '"so imperfectly have I discharged my trust!"' (199). Now possessed of the Delaford estate following his brother's death, not even his home can comfort him, itself a constant reminder of the loss of his soul mate, the cruelty of his male relatives, and the devastating consequences of the socio-economic status quo, with its emphasis on primogeniture to secure capital.

Colonel Brandon is consequently viewed as an object of pity by the characters in the novel. Austen dwells on Elinor's 'compassion' for him: 'she regarded him with respect and compassion' (51), her 'compassion for him encreased, as she had reason to suspect that the misery of disappointed love had already been known by him' (56), and after his testimony he leaves her 'full of compassion and esteem for him' (199). When she learns his personal history Marianne begins to speak to him 'with a kind of compassionate respect' (200) and his 'chief reward for the painful exertion of disclosing past sorrows and present humiliations, was given in the pity-ing eye with which Marianne sometimes observed him' (204). Austen's construction of the Colonel as an object of pity flouts social definitions of masculinity grounded in reputation and personal competence, as well as the vigour, agency and empowerment necessary to the stereotypical ro-mantic hero. The Colonel's duel with Willoughby, which may be regarded as an attempt to regain a sense of self-respect, is cast as an outmoded and frivolous 'fancied necessity' by Elinor (199), anachronous to Austen's redefinition of masculinity as internalised, independent and authentic.[25]

Austen's account of the romantic denouement of Colonel Brandon and Marianne is deliberately obscure. Both characters have already ex-hausted their romance narratives through their failed relationships with Eliza Brandon and John Willoughby. The Colonel's essential passivity continues in his 'courtship' of Marianne — at Delaford, 'he had little to do but to calculate the disproportion between thirty-six and seventeen' (344) — and their relationship is driven by Mrs Dashwood's frequent visits and the 'general consent' that 'Marianne ... was to be the reward of all' (351). Austen refuses to explain why Marianne falls in love with him, though it might be inferred from his capacity to experience and express feeling in a way that is both authentic and socially embedded. Their love is passive, selfless and mutually healing, and their marriage forces the reader to confront some truths rarely represented in courtship romance fiction: that society can break even the best of men, driven by the purest motives; that there is no shame in love that has its genesis in mutual heartbreak; and that damaged men may not be romantic heroes, but they are lovable nonetheless.

Austen's creation of John Willoughby and Colonel Brandon dispels her readers' fantasies regarding conventional literary heroism. As men of 'real Life', however, they are ambivalent reconstructions of masculinity as an individual, internalised identity: in Willoughby, Austen holds out the promise of redemption through psychological insight, only to deny her readers such narrative resolution; and in Colonel Brandon, she illus-trates the traumatic effects of an internalised identity for a man whose socio-economic place renders him incapable of agency and who remains invested in the link between identity and reputation. In Edward Ferrars, however, Austen explores, with measured optimism, the possibilities of rewriting masculinity as a gender identity grounded in integrity, self-belief and authenticity. Edward is as thoroughly unheroic as Colonel Brandon. In his characterisation, however, Austen moves beyond debunking myths of stylised masculinity and offers an alternative conception of masculine identity that is divorced from the overbearing culture of polite sociability and the established socio-economic order. Like Willoughby, Edward is a male heir; unlike Willoughby, he refuses to adopt a masculine gender defined by public performance that, as a matter of birth, he is socially assigned. Austen dramatises the risk faced by men who embody a masculinity grounded in introspection and an internalised sense of self when economic dependence ties them to a social context that does not value or even recognise their gender identity. Edward resists pressure to conform — first passively, then actively — and ultimately chooses family ex-communication and financial punishment over social survival.

For much of *Sense and Sensibility*, Edward is trapped in a social world that only values performative masculine identities. If, as John Tosh argues, masculinity was a social identity 'constructed in three arenas – home, work and all-male association',[26] for much of *Sense and Sensibility* Edward lacks the social status of an adult male. He possesses neither a permanent or temporary home of his own, and 'his mother neither behaved to him so as to make his home comfortable at present, nor to give him any assurance that he might form a home for himself, without strictly attending to her views for his aggrandisement' (24). Nor does Edward pursue a profession, darkly describing himself as an '"idle, helpless being"' and labelling his family's preference for idleness as '"the most advantageous and honourable"' occupation for him (100–01). He also refuses to perform the 'work' of the male heir, living a nomadic existence between London, Plymouth, Sussex and later Devonshire that, in contrast to Willoughby's unshackled pursuit of pleasure, is characterised by loneliness and a sense of personal futility. His mother and sister are relentless in their determination to force him into performing his prescribed role:

> They wanted him to make a fine figure in the world in some manner or other. His mother wished to interest him in political concerns, to get him into parliament, or to see him connected with some of the great men of the day. Mrs John Dashwood wished it likewise; but in the mean while, till one of these superior blessings could be attained, it would have quieted her ambition to see him driving a barouche (17–18).

In contrast to the desires of his family and their value for performance, 'Edward had no turn for great men or barouches. All his wishes centred in domestic comfort and the quiet of a private life' (18).

Austen is particularly attentive to the reputational component of a masculine identity defined by status and display. Edward occupies an inferior status in the opinion of his male relatives. To his brother Robert, who personifies the vacuous performance of fashionable sociability in a manner that exceeds even Willoughby, Edward's inferiority is clear in his ineptness with social performance: 'Edward Ferrars was not recommended to their good opinion by any peculiar graces of person or address.

He was not handsome, and his manners required intimacy to make them pleasing' (17). To Robert, public performer *par excellence*, Edward's '"extreme *gaucherie* which he really believed kept him from mixing in proper society"' results not from any 'natural deficiency' but instead from 'the misfortune of a private education' (235). Robert, by contrast, attributes his assured status to his different education: 'he himself, though probably without any particular, any material superiority by nature, merely from the advantage of a public school, was as well fitted to mix in the world as any other man' (235). Austen, whose childhood home was a private school for boys, distances Edward from the male homosociality and preoccupation with public display she associates with public schooling. John Dashwood also views Edward as his inferior, particularly after he is disinherited: '"Can anything be more galling to the spirit of a man ... than to see his younger brother in possession of an estate which might have been his own? Poor Edward! I feel for him sincerely"' (252). While John may feel compassion for Edward, his remark reflects a loss of status in the estimation of a man who cares for nothing but money.

The Pratt and Steele families in Plymouth, and later the Dashwoods, offer Edward relief from his mother, sister, brother, and their urbane social circle. The question that surrounds Edward throughout *Sense and Sensibility* is whether he will attain the domestic comfort he seeks and needs. His inability to satisfy his family — '"with no inclination for expense, no affection for strangers, no profession, and no assurance"' (89) — tethers him to this liminal position. Unable and unwilling to perform the role of a gentry male heir, Edward is a solitary self in a highly socialised world. He knows that he is incapable of performing for his class:

> I never wish to offend, but I am so foolishly shy, that I often seem negligent, when I am only kept back by my natural awkwardness. I have frequently thought I must have been intended by nature to be fond of low company, I am so little at my ease among strangers of gentility! (93).

Austen is explicit about the effects of Edward's misunderstood and unrecognised model of masculine identity on his wellbeing. It is not only his secret and now regretted engagement to Lucy Steele — itself a result of his social dislocation — that causes his unhappiness and chronic depression, it is also his impossible situation and its relationship to self-fulfilment. Edward truly believes himself to be inferior to his more socially adept male peers: '"Shyness is only the effect of a sense of inferiority in some way or other. If I could persuade myself that my manners were perfectly easy and graceful, I should not be shy"' (93). His low self-esteem is clear in his declaration to Mrs Dashwood that he is determined to raise his sons '"to be as unlike myself as is possible. In feeling, in action, in condition, in every thing"' (101).

The public revelation of Edward's secret engagement to Lucy triggers the rupture needed for him to confront his family and end the stasis that shrouds his existence. His subsequent meeting with his angry mother exposes his independent sense of selfhood and agency in a sharp contrast with Willoughby: "'Edward said very little; but what he did say, was in the most determined manner. Nothing should prevail on him to give up his engagement. He would stand to it, cost him what it might'" (250). Elinor and Marianne reflect on the strength of Edward's integrity, the foundation of his internalised sense of self, despite the high personal costs:

> *They* only knew how little he had to tempt him to be disobedient, and how small was the consolation, beyond the consciousness of doing right, that could remain to him in the loss of friends and fortune. Elinor gloried in his integrity (253).

In *Sense and Sensibility*, Austen locates her modern conception of masculinity in this 'consciousness of doing right'. Edward's self-belief ultimately proves strong enough to resist the extraordinary pressure he faces to adopt a model of masculinity to which he does not subscribe.

Austen presents Mrs Ferrars' subsequent excommunication, first of Edward and then of Robert on the revelation of his elopement with Lucy, as not only cruel but absurd:

> Her family had of late been exceedingly fluctuating. For many years of her life she had had two sons; but the crime and annihilation of Edward a few weeks ago, had robbed her of one; the similar annihilation of Robert had left her for a fortnight without any; and now, by the resuscitation of Edward, she had one again (347).

To Mrs Ferrars and the socio-economic order she symbolises, Edward and Robert are not young men but legal persons capable of being endowed with and therefore denied legal and economic rights. Robert, content to play his prescribed role in this drama, readily accepts his accession to the position of male heir, and Elinor observes 'the happy self-complacency of his manner while enjoying so unfair a division of his mother's love and liberality, to the prejudice of his banished brother, earned only by his own dissipated course of life, and that brother's integrity' (279). Edward, now relieved of the pressure attendant on being the male heir and the economic duress that has dominated his adult life, is liberated to authentically express his own sense of who he is.

The transformation in Edward after his engagement to Elinor is striking: 'He was brought, not from doubt or suspense, but from misery to happiness; – and the change was openly spoken in such a genuine, flowing, grateful cheerfulness, as his friends had never witnessed in him before' (337). Edward's self-realisation through his love for Elinor is also revealed in his refusal to write his mother 'a letter of proper submission' seeking forgiveness for his engagement to Lucy and to confront her in person over his new engagement. Austen rewrites masculinity as an introspective but socially-embedded mode of identity, integral to an alternative model of sociability that focuses on exchange with others rather than self-aggrandisement. In contrast to Edward's hierarchical relationships with Robert and John, he enjoys an equal relationship with Colonel Brandon:

> It would be needless to say, that the gentlemen advanced in the good opinion of each other, as they advanced in each other's acquaintance, for it could not be otherwise. Their resemblance in good principles and good sense, in disposition and manner of thinking, would probably have been sufficient to unite them in friendship, without any other attraction (344).

In his role as a clergyman at Delaford, Edward finds a community that recognises and respects who he is and what he can offer rather than lamenting what he is not:

> if Edward might be judged from the ready discharge of his duties in every particular, from an increasing attachment to his wife and his home, and from the regular cheerfulness of his spirits, he might be supposed no less free from every wish of an exchange (351).

As Edward had told Mrs Dashwood, '"I wish as well as every body else to be perfectly happy; but like every body else it must be in my own way. Greatness will not make me so"' (90).

In *Sense and Sensibility*, Jane Austen debunks stylised literary masculinities through three male protagonists, and demands that her reader embrace the men of 'real Life' in all their unheroic glory. In John Willoughby and Colonel Brandon, Austen overthrows stereotyped literary heroism, and in Edward Ferrars, she presents a nascent vision of masculinity as an individual, internal and authentic gender identity; a prototype for the more psychologically – complex male protagonists of her later novels. In contrast to her determination to debunk literary heroism in *Sense and Sensibility*, in her second published work, *Pride and Prejudice*, Austen creates a male protagonist in Fitzwilliam Darcy who would redefine romantic literary heroism from the Romantic era into the twenty-first century. Austen's dramatic shift suggests that in seeking to overhaul stereotyped literary masculinity in *Sense and Sensibility* — rather an ambitious undertaking for a debut novel — the odds were well and truly stacked against her. Nevertheless, in *Sense and Sensibility*, Austen's piercing critique of the stock masculinities that restrained the development of character, and her advocacy of a model of masculinity that was introspective, authentic, and sociable, forms the foundation of her rewriting of masculinity throughout her career. In *Northanger Abbey* and *Pride and Prejudice*, Austen advances her masculine prototype in Edward Ferrars by exploring the development of male subjectivity through a dialogic relationship to the heroine and the transformative power of romantic love, creating a new vision of literary masculinity that would profoundly influence the courtship romance genre.

2 'I will prove myself a man'
Northanger Abbey

On a walk in Bath with her new friends Henry and Eleanor Tilney, Catherine Morland excitedly anticipates '"something very shocking indeed"' that '"will soon come out in London ... more horrible than anything we have met with yet ... I shall expect murder and every thing of the kind"' (107). Eleanor mistakes Catherine's meaning — the publication of a new Gothic novel — and assumes she is discussing a riot or similar act of public violence. Eleanor hopes that '"proper measures will undoubtedly be taken by government to prevent its coming to effect"' (107). Henry comically elevates his resolution of their misunderstanding to a proof of his manhood:

> I will be noble. I will prove myself a man, no less by the generosity of my soul than the clearness of my head. I have no patience with such of my sex as disdain to let themselves sometimes down to the comprehension of yours (108).

In this exchange, as so often in *Northanger Abbey* (1818), Jane Austen's comedy exposes truths lurking beneath the surface of the witty conversation and sparkling dialogue that brighten this novel. Henry mocks conventional modes of masculinity and the sexual hierarchies that govern polite sociability and courtship rituals. His joke is not on Catherine and Eleanor and their supposedly inferior intellects, but on men whose gender identities are tied to such artificial constructs of masculine superiority and privilege.

Henry Tilney may comically inflate resolving a misunderstanding between Catherine and Eleanor as a proof of manhood, but proving himself 'a man' is precisely what he does in *Northanger Abbey*. He satirises '"such of my sex as disdain to let themselves down to the comprehension of yours"', but through his relationship with Catherine Morland, Henry confronts the danger and corruption of socially-prescribed masculine and feminine gender identities and their reproduction of damaging sexual hierarchies. He may jest about hackneyed gender distinctions in the early days of his romance with Catherine, but in proving himself a man, Henry Tilney changes the very terms on which a masculine identity could be defined.

Henry has perhaps elicited more diverse responses from readers and critics than any of Jane Austen's other male protagonists. He has been cast as 'a male pedagogue in search of female perfection', as a polished bully 'who simply believes that he knows women's minds better than they do', as Austen's 'clever acknowledgment of the feminization of the hero, characteristic of the female gothic', and as 'one of the few Austen heroes invested with his creator's dry humor, flair for words, and ability to mock society'.[1] Such varied interpretations of Henry reflect Austen's diverse and occasionally conflicting agendas in *Northanger Abbey*: to display her talent as an author by parodying the gothic novel and satirising the generic conventions of courtship romance; to advance the novel as a literary form; and to draw the attention of her readers to the dangers presented by everyday English life, particularly for innocent and inexperienced young women. As Jillian Heydt-Stevenson describes it, 'Austen's novel creates a sensation rather like having two tastes on the tongue simultaneously',[2] and Austen deploys Henry to prosecute each of her literary agendas. Readers and critics are left with uncertainty and unease around who he is, and what he represents.

Partial explanations of Henry's character belie his complexity, the depth of his development throughout the novel, and his significance for Austen's rewriting of masculinity. In evaluating Austen's character development in *Northanger Abbey*, the critical focus has been on Catherine's maturation, which has arguably been overstated; as Jan Fergus argues, 'even if Catherine can be said to learn anything from Henry, it does not amount to a moral growth of any kind'.[3] Yet Henry Tilney is the first male protagonist in whom Austen dramatises a psychological change. In contrast to Catherine, his development is fundamentally moral. Henry gradually and reluctantly acknowledges the failure of masculine identities grounded in social performance, reputation and display, embodied in his father and brother. His love for Catherine forces him to confront the inherent deception of masculinities expressed through the public, sociable sphere, and to develop a new conceptualisation of masculinity defined by independence and introspection and measured by authenticity. Critical neglect of Henry's development may result from its subordinated position in the text: his personal growth is tied to the novel's conclusion and almost buried in Austen's satire of the sexual politics of courtship and the conventions of the courtship plot to the very end. Henry's personal transformation through romantic love is nevertheless real; he is a precursor to Austen's more psychologically complex male protagonists in *Pride and Prejudice* and *Persuasion*.

In generic terms, *Northanger Abbey* is often interpreted as Austen's riposte to gothic literature — as matching her critique of sentimental fiction in *Sense and Sensibility* — and the men of the novel are analysed through the lens of the dangerous villain and, to a lesser extent, the sensitive romantic hero. Although gothic literature is an important literary context for *Northanger Abbey*, the stock courtship romance novel is Austen's generic point of departure as she rewrites masculinity through a dialogic process of gender development and formation. The courtship romance genre fictionalised the process by which a young woman identified and accepted a suitable husband, a decision in which she was amply schooled by didactic conduct literature of a moralising stamp addressed to a young female readership. Conduct literature presented a young woman's acceptance of an appropriate husband as a personal duty that would determine not only her individual happiness, but also her capacity to fulfil her social and spiritual roles as a moralising influence within the family and society. As Nancy Armstrong and Leonard Tennenhouse argue, conduct literature was highly influential in creating and regulating desire through culturally-approved models of the desirable woman.[4] Although conduct literature advised a young woman to closely scrutinise male behaviour, her focus on the male was to determine whether he would make a suitable husband, not to fulfil her own desires. Indeed, conduct literature exclusively presented the male as the subject of desire and instructed young women in the arts of presenting themselves as desirably as possible to potential suitors.

By dramatising courtship from the perspective of young women, the courtship romance novel could radically alter the sexual politics of courtship prescribed in conduct literature by positioning the heroine as an agent of desire. The heroine was authorised to scrutinise, critique and evaluate the men she encountered by her need to navigate an economic order that promoted marriage for financial security and a social climate that valued companionate marriage as the best guarantee of individual, familial and social harmony.[5] Privileging the narrative perspective of a single young woman and her evaluation of the desirability — or, more often, the undesirability — of potential suitors, the courtship romance genre valorised female desire and configured the male as a desirable or undesirable object to the heroine. The heroine's judgment of the men around her formed the structural foundation of the narrative, empowering women writers of courtship romance novels to critique masculine identities and offer a uniquely feminine perspective within public debate over the desirable man.[6]

In *Northanger Abbey*, Jane Austen exploits the critical potential of the courtship romance heroine to scrutinise, evaluate, reject and approve different masculine identities through Catherine Morland's appraisal of various suitors. Austen reverses conventional power relationships within courtship, constructing Catherine as an agent of desire and Henry as the object of her relentless pursuit. Austen's comic characterisation of both her leading protagonists shrouds the radicalism of Catherine's agency and Henry's submission to her. Indeed, Henry and Catherine are Austen's most comic protagonists. In her other novels, Austen's protagonists are serious characters and her humour is supplied by the peripheral cast; in *Northanger Abbey* it is the two leads who take the comic roles.[7] Austen layers their comic characterisation to advance her gendered critique:

on one level, they both possess a highly-developed sense of humour about themselves and about each other, which dominates their conversations in Bath; on another, they are tools through which Austen satirises the forms, practices and gendered roles of polite sociability and conventional courtship.

Austen's satire of courtship particularly targets John Gregory's *Legacy to his Daughters* (1774), a popular conduct book that purported to instruct young women in the performance of their roles as modest, self-effacing objects of desire, passively waiting to be courted and married in the context of polite sociability.[8] Lampooning *Legacy to his Daughters* in *Northanger Abbey*, Austen followed Mary Wollstonecraft's attack on Gregory in *A Vindication of the Rights of Woman* (1792), in which she derided his insistence on the sexual difference between men and women and his educational plan as stunting women's development, rendering them dependent on men and unfit for social and national service.[9] The mutual concern of *Rights of Woman* and *Northanger Abbey* with targeting *Legacy to his Daughters* suggests the possibility that Austen was directly influenced by Wollstonecraft in writing this novel. As Diane Hoeveler notes, *Northanger Abbey* 'fictionalizes the major points of Wollstonecraft's treatise' to demonstrate 'that women who are given inadequate educations will be victims of their own folly as well as of masculine hubris, lust, and greed'.[10] Austen's engagement with Wollstonecraft's ideas in *Rights of Woman* extends beyond her characterisation of Catherine, to expose the pernicious effects of sexual hierarchies for both women and men.

From her opening chapter, Austen positions Catherine as a literary heroine in search of a husband: 'when a young lady is to be a heroine [...] Something must and will happen to throw a hero in her way' (18). Anticipating the reader's expectation that Catherine will encounter and evaluate potential suitors, Austen repeatedly draws the reader's attention to this literary device. During Catherine's drive with John Thorpe, Austen constructs female desire as the ultimate arbiter of the desirable man, yet conceals this role reversal through comic understatement and by emphasising Catherine's naivety:

> Little as Catherine was in the habit of judging for herself, and un-
> fixed as were her general notions of what men ought to be, she could
> not entirely repress a doubt, while she bore with the effusions of his
> endless conceit, of his being altogether completely agreeable (65).

Austen frames Catherine as a naive and guileless heroine, deflecting her critical gaze and obsession with judging the men around her, when in reality Catherine thinks of little else.

Catherine immediately identifies Henry Tilney as both a desirable man and a suitable husband and unremittingly pursues him — at times physically chasing him — through the social spaces and public streets of Bath. Austen establishes Henry's desirability through his response to Catherine's determined agency: he is content to allow her to pursue him and does not need to control the relationship. Henry does not subscribe to the dominant role that, as the male, he is prescribed within the typical sexual politics of courtship. Indeed, he explicitly satirises this role on their first meeting:

> I have hitherto been very remiss, madam, in the proper attentions of a partner here; I have not yet asked you how long you have been in Bath; whether you were ever here before; whether you have been at the Upper Rooms, the theatre, and the concert; and how you like the place altogether (25).

He then, 'forming his features into a set smile, and affectedly softening his voice' (26), humorously asks Catherine this series of questions for her entertainment. Henry's suggestion that she should describe him in her journal as '"a queer, half-witted man who would make me dance with him, and distressed me by his nonsense"' (26) — that she should lampoon him — indicates his resistance to the sexual hierarchy of their social environment and its prescriptive terms for their relationship. As Michael Kramp argues, 'Henry recognizes the artifice involved in the genteel code of manners that accompanies this archaic ideal of male sexuality'.[11] Henry's gender identity is plainly not sustained by the social performance of masculine privilege.

Catherine is hooked. She leaves the ball 'with a strong inclination for continuing the acquaintance' (29), and Austen satirically speculates on her thoughts and dreams to consolidate her reversal of the sexual politics of desire:

> Whether she thought of him so much, while she drank her warm wine and water, and prepared herself for bed, as to dream of him when there, cannot be ascertained; but I hope it was no more than in a slight slumber, or a morning doze at most; for if it be true, as a celebrated writer has maintained, that no young lady can be justified in falling in love before the gentleman's love is declared, it must be very improper that a young lady should dream of a gentleman before the gentleman is first known to have dreamt of her (29).

Austen footnotes her reference to 'a celebrated writer' as Samuel Richardson and an essay published in *The Rambler* — 'That a young lady should be in love, and the love of the young gentleman undeclared, is an heterodoxy which prudence, and even policy, must not allow'[12] — anchoring her satire on the gendering of romantic love and courtship rituals to the eighteenth-century origins of the marriage plot.

Throughout their courtship, Austen constructs Catherine as an erotic subject in pursuit of Henry through the gaze, the language, and the enactment of desire.[13] Catherine's eyes constantly seek him out in the public places of Bath, including the Pump-room, the assembly and the theatre. When she finally tracks him down at the next ball, it is unsurprising that John Thorpe's conversation does not 'interest her so much as to prevent her looking very often towards that part of the room where she had left Mr. Tilney' (54). Hampered in her pursuit of Henry by her earlier agreement to dance with John, Catherine concludes that 'to go previously engaged to a ball, does not necessarily increase either the dignity or enjoyment of a young lady' (54). At her next opportunity, she is racked with anxiety that John will ask her to dance again — 'Every young lady may feel for my heroine at this critical moment, for every young lady has at some time or other known the same agitation' (72) — and delights in successfully manipulating the social codes of the ballroom to attract Henry:

> With what sparkling eyes and ready motion she granted his request, and with how pleasing a flutter of heart she went with him to the set, may be easily imagined ... it did not appear to her that life could supply any greater felicity (73).

Thorpe's incessant attempts to thwart Catherine paradoxically offer her more opportunities to expose her desire for Henry. When Thorpe deceives her into driving with him rather than walking with the Tilneys, she explains the mistake: '"I have been quite wild to speak to you, and make my apologies ... if Mr Thorpe had only stopped, I would have jumped out and run after you"' (89). Catherine's imagined pursuit of Henry soon becomes reality when Thorpe again interferes with her plans: she pushes through a crowded public assembly, runs down the street, bursts through Henry's front door, and runs up the stairs, declaring '"I did not care what you thought of me. – I would not stay for the servant"' (97).

Conversations shared by Catherine and Henry, which she occasionally finds perplexing, have led to interpretations of Henry as Catherine's mentor or teacher, as 'the archetypal male pedagogue' who 'is drawn to Catherine for her conditioned deficiencies', and as, at worst, 'indistinguishable from his father'.[14] These conversations, however, advance Austen's satire of conventional courtship and the domineering, self-serving masculinity it prescribes:

> Where people wish to attach, they should always be ignorant. To come with a well-informed mind, is to come with an inability of administering to the vanity of others, which a sensible person would always wish to avoid. A woman especially, if she have the misfortune of knowing any thing, should conceal it as well as she can (106).

Austen is clearly satirising *Legacy to his Daughters*:

> If you happen to have any learning, keep it a profound secret, espe-
> cially from the men, who generally look with a jealous and malig-
> nant eye on a woman of great parts, and a cultivated understanding.
> A man of real genius and candour is far superior to this meanness.
> But such a one will seldom fall in your way.[15]

Austen's satire continues:

> The advantages of natural folly in a beautiful girl have been already
> set forth by the capital pen of a sister author; – and to her treatment
> of the subject I will only add in justice to men, that though to the
> larger and more trifling part of the sex, imbecility in females is a
> great enhancement of their personal charms, there is a portion of
> them too reasonable and too well informed themselves to desire any
> thing more in woman than ignorance. Catherine did not know her
> own advantages – did not know that a good-looking girl, with an
> affectionate heart and a very ignorant mind, cannot fail of attract-
> ing ... (106).

Like Wollstonecraft before her, Austen's target is not Catherine and
young women like her, but men who desire such women.

Austen's satire of Henry — through his lectures on the picturesque, the
enclosure of forests and the machinations of government — strategically
positions him as a foil to men whose gender identities are sustained by
flawed conceptions of masculine privilege and authority and reliant on
female subordination. Henry's conversations with Catherine reveal his
interest in engaging her intellectually and their shared and divergent
views on novels, reading, history and education. This behaviour is at
odds with his later joking remarks about female intelligence, for which
Eleanor rebukes him: "'you may as well make Miss Moreland understand yourself – unless you mean to have her think you intolerably rude
to your sister, and a great brute in your opinion of women in general'"
(108). Catherine openly disagrees with him, establishing a platform of
resistance to Henry's judgment that later serves her well in identifying
dangerous masculinity. On one level Austen frames their relationship
as mentor and gullible student, but on another specifically draws the
reader's attention to Henry's very fallibility:

> It was no effort to Catherine to believe that Henry Tilney could
> never be wrong. His manner might sometimes surprize, but his
> meaning must always be just: – and what she did not understand,
> she was almost as ready to admire, as what she did (109).

Austen's caveat — 'almost' — is significant. It becomes increasingly apparent that when it comes to judging men, Catherine can see what Henry cannot and insists on her own — correct — judgment.

Henry Tilney is not the only man to pass under Catherine's critical eye during her residence in Bath. John Thorpe, General Tilney and Captain Tilney represent models of masculinity associated with 'politeness', an ideal that had, by the time Austen sold her novel to Crosby in 1803, endured sustained public attack. Indeed, Austen's reference to the changing 'manners, books and opinions' (13) in her authorial advertisement to the posthumously published *Northanger Abbey* may have alluded to changes in public discourse concerning male refinement in the Romantic period, which left polite masculinity firmly in the eighteenth century. Polished, urbane and versed in the political, commercial and cultural affairs of the day, in the eighteenth century the ideal of the polite man was extolled as a modern masculinity for a newly civilised English nation.[16] Men could obtain instruction in developing a polite persona through print culture, particularly periodicals such as *The Spectator*,[17] and in conduct literature for men, which emphasised the synthesis of refined conversation and manners with moral integrity, civility and consideration of others. John Harris's *Essay on Politeness* (1775) defined politeness as:

> that temper of mind and tenour of conduct which make persons easy in their behaviour, conciliating in their affection and promoting every one's benefit; that renders reproof palatable, obligation a pleasure, and kind offices never to be slighted or forgotten.[18]

The polite man was inherently sociable, joining other like-minded men in the urban spaces of the coffee-house, club and theatre for 'the informal, thoughtful and genuine sociability central to achieving new standards of "polite" conduct'.[19]

Women had a specific, narrowly-defined role within polite discourse as both the promoters and the beneficiaries of polite masculinity. The polite persona demanded that men be respectful and considerate in their treatment of women, and could not be achieved without their company and conversation. As James Forrester asserted in *The Polite Philosopher* (1734), a conduct book reprinted and extracted countless times throughout the eighteenth century:

> It is the conversation of Women that gives a proper Bias to our inclinations, and, by abating the Ferocity of our passions, engages us to that Gentleness of deportment, which we stile Humanity. The Tenderness we have for them softens the ruggedness of our own nature.[20]

Women ostensibly saved men, and themselves, from raw, aggressive and dangerous masculinity.

In *Northanger Abbey*, Jane Austen rejects politeness as either a masculine ideal or a stable model of masculine identity. Her scepticism is exposed in her early attack on *The Spectator*, which she describes as:

> so often consisting in the statement of improbable circumstances, unnatural characters, and topics of conversation, which no longer concern any one living; and their language, too, frequently so coarse as to give no very favourable idea of the age that could endure it (37).

Twisting critical language typically targeted at novels — 'improbable circumstances, unnatural characters and topics of conversation' — against the flagship periodical of polite masculinity and the newly 'civilised' public sphere,[21] Austen flags her blistering attack on male refinement and its thin relationship to civilisation. John Thorpe, Captain Tilney and General Tilney illustrate, in different ways, the inadequacies of politeness and the dangers it presents to women in courtship and marriage. Where in *Sense and Sensibility* Austen challenges stylised male characterisation, in *Northanger Abbey* she exploits male stereotypes associated with the gothic villain, the rake and the boor to reveal their inherent violence against women.

John Thorpe, a young man from a middle-class family with a comfortable income and a yearning for social advancement, has attempted and failed to cultivate refined masculinity as a path to marriage for wealth and acceptance in higher social echelons. Despite having three sisters to train him, Thorpe wholly misunderstands polite sociability: his manners are confused; he is publicly rude to his mother and sisters; and his conversations with Catherine concern entirely homosocial pursuits, including horses, dogs, hunting, private drinking parties at Oxford, and the objectification of other women. Austen distinguishes Thorpe's egotism and manner from politeness: 'all the rest of his conversation, or rather talk, began and ended with himself and his own concerns' (64). Where in Thorpe Austen represents masculine failure to cultivate politeness, in Captain Tilney she illustrates the slippage between politeness, gallantry and seduction. The Captain's conversation with Isabella Thorpe is constituted by empty flattery and compliment as he seeks to win her affections for his own gratification, and their ensuing liaison results in the severance of her engagement to James Morland. Isabella's willing participation in Captain Tilney's gallantry implies that she is invulnerable to such men, but Catherine's initial inability to identify his deception exposes the dangers of male refinement for inexperienced and trusting young women. General Tilney, who has cultivated a refined persona to gain access to polite sociability and court wealthy partners for his children, represents the third and most insidious failure of polite masculinity. Believing Catherine an heiress, he treats her with a degree of politeness that she finds excessive and uncomfortable: 'in spite of their father's great civilities to her – in spite of his thanks, invitations, and compliments – it had been a release to get away from him' (123). The General's Chesterfieldian politeness is designed to promote self-interest through superficial refinement and empty gestures.

Austen shifts her critique of masculinity from the venues of polite sociability to the domestic space of the home through Catherine's move from Bath to Northanger Abbey. Parodying Catherine as a literary heroine and General Tilney as a gothic villain, Austen shifts Catherine's critical gaze shifts from Henry to his father to explore relationships between masculine identity, authority and domesticity.[22] Austen's portrayal of General Tilney as the patriarchal English gentleman — socially acceptable despite his oppression of his family, his mercenary values, and his callous behaviour to the women under his protection — is equally as dangerous as the mythic European villains of gothic romance.[23] Despite her judgment being warped by her reading of Gothic fiction and Henry's mocking encouragement, Catherine's ready identification of dangerous masculinity serves her well in the domestic environment. It is a skill Henry is yet to learn.

From Catherine's arrival at Northanger Abbey, Austen extends General Tilney's performative approach to masculinity beyond polite sociability to his family and his home. His domestic values lie in his patriarchal role as a landholder, whose house guarantees him wealth and social position, rather than in the modern conception of 'domesticity' defined by John Tosh as 'not just a pattern of residence or a web of obligations, but a profound attachment: a state of mind as well as a physical orientation'.[24] General Tilney controls every aspect of the household; as Eleanor later comments to Catherine, '"you must have been long enough in this house to see that I am but a nominal mistress of it, that my real power is nothing"' (210). Austen reveals the General's mercantile values as he escorts Catherine through the house and grounds, his empty politeness reflected in the style and furnishing of Northanger Abbey. His incessant discussion of the size of the rooms, the modernity of the furnishings and their cost, and his own 'improving' role, together with his nauseatingly false modesty and self-satisfaction in impressing Catherine, reveal his house to be a vehicle for display rather than a home to be shared with his children. The link between General Tilney's masculine identity and his exercise of authority is inscribed in his treatment of his daughter, whose personality and voice he stifles, whose opinion is deemed irrelevant in the pursuit of his own plans, and who is summoned and sent to do his bidding.

Catherine's observations of General Tilney's mental unease and tyrannical approach to family life found her suspicion of his involvement in his wife's death. Henry's speech to Catherine after she reveals her suspicions is often interpreted as encapsulating his essential rationality and his role of mentor.[25] Yet here Austen reveals the depth of Henry's belief in the ideology of the public sphere and its links to civilisation and government, the kind of intercourse practiced by 'polite' men in the venues of public sociability and recorded in the pages of *The Spectator*:

> Dear Miss Morland, consider the dreadful nature of the suspicions you have entertained. What have you been judging from? Remembering the country and the age in which we live. Remember that we are English, that we are Christians. Consult your own understanding, your own sense of the probable, your own observation of what is passing around you – Does our education prepare us for such atrocities? Do our laws connive at them? Could they be perpetrated without being known, in a country like this, where social and literary intercourse is on such a footing; where every man is surrounded by a neighbourhood of voluntary spies, and where roads and newspapers lay every thing open? (186).

Henry's speech reveals much more about his own lack of judgment than Catherine's. Henry remains personally invested in an ideology of civilisation and refinement that supports the martial ambitions of men like John Thorpe, Captain Tilney and General Tilney. Although his faith in the power of public institutions to guarantee civility, stability and justice may be commendable, Henry naively assumes that other men, including his father and brother, execute public responsibilities and private duties with his own sense of goodwill.

Austen soon reveals that Henry's faith in other men is misplaced, with the news that James Morland has severed his engagement to Isabella Thorpe because of her liaison with Captain Tilney. In Bath, Henry resisted Catherine urging him to counsel Captain Tilney about the pain he was inflicting on James and — as she thought — himself, declaring that James had nothing to fear from his brother, only from his fiancée, and insisting that Captain Tilney '"knows what he is about, and must be his own master"' (142). When Catherine receives her letter from James, she specifically recalls Henry's incorrect judgment: '"when we talked about it in Bath, you little thought of its ending so"'. Henry responds only by saying, '"I hope he has not had any material share in bringing on Mr Morland's disappointment"' (192), deflecting self-reflection and directing his wit and ire at Isabella instead. Henry again condones his brother's behaviour, a judgment Catherine resists:

> I must say I do not like him at all. Though it has turned out so well for us, I do not like him at all ... suppose he had made her very much in love with him? ... It is very right that you should stand by your brother (204–05).

Catherine sees what Henry still cannot.

Ultimately, however, Henry awakens to his father's true character, the actions of which he is capable, and the polite persona he has cultivated as a subterfuge. Austen links General Tilney's 'deception' regarding Catherine's status as an heiress to his connection to John Thorpe, a relationship established in the signature venues of polite sociability, the terms of which are set by its values. Meeting in the Bedford coffee-house, an all-male venue in Covent Garden, at the theatre in Bath, and later by chance in London, it is private conversations between these men in public spaces that prompt both Catherine's invitation to Northanger Abbey and her expulsion from it. Thorpe, 'most happy to be on speaking terms with a man of General Tilney's importance', amplifies Catherine's wealth and social status to gratify his own vanity, and later casts the Morlands as 'a forward, bragging, scheming race' (228–30) as vengeance for the breakdown in the relationship between the two families. Catherine becomes a pawn in a competitive world of male brinkmanship. Austen reveals the polite masculinity championed by *The Spectator* and presumed by conduct literature such as *Legacy to his Daughters* as misogyny by another name. She exposes the openness and transparency of the public sphere Henry trumpets as a sham, vulnerable to the machinations of men like General Tilney and John Thorpe, for whom women are economic property to be exchanged, collateral damage in the battle of macho one-upmanship in which they are embroiled.

Henry's awakening to his father's real character triggers his rejection of performative masculine identities and his development instead of an independent, internalised sense of self founded on his love for Catherine and their domestic life together. Throughout *Northanger Abbey* Henry's lack of independence from his father means that like Edward Ferrars before him he is not, to use John Tosh's phrase, 'an adult, fully masculine person'.[26] Despite his financial independence — he has his own home, a secure fortune, and a profession that provides 'an income of independence and comfort' (245) — Henry lacks moral independence: 'the condition in which self-mastery, conscience and individual responsibility could be exercised'.[27] At twenty six and financially secure, Henry remains under the General's control: he visits Bath to find his father accommodation, his stay there is determined by his father's wishes, the General continues his command even in Henry's own home at Woodston, and he is instructed by his father first to court and then to abandon Catherine.

When General Tilney expels Catherine from Northanger Abbey, Henry can no longer remain under the control of a man of such repugnant and dangerous values and behaviour. In turmoil on his arrival at Fullerton, Austen recalls Henry's encounter with Catherine at the Abbey: the 'embarrassment of real sensibility' (225) as he apologises for his appearance at Fullerton, and his blush 'for the narrow-minded counsel which he was obliged to expose' (230), echo Catherine's own shame and embarrassment. Austen allows her heroine 'a triumphant delight' when she hears 'enough to feel, that in suspecting General Tilney of either murdering or shutting up his wife, she had scarcely sinned against his character, or magnified his cruelty' (230). Henry's response to 'hearing how Catherine had been treated ... had been open and bold' and he resolves to pursue her despite his father's disapproval. Henry was 'sustained in his purpose by a conviction of its justice' and:

> felt himself bound as much in honour as in affection to Miss Morland, and believing that heart to be his own ... no unworthy retraction of a tacit consent, no reversing decree of unjustifiable anger, could shake his fidelity, or influence the resolutions it prompted (231).

Although Kramp favourably contrasts Henry's rational approach to romantic love with 'unmanaged males' who are 'vulnerable to the irrational power of amorous emotions',[28] it is precisely because of his love for Catherine and not despite it that Henry is able to break from his father and forge an independent adult male identity. Drawing on the language of justice, honour and fidelity, Austen grounds Henry's identity in the qualities that ideally guarantee the public sphere, relocating them to the authentic, internalised male self secured by romantic love. Austen's concluding statement underlines the significance of Henry's transformation and severance from his father: 'I leave it to be settled by whomsoever it may concern, whether the tendency of this work be altogether to recommend parental tyranny, or reward filial disobedience' (235).

In proving himself 'a man', Henry Tilney not only discards masculine 'ideals' reflected in his father and brother, but also develops a new definition of masculine identity that is private, internal and authentic. Austen links Henry's transformation to his pursuit of a companionate marriage with Catherine that complements her strong sense of agency and desire. In the final chapter of *Northanger Abbey*, Austen returns to her satire and reversal of the sexual politics of courtship as it is Catherine — 'the anxious, agitated, happy, feverish Catherine' — whose passion takes the lead (226). Henry is passive even in his proposal — 'that heart was solicited, which, perhaps, they pretty equally knew was already entirely his own' — and Austen ascribes his love for her to his realisation that she was attracted to him:

> though Henry was now sincerely attached to her, though he felt and delighted in all the excellencies of her character and truly loved her society, I must confess that his affection originated in nothing better than gratitude, or, in other words, that a persuasion of her partiality for him had been the only cause of giving her a serious thought (227).

Austen ridicules prescriptive approaches to desire, love and romance in a parting blow against *Legacy to his Daughters*:

> Some agreeable qualities recommend a gentleman to your common good liking and friendship. In the course of his acquaintance, he contracts an attachment to you. When you perceive it, it excites your gratitude; this gratitude rises into a preference, and this preference perhaps at last advances to some degree of attachment.[29]

Austen's narrator underscores her satiric portrayal of courtship and inversion of the sexual politics of desire: 'It is a new circumstance in romance, I acknowledge, and dreadfully derogatory of an heroine's dignity; but if it be as new in common life, the credit of a wild imagination will at least be all my own' (227).

Jane Austen's famous defence of the novel — that literary form in which 'the greatest powers of the mind are displayed, in which the most thorough knowledge of human nature, the happiest delineation of its varieties, the liveliest effusions of wit and humour are conveyed in the best chosen language' (37) — resonates as she rewrites masculinity in *Northanger Abbey*. As Henry Tilney and Catherine Morland are 'hastening together to perfect felicity' (233), Austen satirises prescriptive masculine and feminine roles regulating desire, romance and courtship. She exposes the duplicity, corruption and brinkmanship that lie at the heart of the public sphere and the masculine 'ideals' it celebrates. In charting Henry's development to manhood, Austen offers an alternative definition of masculinity: an internalised, individual and authentic identity that enables respectful, equal relationships with women of which his father and brother are wholly incapable. By consulting 'her own understanding', Catherine, however unconsciously, pushes Henry to develop a masculine identity that, freed from the need to public perform a sexual hierarchy, complements her determined agency. Austen's dramatisation of the romance between Catherine and Henry in *Northanger Abbey* is a comic preface to the dialogic process of masculine and feminine gender formation she pursues with greater depth and complexity in *Pride and Prejudice*.

3 'A man violently in love'

Pride and Prejudice

When Jane Austen published *Pride and Prejudice* in January 1813, she knew she had created something special. The letters she wrote in the six months after her 'own darling Child' entered the world,[1] which Cassandra left comparatively intact, reveal an excitement about the publication of *Pride and Prejudice* that is unmatched for any of her other novels. Austen's elation illuminates her identity as a professional author as she dwells on the details of the novel's publication: the distribution of the earliest sets of volumes, advertisements in the newspaper press, the price of the work, and typographical issues in the printing. Although Austen appears self-critical, famously describing *Pride and Prejudice* as 'rather too light & bright & sparkling',[2] her authorial pride is clearly exposed in the tension between her commitment to anonymity and her desire for acclaim. Her authorship of the novel she describes as 'such a Work in the World!'[3] publicly shrouded in secrecy, Austen is eager for all the private praise she can get, writing to Cassandra: 'I am much obliged to you all for your praise' and later, 'I am exceedingly pleased that you can say what you do, after having gone thro' the whole work – & Fanny's praise is very gratifying'.[4] Austen's response to her brother Henry's public revelation of her authorship registers both mortification and delight:

> Henry heard P. & P. warmly praised in Scotland, by Lady Robt Kerr & another Lady; – & what does he do in the warmth of his Brotherly vanity & Love, but immediately tell them who wrote it! – A Thing once set going in that way – one knows how it spreads! – and he, dear Creature, has set it going so much more than once. I know it is all done from affection & partiality.[5]

Austen's transcription of Lady Robert Kerr's praise in her 'Opinions of *Mansfield Park*', however, suggests that she later exploited this connection for her own gratification.

Austen's correspondence regarding *Pride and Prejudice* is the only surviving source in which she comments on her characters beyond the scope of the novels themselves. Her letters reveal the strength of her personal investment in the people she created. On reading aloud the first set of volumes to arrive at Chawton, she records her neighbour

Miss Benn's amusement: '*that* she c^d not help you know, with two such people to lead the way; but she really does seem to admire Elizabeth. I must confess that *I* think her as delightful a creature as ever appeared in print, & how I shall be able to tolerate those who do not like *her* at least, I do not know'.[6] Austen reveals not only her admiration for Elizabeth Bennet, but also how she saw her male protagonist. Austen's emphasis — '*her* at least' — reveals a suspicion or concern that her readers may not 'like' *him*: that they might prefer Elizabeth to Darcy, fail to value and appreciate him in the way Austen clearly does, or misunderstand or actively resist him. Austen's own interpretation of Fitzwilliam Darcy is revealed in a letter from London the following May: 'We have been both to the Exhibition & Sir J. Reynolds', – and I am disappointed, for there was nothing like Mrs D. at either. – I can only imagine that Mr D. prizes any Picture of her too much to like it should be exposed to the public eye. – I can imagine he w^d have that sort [of *omitted*] feeling – that mixture of Love, Pride & Delicacy'.[7]

With the benefit of two hundred years of hindsight, it is apparent that Jane Austen need not have been concerned about the public reception of her stellar male protagonist. Her description of Darcy as possessing 'that mixture of Love, Pride & Delicacy' captures his psychological complexity and its inextricable connection to his consuming love for Elizabeth Bennet. For most of *Pride and Prejudice* Darcy is, as Austen describes him late in the novel, 'a man violently in love' (346). He is attracted to Elizabeth from chapter six and his love for her motivates virtually all his behaviour throughout the novel. Although recent accounts of Darcy emphasise his eroticism, particularly in the wake of screen adaptations privileging that aspect of his characterisation,[8] Austen's creation of Darcy as an eroticised masculine ideal is more than matched by her exploration of the transformative power of romantic love on the male self. An ingenious combination of psychological depth with a passion for the woman he loves that threatens to engulf him, Darcy is a remarkable literary creation who has driven the enduring popularity of *Pride and Prejudice*, and arguably of Austen herself. In writing Fitzwilliam Darcy in 1813, Austen profoundly influenced the literary men that women writers would create throughout the nineteenth century, including Emily Brontë's Heathcliff, Charlotte Brontë's Rochester, Elizabeth Gaskell's Thornton and George Eliot's Lydgate, leaving a stamp on the courtship romance genre that resonates in the modern era.[9]

Nevertheless, Austen clearly experienced at least some anxiety about what her readers would make of Darcy. He represents both a technical innovation and an ideological advancement in literary masculinity and his originality may account for Austen's concern regarding his reception. Darcy is Austen's first male protagonist to embody the interiority, consciousness and layering of characterisation that emerged in the fiction of the Romantic era; the first male protagonist through whom Austen interrogates the male self as a subject in his own right; and her only male protagonist to consciously change himself for the woman he loves. In Darcy, Austen charts a psychological transformation through the power of romantic love, as he develops a wholly new conception of masculine identity. His change is critical to the essential drama and narrative structure of the novel. Furthermore, despite his status as a beacon of gentry masculinity, he consciously changes himself for the sole purpose of becoming desirable to a woman who is the very embodiment of Romantic feminine rationality, individualism and agency.

In *Pride and Prejudice*, Austen changes the terms of her engagement with the courtship romance genre to succeed with this ambitious literary project. Leaving behind her critique of eighteenth-century fictional genres that framed her rewriting of masculinity in *Sense and Sensibility* and *Northanger Abbey*, in *Pride and Prejudice* she explores the power of the courtship romance genre to rewrite masculinity and femininity through a dialogic process of gender formation. Elizabeth and Darcy and the complicated relationship between them dominate *Pride and Prejudice* in a way that is unmatched by the central couples in Austen's other works. They command the page in a way that leaves the peripheral characters of this novel much less developed than their counterparts in *Sense and Sensibility*, *Mansfield Park* and *Emma*. Austen's almost exclusive focus on the romance of her dual protagonists also distances their relationship from the social and political contexts that influence both her earlier and her later novels. Across the spectrum of Austen's work, *Pride and Prejudice* represents the courtship romance plot in its purest form.

Austen herself recognised this aspect of the novel when she described it as 'rather too light & bright & sparkling'.[10] Its fairy-tale quality has enabled it to be endlessly adapted across time, place and textual form. Despite its ostensible timelessness, however, Austen anchors *Pride and Prejudice* within a Romantic literary and cultural context that is critical to the dialectical relationship she constructs between masculinity and femininity.[11] Darcy, who is '"always buying books"', remarks that he '"cannot comprehend the neglect of a family library in such days as these"' (38), locating the novel within a vibrant and contemporary literary culture. Elizabeth's planned tour to the Lakes with the Gardiners, only later truncated to Derbyshire, implicitly references Wordsworth and Coleridge, and links her to the appreciation of nature central to the Romantic movement and enabled by a burgeoning domestic tourism market. In Elizabeth's exclamation '"What are men to rocks and mountains?"' (152), Austen both exploits Romantic ideology to register her heroine's disenchantment with the men who surround her — the arrogant and interfering Darcy, the weak Bingley, the unctuous Collins and the mercenary Wickham — and satirises its promise of self-fulfilment through an emotive response to nature.

Austen forecasts an alternative, though no less Romantic, vision for the realisation of the individual self. The 'two such people' who 'lead the way' are, of all Austen's characters, the most individualistic and the most sceptical of the forms and practices that dictate polite sociability. Austen questions whether and how Elizabeth and Darcy can achieve personal fulfilment within a social context they each find so odious. Her solution lies not in the realisation of the individual self through solitary reflection or the emotions excited by the natural sublime, but instead in the powerful effects of romantic love. Austen explores the consequences of romantic love for the male and female self respectively, locating the process of gender formation at the heart of the novel's trajectory and staking a claim for the courtship romance as a key genre of Romanticism.

Austen's development of innovative narrative techniques in *Pride and Prejudice* draws out the depth and complexity of her male protagonist and projects the courtship romance into Romantic literary culture. In the first half of the novel, Austen's narrative focus frequently roams away from Elizabeth to offer the reader an omniscient perspective on Darcy. Austen exploits this narrative freedom through free indirect discourse, dialogue and focalisation to endow Darcy with his own narrative point of view. Her split narrative perspective between Elizabeth and Darcy creates a dissonance between the heroine and a critically-engaged reader, who knows more about Darcy than Elizabeth does, to whom alternative interpretations of his behaviour are available, and who can see the unfolding events through his eyes. The reader's glimpses of Darcy's interiority are a remarkable exception in the work of a writer who, as E. J. Clery notes, generally 'denies direct access to the unspoken thoughts and views of her heroes'.[12] The effectiveness of Austen's strategies depends, however, on the acuity of her reader. Austen's expectations of her readers are illuminated by her famous remark on the publication of *Pride and Prejudice* that '"I do not write for such dull Elves" "As have not a great deal of Ingenuity themselves"'.[13] Austen's nuanced and sophisticated textual representation of masculinity in this novel reflects her expectations of 'a growing phalanx of clever, curious and "judicious" readers whose taste for more complex literary fare has been nurtured since childhood'.[14]

Austen focuses Darcy's narrative perspective exclusively on revealing to the reader his growing attraction to and love for Elizabeth Bennet and the torment it costs him. The glimpses she offers the reader into his interiority reveal him to be consumed by his fascination with and desire for the heroine, as we see him fall further and further in love. For Darcy, falling in love with Elizabeth is far from a welcome experience. He becomes a site of contest between two alternative and competing masculine identities. His individualism, highly introspective personality and self-containment, which are enhanced by Austen's strategies for revealing his interiority and psychological complexity, align him with a masculine identity that is grounded in a sense of individual, internalised subjectivity and selfhood. Yet the pride that dominates his way of thinking about himself and others signifies his ongoing investment in a masculinity defined externally by public reputation. Darcy may appear intellectually and emotionally detached from the people and society around him, but how he sees himself as a man is dominated by status, wealth, codes of social propriety and above all reputation, the lynchpins of an adult male identity defined by social performance rather than an internalised sense of self.

Austen reveals Darcy's split masculine identity through his perennially contradictory opinions and behaviour. He apparently values fashionable sociability and social propriety, criticising the Meryton assembly as 'a collection of people in whom there was little beauty and no fashion, for none of whom he had felt the smallest interest, and from none received either attention or pleasure' (18), but refuses to participate in either dancing or conversation, the signature graces of polite sociability for a single man of his social class. His relationships with Lady Catherine de Bourgh and Caroline Bingley, representatives of the socio-economic establishment and the fashionable world, are ambivalent and occasionally hostile. Darcy knows that both these women view him as a marriage prospect — Lady Catherine for her daughter and Caroline for herself — and they assume their shared values for wealth and status will dictate his marital choice. Darcy treats these women at turns with respect and disdain, mirroring his own internal conflict between a gender identity defined by social performance and the appeal of an authentic, internalised male subjectivity to which he is more suited. Darcy appears to spurn the opinions of others, yet performs two of the most damaging acts in the novel — refusing to publicise the truth about George Wickham, and separating Charles Bingley from Jane Bennet — solely to protect status and reputation.

For Darcy, falling in love with Elizabeth intensifies the conflict between these two mutually-exclusive approaches to masculine identity. Austen's focalisation through Darcy's erotic gaze as he is increasingly drawn to her exposes the battle between his conscious pride and the attraction of a woman whose agency lies beyond her sexualised role within polite sociability:

> Mr. Darcy had at first scarcely allowed her to be pretty; he had looked at her without admiration at the ball; and when they next met, he looked at her only to criticise. But no sooner had he made it clear to himself and his friends that she had hardly a good feature in her face, than he began to find it was rendered uncommonly intelligent by the beautiful expression of her dark eyes. To this discovery succeeded some others equally mortifying. Though he had

detected with a critical eye more than one failure of perfect symmetry in her form, he was forced to acknowledge that her figure to be light and pleasing; and in spite of asserting that her manners were not those of the fashionable world, he was caught by their easy playfulness (24).

Austen's focalisation through Darcy's narrative perspective reveals both his erotic attraction to Elizabeth and his resistance to it. This conflict continues during her stay at Netherfield, as he realises that he has fallen in love with a woman who is his social and economic inferior and brings with her a family that exposes him to public embarrassment. Elizabeth presents a threat to Darcy's reputation and therefore to the externalised masculine identity in which he remains invested. His initial response is denial: 'He really believed, that were it not for the inferiority of her connections, he should be in some danger' (51). When denial is no longer plausible, he acknowledges his attraction and resolves to extinguish it:

> She attracted him more than he liked – and Miss Bingley was uncivil to *her*, and more teasing than usual to himself. He wisely resolved to be particularly careful that no sign of admiration should *now* escape him, nothing that could elevate her with the hope of influencing his felicity; sensible that if such an idea had been suggested, his behaviour during the last day must have material weight in confirming or crushing it. Steady to his purpose, he scarcely spoke ten words to her throughout the whole of Saturday, and though they were at one time left by themselves for half an hour, he adhered most conscientiously to his book, and would not even look at her (59).

Matching Darcy's conflict between alternative masculine identities is the battle between the mind and the body as he seeks to control his desire: 'He wisely resolved', 'Steady to his purpose', and 'he adhered most conscientiously to his book'. Where Austen earlier reveals Darcy's attraction through the gaze, his resistance is signified through its absence: he 'would not even look at her'.

While Darcy is consumed by Elizabeth she avoids thinking about him at all: 'to her he was only the man who made himself agreeable no where, and who had not thought her handsome enough to dance with' (24). Unlike the women with whom he usually associates, typified in Caroline Bingley, Elizabeth is uninterested in attracting the notice of either Darcy or any other man. In her portrayal of these alternative models of womanhood, Austen advances a debate that had preoccupied women writers across the political spectrum throughout the post-Revolutionary era. Despite their philosophic differences, writers as diverse as Mary Wollstonecraft, Priscilla Wakefield and Hannah More were united in their resistance to the persistent definition of the female body and mind in terms of sexuality. They critiqued the focus of female education on attracting male attention through sexual allure and the acquisition of otherwise useless 'accomplishments' and advocated instead an education that would expand the mind and prepare women for a life of family, social and national service.[15] Caroline embodies a sexualised feminine subjectivity that defers to Darcy's judgment and persistently draws his notice but to which he refuses to respond, at one point declaring that '"there is meanness in *all* the arts which ladies sometimes condescend to employ for captivation"' (40). Elizabeth, by contrast, embodies the active, rational feminine ideal championed by Austen among other women writers throughout the Romantic era. Physically energetic, intellectually astute, outspoken, caring of her family and friends, and deeply interested in the moral questions of her social world, Elizabeth Bennet is the image of 'the new ideal of the rational, maternal, bourgeois, female citizen'.[16]

Austen repeatedly and explicitly links Darcy's love for Elizabeth to her unconventional feminine subjectivity. After she verbally disarms him one evening, Austen focalises through Darcy to reveal that he 'had never been so bewitched by any woman as he was by her' (51). Elizabeth's resistance to his half-hearted attempts at playing the male lover — refusing to dance with him and satirising his attempts at predictable, clichéd conversation — only make her more intriguing, despite her sympathy with George Wickham: 'in Darcy's breast there was a tolerable powerful feeling towards her, which soon procured her pardon' (92–93). Elizabeth refuses to pander to Darcy in their exchange over women's musical accomplishments when they next meet at Rosings. When Darcy 'stationed himself so as to command a full view of the fair performer's countenance' (170), she derides her own performance in comparison with his sister, accuses him of trying to intimidate her and actively resists the idea that she is using music to attract male attention.[17] Throughout their stay in Kent, Elizabeth's physical exertion, witty conversation and verbal sparring — what Darcy would later describe as 'the liveliness of your mind' — only increase his attraction to her in contrast to the sickly, colourless Anne be Bourgh, his intended bride. His attempts at reconciling the conflict between his desire for Elizabeth and resistance to a relationship with her result in his more than usually awkward social behaviour: staring at her in social company, visiting her without speaking, and pursuing her on walks in the countryside without being able to hold a conversation.

The tension between Darcy's divided masculine identity — the externalised value for reputation, status and wealth and the internalised, authentic self that is captivated by Elizabeth — explodes spectacularly when he asks her to marry him. In Darcy's first proposal, Austen constructs the transformative effects of romantic love on the male protagonist very differently than for Edward Ferrars in *Sense and Sensibility* and Henry Tilney in *Northanger Abbey*. The love these men feel for Elinor Dashwood and Catherine Morland triggers a shift in masculine identity when events over which they have no control threaten their relationships to the women they love. Darcy, by contrast, is under no such pressure. His moment is of his own choosing, and the manner of his proposal reveals that his desire for Elizabeth has, at this stage, produced no self-examination or reflection whatsoever. His elaboration on his 'sense of her inferiority – of its being a degradation – of the family obstacles which judgment had always opposed to inclination' (185) reveals that the challenge Elizabeth poses to his status and reputation, and thus to his gender identity, have protracted and all but prevented his proposal. He describes such feelings as '"natural and just"', asking: '"Could you expect me to rejoice in the inferiority of your connections? To congratulate myself on the hope of relations whose condition in life is so decidedly below my own?"' (188).

Despite his cruelty, Darcy's proposal reveals the foundation of the marriage that will eventually conclude the novel. He is open and honest with his intended wife: '"disguise of every sort is my abhorrence"' (188). He is obviously attracted to Elizabeth but refuses to sexualise her through flattery and compliment, determined instead to treat her as an intellectual equal rather than a sexual subordinate. Austen consolidates this approach in his letter, in which Darcy appeals to Elizabeth's sense of justice and engages her as a rational person with a moral compass of her own. Elizabeth may unequivocally reject Darcy for his '"arrogance"', '"conceit"' and '"selfish disdain of the feelings of others"' (188) — the damaging consequences of a masculine identity defined by the pride of public reputation — but chauvinistic he is not.

Elizabeth's rejection triggers Darcy's realisation that his adherence to a masculine identity defined by reputation has wholly alienated the woman with whom he is passionately in love. Elizabeth not only declines his proposal of marriage, but also declares an abhorrence of him and everything he represents. Confronted with the knowledge of '"how insufficient were all my pretensions to please a woman worthy of being pleased"' (349) and reflecting on the behaviour that such pretensions produced, Darcy is forced to acknowledge the thinness of a masculine identity defined by social performance and its justifiable repugnance to a woman like Elizabeth. He had assumed that Elizabeth would share his value for wealth, status and reputation, and that his credentials as a beacon of gentry masculinity would be sufficient; as he later tells her, '"I came to you without a doubt of my reception"' (349). In the wake of Elizabeth's rejection, Darcy finally discards a masculine identity defined by status and reputation, and accepts an internalised, authentic identity, heedless of the demands of the establishment and the fashionable world. His change has been interpreted as a development from self-restraint to emotional display, as an essentially behavioural change from rudeness to politeness, and as a shift in values from social exclusivity to inclusiveness.[18] These are, however, the effects of a change in his gender identity: how Darcy sees himself as a man.

Darcy's development is triggered not by his desire for Elizabeth but instead by his fundamental need to be desirable to her. Female desire is a powerful force in *Pride and Prejudice* not only because of Austen's construction of Elizabeth Bennet as an erotic subject,[19] but also because Austen explicitly presents female desire as a catalyst that can and should change how men understand themselves *as men*. Championing female desire as a positive force for male self-improvement, Austen rejects the dominant discourses that motivated men to be what society demanded, what their (male) peers and professions respected, and what the nation needed. In place of such social and political causes, Austen privileges the personal and the intimate, dramatising this a bastion of idealised gentry manhood changing himself for the sole purpose of becoming desirable to the woman he loves. Darcy tells Elizabeth quite plainly at the end of the novel that his return to Hertfordshire was '"to judge, if I could, whether I might ever hope to make you love me"' (361). This becomes Darcy's mission.

The question that dominates the second half of *Pride and Prejudice* becomes, then, what does Elizabeth want? Austen contrasts Elizabeth, like Darcy, with her predecessors. Unlike Marianne and Catherine, Elizabeth actively resists fantasising about an imagined masculine ideal. To Elizabeth, desire is a profoundly intellectual process rather than an emotional revelation or a sexual awakening,[20] reflected in Austen's placement of Elizabeth's cognition at the centre of the narrative in the second half of the novel. Her focus narrows further to Elizabeth's point of view during her visit to Derbyshire and by the time Darcy returns to Hertfordshire, Austen completely dispenses with all other narrative strategies, including her roaming narrator and the glimpses she earlier offered the reader into his interiority.

Austen's dramatic shift in narrative approach to focus exclusively on Elizabeth in the second half of the novel has generated a perception that Darcy is mysterious or inscrutable, which Sarah Wootton argues lends a Byronic quality to his character, as he presents 'a romantic "challenge" or conundrum for the heroine to "solve"'.[21] His perceived inscrutability is an effect, but not the purpose, of Austen's narrative strategies. Her constricted focus on Elizabeth's point of view foregrounds the dialogic process of masculine and feminine gender formation that is critical to her rewriting of masculinity in this novel. The Romantic feminine agency Elizabeth expresses in the first half of the novel is fully realised in the second, in the profoundly intellectual process by which she selects a husband; indeed, after Darcy's marriage proposal, the novel's central dilemma is not whether he will choose her, but whether she will choose him. Austen positions her reader as reading Elizabeth in her attempts to read Darcy, dramatising Elizabeth's cognition, foregrounding Darcy's transformation and linking it to his need to become desirable to her.

Indeed, throughout *Pride and Prejudice* Austen is preoccupied with the question of whether and how a person can be 'read'. Her inquiry relies on an essentially Romantic idea of the individual as possessing an internalised 'self' that, Elizabeth maintains, may be discerned, scrutinised and understood by the shrewd observer. Priding herself on her capacity to read others, Elizabeth immediately sees through the Bingley sisters, tells Charles Bingley '"I understand you perfectly"' (42), and experiences her first moment of self-discovery when she realises how wrongly she has read Wickham. After Darcy's marriage proposal, Elizabeth's power as a reader of others moves well beyond amusing herself in the context of polite sociability and becomes critical to her self-fulfilment. Despite declaring to Bingley that '"intricate characters are the *most* amusing"' (42), she finds the task of reading Darcy agonisingly difficult until the novel's end (and, one suspects, beyond). Having refused to heed his advice — '"I could wish, Miss Bennet, that you were not to sketch my character at the present moment, as there is reason to fear that the performance would reflect no credit on either"' (92) — Elizabeth has already misread Darcy once. In Austen's denouement, both Elizabeth and the reader must rely solely on her judgment, when the stakes are so much higher.

Elizabeth's rereading of Darcy is ignited by her travels in Derbyshire. Her cognitive responses to his house, grounds, portrait, and eventually the man himself reveal his changed identity and its relationship to romantic love.[22] Having surveyed Pemberley and developed a new appreciation of its owner, Elizabeth's reflections on his portrait specifically recall his love for her and its erotic expression through his gaze:

> she beheld a striking resemblance of Mr. Darcy, with such a smile over his face, as she remembered to have sometimes seen, when he looked at her [...] as she stood before the canvas, on which he was represented, and fixed his eyes on herself, she thought of his regard with a deeper sentiment of gratitude than it had ever raised before; she remembered its warmth, and softened its impropriety of expression (240).

Elizabeth's contemplation of the portrait is immediately followed by their mortifying surprise encounter. She is astonished by his openness and generosity despite their mutual embarrassment:

> his behaviour, so strikingly altered, – what could it mean? That he should even speak to her was amazing! – but to speak with such civility, to enquire after her family! Never in her life had she seen his manners so little dignified, never had he spoken with such gentleness as on this unexpected meeting (242).

In disclaiming her own role in triggering this change, Elizabeth paradoxically connects it to his love for her:

> Why is he so altered? From what can it proceed? It cannot be for *me*, it cannot be for *my* sake that his manners are thus softened. My reproofs at Hunsford could not work such a change as this. It is impossible that he should still love me (244).

When they meet in Lambton, Austen focalises through Elizabeth to raise issues of class, wealth and status, the foundation of Darcy's previous identity, in the context of his change:

> When she saw him thus seeking the acquaintance, and courting the good opinion of people, with whom any intercourse a few months ago would have been a disgrace; when she saw him thus civil, not only to herself, but to the very relations whom he had openly disdained, and recollected their last lively scene in Hunsford Parsonage, the difference, the change was so great, and struck so forcibly on her mind, that she could hardly restrain her astonishment from being visible (251).

Darcy confirms the accuracy of Elizabeth's suspicions at the end of the novel:

> My object *then* ... was to shew you, by every civility in my power, that I was not so mean as to resent the past; and I hoped to obtain your forgiveness, to lessen your ill opinion, by letting you see that your reproofs had been attended to (349–50).

Darcy's openness and honesty in how he now presents himself to others are hallmarks of a masculine identity that is stable, internalised and authentic. With nothing to either prove or hide, his enduring love for Elizabeth becomes obvious to those around him. In Hertfordshire and Kent, his devotion to her had only been suspected by Charlotte, and then with hesitation; in Derbyshire, it is obvious to the Gardiners:

> The suspicions which had just arisen of Mr. Darcy and their niece, directed their observation towards each with an earnest, though guarded, enquiry; and they soon drew from those enquiries the full conviction that one of them at least knew what it was to love. Of the lady's sensations they remained a little in doubt; but that the gentleman was overflowing with admiration was evident enough (249).

When Elizabeth returns to Pemberley, his admiration is apparent: 'she saw that the suspicions of the whole party were awakened against them, and that there was scarcely an eye which did not watch his behavior when he first came into the room' (256–57). In Austen's final narrative diversion from Elizabeth to Darcy, taking the reader into the Pemberley drawing room, Darcy discards the frivolous banter of his earlier conversations with Caroline Bingley and openly declares '"it is many months since I have considered her as one of the handsomest women of my acquaintance"' (259).

Elizabeth attempts to rationalise Darcy's change and understand her feelings for him. Austen's language to describe this process could have been lifted from Mary Wollstonecraft's prescription for a successful companionate marriage in *A Vindication of the Rights of Woman*: 'She respected, she esteemed, she was grateful to him' (253). Austen explicitly links his change to his love for Elizabeth: 'a change in a man of so much pride, excited not only astonishment but gratitude – for to love, ardent love, it must be attributed' (253). Austen reveals Elizabeth's contemplations through a muted language of mutual happiness rather than the passion that drives Darcy's feelings for her:

> she felt a real interest in his welfare; and she only wanted to know how far she wished that welfare to depend upon herself, and how far it would be for the happiness of both that she should employ the power, which her fancy told her she still possessed, of bringing on the renewal of his addresses (253).

Austen's narrator intervenes to specifically draw the reader's attention to the wholly rational basis of Elizabeth's change of opinion about Darcy, lest they should miss the point:

> If gratitude and esteem are good foundations of affection, Elizabeth's change of sentiment will be neither improbable nor faulty. But if otherwise, if the regard springing from such sources is unreasonable or unnatural, in comparison of what is so often described as arising on a first interview with its object, and even before two words have been exchanged, nothing can be said in her defence, except that she had given somewhat of a trial to the latter method, in her partiality for Wickham, and that its ill-success might perhaps authorise her to seek the other less interesting mode of attachment (265–66).

The possibility of their marriage vanishes, Elizabeth fears, with the revelation of Lydia's elopement with Wickham, prompting her circumscribed reflection that 'never had she so honestly felt that she could have loved him, as now, when all love must be in vain' (264). As she quietly contemplates what she believes she has lost, Elizabeth realises that 'she could have been happy with him' at precisely the moment when there appears to be a 'gulf impossible' between them (295).

Austen is adamant that the 'happy marriage' that, Elizabeth reflects, could have taught 'the admiring multitude what connubial felicity really was' (296) would have resulted not from her suitability as Darcy's wife, but instead from his compatibility with her:

> She began now to comprehend that he was exactly the man, who, in disposition and talents, would most suit her. His understanding and temper, though unlike her own, would have answered all her wishes. It was an union that must have been to the advantage of both; by her ease and liveliness, his mind might have been softened, his manners improved, and from his judgment, information, and knowledge of the world, she must have received benefit of greater importance (295).

The dynamic relationship between these two highly individualistic people reflects the 'civilizing process' with which, Enit Karafili Steiner argues, Austen links her 'reformulation of female subjectivity, voicing transformations that establish a continuous dialogue between the personal and the political, the private and the public'.[23] Although Elizabeth could have — arguably, already has had — a 'civilizing' effect on Darcy, from him she would receive 'benefit of greater importance': the tools she needs to develop a subjectivity beyond the familial and the domestic, to assume a position of agency as a citizen with the potential for social and political engagement and influence.

The events that, Elizabeth fears, will terminate their relationship, provide Darcy with an opportunity to prove both the extent of his change and the social power of an internalised, authentic masculine identity. Before uniting him to Elizabeth, Austen subjects her male protagonist to personal trials that, to his former self, would have been nothing less than mortifying. Darcy's investment in an externalised masculine identity has inflicted harm on others for which he must atone through measures that test the authenticity of the internalised male subjectivity he appeared to have embraced in Derbyshire. Recognition of his own culpability drives him to locate Wickham and Lydia and negotiate a financial settlement for their marriage. Austen reveals his motivations through Mrs Gardiner's letter to Elizabeth:

> his conviction of its being owing to himself Wickham's worthlessness had not been so well known ... He generously imputed the whole to his mistaken pride, and confessed that he had before thought it beneath him, to lay his private actions open to the world (304–05).

No longer beholden to social performance, Darcy insists that 'his character was to speak for itself' (305). In Elizabeth's reflection that she felt 'proud of him ... that in a cause of compassion and honour, he had been able to get the better of himself' (309), Austen reveals that Darcy's change is not of manner or behaviour, but a conscious development in understanding the self.

Darcy may wish for his character to speak for itself, but Elizabeth experiences her greatest frustration in her attempts to read him on his return to Hertfordshire. Austen's absolute narrative focus on Elizabeth's point of view generates, as Clery argues, a psychological distance between Darcy, Elizabeth, and the reader that drives the narrative suspense building to the novel's conclusion, and cements Austen's place as 'the founder of the modern romance narrative, as the first to recognize the extraordinary narrative power of keeping the hero's point of view in reserve'.[24] Austen's focus on Elizabeth's cognition in the context of the conventional, highly-regulated social forms and practices of her family circle — a morning visit, a dinner at Longbourn — highlights the extreme restrictions under which both she and Darcy labour in the advancement of their relationship within spaces of polite sociability. The distaste they share for the society of Hertfordshire, which he bears 'with admirable calmness' and in which she 'was ever anxious to keep him to herself, and to those members of her family with whom he might converse without mortification' (362–63), resists an interpretation of their union as signifying social inclusiveness for either. Instead, 'the comfort and elegance of their family party at Pemberley', the place where Elizabeth has read Darcy as most himself, suggests their retreat into a private oasis in which these Romantic individuals can realise personal fulfilment in each other.

In the closing chapters of *Pride and Prejudice*, Austen affirms that Darcy's new sense of masculine selfhood has emerged from his love for Elizabeth. He attributes his pride, and with it a masculine identity defined by status and reputation, to a defective upbringing:

> I have been a selfish being all my life, in practice, though not in principle. As a child I was taught what was *right*, but I was not taught to correct my temper. I was given good principles, but left to follow them in pride and conceit. Unfortunately an only son, (for many years an only *child*) I was spoilt by my parents, who though good themselves, (my father particularly, all that was benevolent and amiable,) allowed, encouraged, almost taught me to be selfish and overbearing, to care for none beyond my own family circle, to think meanly of all the rest of the world, to *wish* at least to think meanly of their sense and worth compared with my own (349).

Darcy has changed this conceited way of understanding himself, a change he attributes directly to Elizabeth: "'such I might have been but for you, dearest, loveliest, Elizabeth! What do I not owe you! You taught me a lesson, hard indeed at first, but most advantageous. By you, I was properly humbled"' (349). Elizabeth herself accounts for the circumstances in which he fell in love with her, critiquing sexualised models of the desirable woman and advocating for her own feminine agency:

> The fact is, you were sick of civility, of deference, of officious attention. You were disgusted with the women who were always speaking and looking, and thinking for *your* approbation alone. I roused, and interested you, because I was so unlike *them* (359).

In *Pride and Prejudice*, Jane Austen dramatises a dialogue between a woman who embodies a rational, individualistic, and potentially disruptive Romantic feminine subjectivity, and a man who, though otherwise a conservative gentry ideal, develops psychologically to become the man she needs him to be. Austen exploits the wide narrative capabilities of the courtship romance genre to explore masculine identity as a subject in its own right, to foster complexity in male characterisation, and to chart the development of male selfhood through an explicitly feminine and feminist lens. *Pride and Prejudice* is the culmination of the first phase of Austen's rewriting of masculinity, drawing the Romantic championing of individualism, emotion, and self-realisation into the courtship romance genre and celebrating the fulfilment of the male self through romantic love. Austen dwells on this fulfilment when Darcy's love for Elizabeth is finally reciprocated:

> The happiness which this reply produced, was such as he had probably never felt before; and he expressed himself on the occasion as sensibly and as warmly as a man violently in love can be supposed to do. Had Elizabeth been able to encounter his eye, she might have seen how well the expression of heartfelt delight, diffused over his face, became him (346).

In Darcy and his transformation of the male self through romantic love Austen would seem, then, to have devised a solution to the insidious problem of defining masculinity as the social performance of a sexual hierarchy inherently oppressive to women like Elizabeth Bennet. Never again, however, would Austen offer such an idealised, apparently uncomplicated vision of heterosexual love and companionate marriage. In real terms, the 'connubial felicity' that Elizabeth foresees is possible only by Darcy's wealth, status, and access to the utopian Pemberley. In Austen's final three novels, she problematises and even resists such solutions. *Mansfield Park* and *Emma* bear the burden of external events — the Napoleonic Wars, the Regency, and an increasingly fraught domestic political situation — from which *Pride and Prejudice* is largely removed. These novels are imbued with an anxiety over masculinity that, in terms of both gender and genre, is new to Austen's fiction.

That anxiety precludes the pure celebration of romantic love and its liberating possibilities for men and women in *Pride and Prejudice*, but presents opportunities for Austen to ask new questions in her rewriting of masculinity and its relationship to genre. It is not until the post-war era that Austen returns to exploring the effects of romantic love on the male self, offering a uniquely complex vision of relationships between feminine agency and masculine emotional authenticity in *Persuasion*.

4 'You will make him everything'

Redeeming Masculinity
in *Mansfield Park*

When *Pride and Prejudice* was published in 1813 and the world was meeting the man who would redefine desirable literary heroism, Jane Austen was at work on *Mansfield Park* (1814) and rewriting masculinity from a wholly new perspective. In *Mansfield Park* and *Emma* (1815), Austen explores masculine gender identities through the lens of national, imperial and international events and their influence on gender and genre. Leaving behind her celebration of male self-fulfilment through romantic love in her earlier novels, in *Mansfield Park* and *Emma* Austen turns her attention away from individual male subjectivity and focuses instead on exploring masculine identities in relation to men's power and responsibilities within social, economic and political contexts. Even within such a heightened political climate, however, Austen privileges men's relationships with women over their responsibilities to their communities and the nation.

Austen's rewriting of masculinity in connection with feminine agency in *Mansfield Park* and *Emma* is sharpened by her responses to developments in the fiction marketplace in the years she became a professional writer. The surge of nationalism and reactionary conservative ideologies in the post-Revolutionary era influenced the development of the novel through the emergence of new genres, including Evangelical fiction, the national tale and the historical novel. The complex political context to which Austen clearly responds in these novels encompasses not only the major events of the era, but also the rapid and rising popularity of these genres, which Austen judges in terms of the masculine ideals they champion and their relationship to feminine agency. It is apparent in *Mansfield Park* and *Emma* that Austen critiqued both Evangelical fiction and the national tale for reinscribing into the novel the conservative gender identities against which she had written in *Northanger Abbey* and *Pride and Prejudice*, and threatening the courtship romance's generic power to rewrite masculinity as aligned to feminine agency.

Whereas in *Pride and Prejudice* Austen celebrates Fitzwilliam Darcy's transformation through romantic love and valorisation of Elizabeth Bennet's agency and selfhood, in *Mansfield Park* she presents three men, Sir Thomas Bertram, Edmund Bertram and Henry

Crawford, who are incapable of comprehending feminine agency, and who are therefore also incapable of romance itself. These men treat her heroine Fanny Price not as a woman in her own right, but instead as the embodiment of a conservative feminine ideal. Each of these men views Fanny as a moral salve who can serve his own needs, attempting to claim her and the redemption she offers at the precise moment that he realises the failure of his masculine identity. Edmund perversely celebrates this exchange when he urges Fanny to accept Henry's marriage proposal:

> a most fortunate man he is to attach himself to such a creature – to a woman, who firm as a rock in her own principles, has a gentleness of character so well adapted to recommend them ... He will make you happy, Fanny, I know he will make you happy; but you will make him everything (325).

Fanny vehemently disclaims such a role: '"I would not engage in such a charge ... in such an office of high responsibility!"' (325). Misinterpreting the situation before him, Edmund cannot see that Fanny's refusal arises not from a belief that she is unfit to guide Henry, but because she does not see it as her role to do so. When Fanny tells Henry, '"We all have a better guide in ourselves, if we would attend to it, than any other person can be"' (383), Austen disclaims a sexual exchange in which the feminine role is to redeem for masculine failure.

Austen's characterisation of the heroine, the patriarch and alternative suitors in *Mansfield Park* reproduces and denounces conservative masculine and feminine gender identities and the sexual hierarchy between them. *Mansfield Park* is Jane Austen's rejoinder to the rise of Evangelical fiction as a major literary force in the late 1800s and early 1810s. The Evangelical novel emerged as part of a broader conservative, anti-Revolutionary agenda to exploit the popularity of the novel and transform it into a respectable literary form; as Lisa Wood argues, to novelists such as Mary Brunton and Jane West, 'the counterrevolutionary project will be effected ... not through the cessation of consumption, but through the purification of the product consumed'.[1] The rise of the Evangelical novel was not merely coincident with the emergence of Evangelicalism as a theological and political movement, but a deliberate strategy by novelists who either identified as Evangelicals or were sympathetic with the movement's concerns. As Anthony Mandal contends, Evangelical writers sought 'to tame the novel and to educate its readers', 'to infuse respectability into the unruly novel from the late 1800s onwards' and had 'the aim of reforming fiction and using the medium to instil rectitude into a wayward audience'.[2] The vantage point of historical reflection reveals that such strategies may have contributed to the consolidation of the novel as a respectable and inherently valuable literary form.[3] Although Austen was clearly dedicated to the advancement of the novel, writing within the 1810s she is sceptical, at the very least, of this new generic development.

Austen's interrogation of masculinity in *Mansfield Park* is framed by Evangelicalism and its associated fictional genres. Austen draws the movement's focus on an individual relationship with God and on the spiritual life of the inner self as a path to morality into her overt concern with the moral behaviour of her characters and its consequences.[4] In her scrutiny of men's execution of public duties, Austen raises several issues of concern to Evangelicals, including 'the abandonment of plurality (clergymen holding more than one living at the same time), a return to Scripture as the basis of Anglican practice, and, more topically, the abolition of the slave trade'.[5] As Mandal remarks, the attention Evangelical women turned to such issues may have been particularly useful to Austen in writing 'a work concerned with so many issues topical at the time'.[6] *Mansfield Park* is Austen's first politically explicit critique of masculinity, and the men of this novel have long been interpreted as agents who carry meaning well beyond the immediate scope of the narrative.[7] Austen allegorically, metaphorically and literally interrogates the power men wield through the two most entrenched institutions in the country — the state and the church — by projecting masculine identity into a debate with local, national and international ramifications. She defines the men of *Mansfield Park* through their public and professional roles with a depth unmatched in her other novels. A condition-of-England novel, an allegory of the Regency and a critique not only of the Atlantic slave trade, but also of Britain's imperial project more broadly,[8] Austen's textual construction of masculinity in *Mansfield Park* resists the recurring interpretation of her men as limited in scope to the private and domestic. She amply demonstrates that her authorial range extended to critiquing masculinity through male power and authority.

Even in *Mansfield Park*, however, the true test of masculine worth lies in men's relationships with women rather than in their public and professional responsibilities. In her characterisation of Fanny Price, Sir Thomas Bertram, Edmund Bertram and Henry Crawford, Austen challenges relationships Evangelical fiction constructs between a spiritual masculine ideal and a conservative, submissive and modest vision of desirable femininity. Conservative women writers, including Austen's contemporaries Hannah More, Mary Brunton and Jane West, exploited the feminine agency emerging in the Romantic era to didactically celebrate domestic femininity and its critical role in countering revolutionary ideologies.[9] Within the narrower genre of Evangelical fiction, novelists championed a modest and pious, yet educated and rational, model of femininity that could complement a domesticated, spiritual masculine ideal and support the male in the proper execution of public, professional responsibilities. In *Mansfield Park*, Austen replicates and rejects this dynamic in the relationships she constructs between the heroine, the patriarch, and alternative suitors, challenging Evangelical ideologies of sexual difference and their curtailing of feminine agency.

In *Coelebs in Search of a Wife* (1808), the founding work of Evangelical fiction, Hannah More dramatises the quest by the central male protagonist, Charles, for a woman who personifies an Evangelical feminine ideal. He critiques and discards alternative approaches to femininity aligned with revolutionary ideologies before identifying the modest, demure and voiceless Lucilla Stanley as his perfect mate. Charles' feminine ideal is, as Peter Knox-Shaw remarks, one who can 'complement (and compliment) his male virtues'.[10] In January 1809, Austen resisted Cassandra's attempt to interest her in *Coelebs* shortly after it was published:

> You have by no means raised my curiosity after Caleb; – My disinclination for it before was affected, but now it is real; I do not like the Evangelicals. – Of course I shall be delighted when I read it, like other people, but till I do, I dislike it.[11]

Austen's retort — 'I do not like the Evangelicals' — is unequivocal, yet softened by her reflection on her own prejudice and the fickle nature of the reading public: readers who prejudge a work and change their minds when they read it. Her unflinching aversion to the novel is clear, however, when she satirises its title:

> I am not at all ashamed about the name of the Novel, having been guilty of no insult towards your handwriting; the Dipthong I always saw, but knowing how fond you are of adding a vowel wherever you could, I attributed it to that alone – & the knowledge of the truth does the book no service; – the only merit it could have, was in the name of Caleb, which has an honest, unpretending sound; but in Coelebs, there is pedantry & affectation. – Is it written only to Classical Scholars?[12]

Austen's remark that 'the only merit it could have, was in the name of Caleb' and her association of the novel with pedantry mark her scepticism of the literary value of this emerging genre.

Although it is unknown whether Cassandra was able to persuade her sister to read *Coelebs*, Austen looked forward with anticipation to the publication of Mary Brunton's 'Evangelical romance'[13] *Self-Control* in 1811:

> We have tried to get Self-controul, but in vain. – I *should* like to know what her Estimate is – but am always half afraid of finding a clever novel *too clever* – & of finding my own story & my own people all forestalled.[14]

Anticipating the publication of *Sense and Sensibility* in October the same year, Austen reveals her conscious engagement with the literary marketplace and the work of her contemporaries even before she was a published novelist. Where Austen charges More with 'pedantry and affectation' in *Coelebs*, she accuses Brunton of implausibility in *Self-Control*. She need not have been concerned about 'finding my own story & my own people all forestalled': Brunton's exemplary Evangelical heroine, Laura Montraville, overcomes a series of personal and financial hardships through a melodramatic plot, and didactically learns to identify and desire the deserving suitor. Relentlessly pursued by the desirable but morally corrupt Colonel Hargraves, Laura eventually escapes his sexual harassment and violence and is united with the principled, responsible Montague de Courcy, who can offer her the settled domesticity she needs to fulfil her feminine purpose. In October 1813, shortly after she completed *Mansfield Park*, Austen reveals her scepticism about the novel's melodrama:

> I am looking over Self Control again, & my opinion is confirmed of its' being an excellently-meant, elegantly-written Work, without anything of Nature or Probability in it. I declare I do not know whether Laura's passage down the American River, is not the most natural, possible, every-day thing she ever does.[15]

In a retort to an unknown critic of *Mansfield Park*, Austen exposes her enduring distaste for the melodrama of Brunton's novel and the appetite of the reading public:

> I will redeem my credit with him, by writing a close Imitation of "Self-control" as soon as I can; – I will improve upon it; – my Heroine shall not merely be wafted down an American river in a boat by herself, she shall cross the Atlantic in the same way, & never stop till she reaches Gravesent.–[16]

Austen's letters reveal her disdain for the two genre-defining works of Evangelical fiction published before *Mansfield Park*. Although her 1814 remark — 'I am by no means convinced that we ought not all to be Evangelicals'[17] — has sparked scholarly debate concerning her possible affinity with Evangelicalism,[18] her enthusiasm was expressed in the context of offering courtship advice to her niece Fanny Knight rather than the emergence of Evangelicalism as a literary force. *Mansfield Park* is Austen's rejoinder to the movement's influence on the literary marketplace and specifically on the novel as a literary form. Austen's challenge to Evangelicalism, however, is not to the pedantry of Hannah More or to the melodrama of Mary Brunton, but to the masculine and feminine ideals and the hierarchy between them that Evangelical writers sought to reinscribe into the novel and, through it, into British society.

Evangelical fiction extolled virtues including self-examination and regulation, domesticity, principled morality and the integration of self with community, for both women and men. In remodelling feminine and masculine gender identities, however, Evangelical fiction left the sexual hierarchy between them unchanged.[19] Although More and West sought to expand women's social roles by recognising their moral and spiritual authority, they also 'endorse a hierarchical structuring of the domestic sphere and rigid prescriptive limitations on what constitutes the feminine character'.[20] In *Self-Control*, Brunton constructs Laura's agency as necessitated by economic need and a lack of male protection; her independence is happily circumscribed by her marriage into settled domesticity and motherhood at the novel's conclusion. Women function, ideally, as 'helpmeets for men' in their performance of an idealised Christian manhood characterised by 'piety, domesticity, a proper sense of responsibility about business'.[21] A paradoxical male subjectivity emerges in Evangelical fiction: the male is both naturalised as superior to the heroine, yet remains dependent on her as a moral and spiritual guide.[22] Evangelicalism's contingent masculine identity, sustained by a necessarily circumscribed feminine role, was anathema to Austen's celebration of authentic, internalised masculinity and its unique power to realise feminine agency.

Austen's challenge to Evangelical masculinity in *Mansfield Park* recalls her split narrative perspective across three male protagonists in *Sense and Sensibility*. Her breadth of male characterisation, across Sir Thomas Bertram, Edmund Bertram and Henry Crawford, as well as peripheral male characters including Tom Bertram, James Rushworth, Mr Yates and William Price, scrutinises male roles within courtship and links masculine identity to a range of political, social and economic issues. The lynchpin of each male protagonist's characterisation is his relationship to Fanny, who Austen constructs to serve several political and literary agendas. Fanny's location within the courtship plot is unique among Austen's heroines: she has loved Edmund since childhood and, her heart already his, she critiques men less as potential suitors than as social and political actors. Austen replicates the modest, principled and moral feminine ideal celebrated in Evangelical fiction; her almost absolute focus on Fanny's consciousness and interiority, her moral rectitude and her domesticity are hallmarks of the Evangelical heroine.[23] As a judge of the morality of others, who develops little herself, Fanny reflects a pattern of conservative heroines in novels by More and West. She functions in *Mansfield Park* in the same manner as Evangelical heroines described by Wood:

> the exemplary protagonist's valorized qualities are generally established in early childhood in the home, and contact with the world ... becomes an opportunity for the protagonist to resist

corruption, rather than to gain experience. In general, antirevolutionary novels focus less on personal psychological and emotional development than on an individual's propriety of action within a social setting.[24]

Modest and submissive yet educated, principled and rational, Fanny Price embodies the Evangelical feminine ideal.[25]

In Fanny's courtship narrative, Austen recreates relationships between the Evangelical heroine and three men who represent different facets of Evangelical masculinity, exposing their conservative vision of feminine agency and the ideology of sexual difference that lies at the heart of Evangelicalism. Neither Sir Thomas, nor Edmund, nor Henry views Fanny as a woman possessing individualism, agency and selfhood, but instead as a feminine ideal he seeks to claim as a path to atonement for his failures. Fanny is the wife who will domesticate and guide Henry, the wife who will console and advise Edmund, and the daughter that Sir Thomas, realising his paternal failure to his own children, belatedly discovers he wanted all along. As each man attempts to acquire or trade Fanny for the principled morality and spiritual guidance she offers, Austen refuses to allow her heroine to participate in a sexual exchange that is defined by masculine need.

Austen's challenge to Evangelical literary heroism crosses masculine identities defined by both social performance and an internalised and authentic sense of self. Austen contrasts the introspective, spiritual Edmund with the performative Sir Thomas, Tom, Henry and Rushworth through recurring discussions of professionalism and its relationship to domesticity.[26] Drawing on Evangelical ideology, Austen links men's public and private lives and ascribes their professional failures to externalised approaches to masculinity, which Evangelicalism also resisted. These men are captive to a demand for social display that depends on the accumulation of wealth, the maintenance of status and reputation, the pursuit of ambition and the indulgences of fashionable sociability. Such lures distract them from the proper discharge of their responsibilities in a neglect that wreaks havoc on the Bertram family and threatens the destruction of the Mansfield Park estate. Sir Thomas' Antiguan estates underwrite his masculine identity, economically sustaining his social status and justifying his extended absence from family and home. He tacitly allows his empire to be ruled by the son he knows to be 'careless and extravagant' (21) in a way that has already drained the family's resources. Tom is also an absentee landlord and prefers watering places such as Ramsgate and Weymouth to the estate he will inherit.[27] To Tom, Mansfield Park is a venue for hunting, dancing, theatre and other pleasures to bolster his standing with his male peers; when the 'season and duties' of September bring him back to the estate, his arrival is announced 'first in a letter to the gamekeeper, and then in a letter to Edmund' (107).

Austen highlights the limits of masculinities grounded in social performance among the younger landowners through their attitudes to estate management, improvement and connection to local communities. Conversations about the purpose and aesthetics of estate improvement recur throughout the novel, reflecting the Romantic-era debate between Humphry Repton, a landscape improver who pursued a tradition of formal garden design, and Uvedale Price and Richard Payne Knight, who preferred a less ornate and more natural style of landscape associated with the picturesque. Rushworth, recently returned from a friend's estate that had altered so much that "'I told Smith I did not know where I was'" (51), becomes obsessed with embarking on a similar 'improvement' of Sotherton Court. Such extreme alterations were associated with Repton, whose style 'was in every way one of disconnection' and was 'dependent upon the eradication of commons, of signs of commerce, and of laborers' homes'.[28] Henry Crawford's captivation with estate improvement — "'I had not been of age three months before Everingham was all that it is now'" (58) — reflects a similarly Reptonian value for extreme change. To Rushworth and Crawford, estates provide opportunities for the display of wealth and taste to boost their status among their peers and sustain the performative masculinity they embody.

Austen presents masculinities grounded in social display as particularly troubling because these men are invested with actual political power over the nation at large. Sir Thomas's professional responsibilities are spread between his home estate, his imperial venture in Antigua and his role as a member of parliament. Austen's silence on Sir Thomas's role as a lawmaker — other than to mention that Lady Bertram and his children no longer accompany him to London 'to attend his duty in Parliament' (20) — implies that his absenteeism is also from the institutions and apparatus of state. More disturbing still is the possibility that the 'inferior young man' (185) Rushworth may join him; as Mary Crawford and Mrs Grant speculate, "'When Sir Thomas comes, I dare say he will be in for some borough'" (149).[29] Indeed, it is the political interest that Rushworth shares with Sir Thomas that recommends his engagement to Maria:

> Sir Thomas ... was truly happy in the prospect of an alliance so unquestionably advantageous ... It was a connection exactly of the right sort; in the same county, and the same interest; and his most hearty concurrence was conveyed as soon as possible (38).

Even when he suspects his daughter's indifference, and indeed hostility, to her future husband, Sir Thomas remains 'happy to secure a marriage which would bring him such an addition of respectability and influence' (187) and consolidate the status that supports his externalised masculine identity.

Edmund Bertram's resistance to a masculine identity defined by the social display of wealth and status sets him apart from his male counterparts in *Mansfield Park*. In Edmund, Austen reflects the Evangelical focus on the inner self and its regulation in a way that would seem to complement her overarching concern with rewriting masculinity as an internalised, individual and authentic gender identity. As John Tosh argues, Evangelical models of ideal Christian manliness sought to replace the definition of masculinity as public reputation with the concept of '*character* – by which they meant the inner resources of heart and mind transformed by God's saving grace'.[30] Edmund reflects the Evangelical masculine ideal: 'the serious Christian was urged to listen only to the inward monitor of conscience, and to appear to the world as he really was'.[31] Like Darcy before him, Edmund possesses a highly introspective personality; unlike Darcy, however, Edmund is committed to a persistent, almost debilitating self-examination that 'could only be achieved by means of unremitting self-scrutiny through private prayer and contemplation'.[32]

Austen reflects Edmund's internalised, strongly Evangelical sense of self in his commitment to his professional role as a clergyman. Responding to Mary Crawford's dismissal of a clergyman as '"nothing"' (86), Edmund declares his personal investment in the social and religious reform attendant on his profession:

> I cannot call that situation nothing, which has the charge of all that is of the first importance to mankind, individually or collectively considered, temporally and eternally, – which has the guardianship of religion and morals, and consequently of the manners which result from their influence. No one here can call the *office* nothing. If the man who holds it is so, it is by neglect of his duty, by foregoing its just importance, and stepping out of his place to appear what he ought not to appear (86).

Edmund projects the influence of the clerical role from local parishes to the national well-being — '"*You* are speaking of London. *I* am speaking of the nation at large"' (87) — and links the conduct of a nation's clergymen to its character and morality:

> The *manners* I speak of, might rather be called *conduct*, perhaps, the result of good principles; the effect, in short, of those doctrines which it is their duty to teach and recommend; and it will, I believe, be every where found that as the clergy are, or are not what they ought to be, so are the rest of the nation (87).

Austen unites Edmund's commitment to the clerical profession to his value for rural domesticity, ironically contrasting this second son's attachment to

home with his absentee landowning peers: he has '"no idea but of residence"' at Thornton Lacey (228). Unfettered by a performative masculinity dependent on display, Edmund prefers to improve his parish residence
through '"an inferior degree of beauty, of my own choice, and acquired
progressively"' than to '"put myself into the hands of an improver"' (54).
Edmund resists Henry's recommendation that he improve Thornton Lacey
to privilege fashion over community integration — '"The farm-yard must
be cleared away entirely, and planted up to shut out the blacksmith's shop"'
(223) — and make the house '"the residence of a man of education, taste,
modern manners, good connections"' (225). This would create, according
to Henry, an elevated yet false public appearance:

> All this may be stamped on it; and that house receive such an air as
> to make its owner be set down as the great land-holder of the parish,
> by every creature travelling the road; especially as there is no real
> squire's house to dispute the point (225).

Uninterested in pretending to be someone he is not, Edmund declares:

> I must be satisfied with rather less ornament and beauty. I think the
> house and premises may be made comfortable, and given the air of
> a gentleman's residence without any very heavy expense, and that
> must suffice me; and I hope may suffice all who care about me (224).

Austen crystallises the conflict between the internalised sense of masculine self embodied in Edmund, and his externally-focused counterparts,
through the amateur home theatricals. The demands of role-playing expose Edmund's struggle to maintain a stable, introspective subjectivity
in a highly performative world.[33] As William H. Galperin argues, the
home theatricals drive Austen's interrogation of the idea of subjectivity
itself, revealed in her choice of play: 'Where the original *Lovers' Vows*
may be regarded as a play in which a more natural and authentic identity asserts its claim over a selfhood forged by culture and society ... the
"English" *Lovers' Vows* is far less sanguine about a selfhood seemingly
impervious to anything but itself'.[34] Henry, who at this point in the
novel is yet to contemplate the idea of an alternative mode of subjectivity, relishes the opportunity for his highly performative self to even more
self-consciously perform. To Edmund, however, the theatricals present
a twofold challenge: they are a moral dilemma in themselves and will
ultimately force him into public performance.

Edmund openly objects to the home theatricals on the grounds of his
father's absence, the impropriety of his sisters acting and the disruption
caused by the construction of a theatre that '"would be taking liberties with
my Father's house in his absence which could not be justified"' (118). Unlike his predecessor Edward Ferrars, whose family situation and personal

circumstances repeatedly thrust him into the whirl of polite sociability, Edmund generally avoids such confrontations and their personal costs. His access to a comfortable home in the country, his profession, and the prospect of domestic independence with his own rural parish shield him from the excesses of masculinities defined by the fashionable world. To Edmund, the theatricals are an unwelcome incursion into the domestic tranquillity that accommodates his introspective, internalised subjectivity, possessing neither the talent nor the taste for performance.

Edmund's refusal to participate triggers the recruitment of an outsider to play a lover to Mary Crawford. Unable to countenance such a mortification to Mary, he deplores the public exposure of his family's licentiousness: "'This is the end of all the privacy and propriety which was talked about at first ... it does appear to me an evil of such magnitude as must, *if possible*, be prevented"' (142). His decision to participate is a personal sacrifice to his sense of self to prevent what he perceives as a greater evil. His appeal to Fanny reveals the moral dilemma he confronts: "'Can you mention any other measure by which I have a chance of doing equal good?"' (143–44). Despite recognising his dilemma and offering him no alternative, Fanny judges him harshly for his decision: 'Her heart and her judgment were equally against Edmund's decision; she could not acquit his unsteadiness; and his happiness under it made her wretched. She was full of jealousy and agitation' (147). Austen's focalisation through Fanny reveals her envy and self-pity:

> Miss Crawford came with looks of gaiety which seemed an insult, with friendly expressions towards herself which she could hardly answer calmly ... She alone was sad and insignificant; she had no share in any thing; she might go or stay, she might be in the midst of their noise, or retreat from it to the solitude of the east room, without being seen or missed (147).

On Sir Thomas's return, Austen exposes the high personal cost to Edmund for his attempts to maintain a coherent, secure selfhood in a social context dominated by fashionable display and moral heedlessness. Despite his attempts to make the right decision, Edmund bears greater punishment than the siblings who do not even try, as Sir Thomas

> looked with inquiring earnestness at his daughters and Edmund, dwelling particularly on the latter, and speaking a language, a remonstrance, a reproof, which *he* felt at his heart ... Such a look of reproach at Edmund from his father she could never have expected to witness (172).

Sir Thomas's return not only terminates the home theatricals; it also triggers the commencement of Fanny Price's courtship narrative. From his initial reflection 'that any one in the habit of such idle observations *would have thought* that Mr. Crawford was the admirer of Fanny Price' (220), to staging her ball, evicting her to Portsmouth and eventually offering the 'joyful consent which met Edmund's application' (438), Sir Thomas is the superintendent of Fanny's courtship plot. His role as family patriarch is inscribed in his attempts to trade Fanny between Henry and Edmund, who Austen characterises to reflect Charles, the male protagonist of Hannah More's *Coelebs*: both men have preconceived notions of what they want in a wife and identify Fanny, among a range of alternatives, as the woman best able to fulfil the role as they understand it. In striking contrast to their predecessor Mr Darcy and their successor Mr Knightley, neither Edmund nor Henry is interested in what he can offer Fanny; on the contrary, each man views his relationship with her solely in terms of what, as an Evangelical feminine exemplar, he believes she can do for him. Although Edmund and Henry represent vastly different masculine identities, their failures as men are identical; they view women through an ideology of sexual difference that judges them according to their fulfilment of a socially-prescribed role defined by male need. Both men become attracted to Fanny as they realise their failures as men, and both identify her as a path to self-improvement and redemption. Austen denies both men this narrative resolution, in different ways.

Henry is the first man to recognise his shortcomings, a realisation triggered by the arrival of William Price and his tales of patriotic adventure: 'He longed to have been at sea, and seen and done and suffered as much ... The glory of heroism, of usefulness, of exertion, of endurance, made his own habits of selfish indulgence appear in shameful contrast' (218–19). Though Austen remarks that his wish 'was rather eager than lasting' (219), Henry's efforts to befriend William and secure his promotion arise from his increasing awareness that his social position brings with it a responsibility to help others. Henry fixates on Fanny in his desire for self-improvement. Initially, she presents a conundrum he must solve: '"I do not quite know what to make of Miss Fanny. I do not understand her ... What is her character? – Is she solemn? – Is she queer? – Is she prudish? ... I must get the better of this"' (213). Although Henry attempts to charm Fanny and make her fall in love with him, the reverse happens and he finds himself falling in love instead.

Of all Austen's male protagonists, Henry is the most expressive in what he loves about the heroine. Drawing on the rhetoric of the modest woman championed by Evangelical ideology, Henry extols Fanny's '"beauty of face and figure"', '"graces of manner and goodness of heart"', '"gentleness, modesty, and sweetness"' of character, '"understanding ... quick and clear"', and '"modest and elegant mind"' (270–71). Henry's courtship of Fanny reflects the 'man of sense' endorsed by conservative male conduct literature: 'According to the conventional wisdom, a man might flirt with a coquette, but when he had marriage in mind he always looked for a modest woman ... the exemplary hero will always marry the blushing heroine'.[35] Mary congratulates him on the prospect of '"a sweet little wife, all gratitude and devotion"' (269). Henry values Fanny not for herself but the kind of wife he believes she would be:

> Henry Crawford had too much sense not to feel the worth of good principles in a wife ... when he talked of her having such a steadiness and regularity of conduct, such a high notion of honour, and such an observance of decorum as might warrant any man in the fullest dependence on her faith and integrity, he expressed what was inspired by the knowledge of her being well principled and religious (271).

Austen is explicit that to Henry, Fanny is a path to his own self-improvement: '"I could so wholly and absolutely confide in her ... and *that* is what I want"' (271). His declaration '"I am quite determined to marry Fanny Price"' (268) assumes that, as Fanny personifies a submissive feminine ideal, she will acquiesce to her socially-prescribed role and accept him.

Sir Thomas shares Henry's assumptions about Fanny and is outraged by her refusal. To him, Fanny's 'no' is incomprehensible because Henry so thoroughly embodies the performative masculinity he values:

> Here is a young man wishing to pay his addresses to you, with every thing to recommend him; not merely situation in life, fortune, and character, but with more than common agreeableness, with address and conversation pleasing to every body. And he is not an acquaintance of to-day, you have now known him some time. His sister, moreover, is your intimate friend, and he has been doing *that* for your brother, which I should suppose would have been almost sufficient recommendation to you, had there been no other (291).

Austen exposes the pernicious foundation of performative masculinity in an ideology of sexual difference that denies feminine agency. To Sir Thomas, daughters are chattels to be exchanged between men defined by wealth, status and reputation: '"Gladly would I have bestowed either of my own daughters on him ... had Mr Crawford sought Julia's hand, I should have given it to him with superior and more heartfelt satisfaction than I gave Maria's to Mr. Rushworth"' (294). Fanny's refusal presents a resistance to the passive, modest womanhood upon which such an exchange relies:

> I had thought you peculiarly free from wilfulness of temper, self-conceit, and every tendency to the independence of spirit, which prevails so much in modern days, even in young women, and which in young women is offensive and disgusting beyond all common offence (293).

Austen highlights Fanny's quiet, determined agency throughout Sir Thomas's violent excoriation of her conduct:

> you have now shewn me that you can be wilful and perverse, that you can and will decide for yourself, without any consideration or deference for those who surely have some right to guide you – without even asking their advice (293–94).

Qualities that Austen celebrates in Marianne Dashwood, Catherine Morland, Elizabeth Bennet and Emma Woodhouse are, to Sir Thomas, "'a gross violation of duty and respect'" (294).

Fanny's rejection prompts Henry, like Darcy before him, to recognise his own need to change to become desirable to her. The question Austen poses in the final volume of *Mansfield Park* is whether Henry can establish the stable, authentic and internalised masculinity identity that will be acceptable to Fanny. Reluctant to divulge her misgivings, Fanny is eventually badgered into revealing her scepticism of Henry's instability: "'I thought it was a pity you did not always know yourself as well as you seemed to do at that moment'" (317). Self-knowledge is critical to Henry becoming the man Fanny desires and who he believes he can be: "'It is not by protestations that I shall endeavour to convince you I am wronged, it is not by telling you that my affections are steady. My conduct shall speak for me'" (318). Even as he forms this resolution, however, Henry remains captive to the idea of what Fanny represents rather than the woman who stands before him: "'You have some touches of the angel in you, beyond what – not merely beyond what one sees, because one never sees any thing like it – but beyond what one fancies might be'" (318).

Henry's attempts to forge an independent, authentic sense of self are real. He discards his absentee approach to estate management, visiting Everingham to attend the business of his estate in person and anticipating a life of settled domesticity. When he visits Fanny in Portsmouth to meet her family and reassure her of his enduring love, he foresees their future partnership in managing his estate for the benefit of the local community, expressing his hope "'soon to have an assistant, a friend, a guide in every plan of utility or charity for Everingham, a somebody that would make Everingham and all about it, a dearer object than it had ever been yet'" (376). Even now, Henry defines Fanny's role according to his wants and needs. Henry's efforts, however, are not without effect. Fanny's opinion of him grows steadily more favourable: "'It was pleasing to hear him speak so properly; here, he had been acting as he ought to do. To be the friend of the poor and oppressed! Nothing could be more grateful to her'" (376). She is persuaded that 'he might have more good qualities than she had been wont to suppose. She began to feel the possibility of his turning out well at last [...] He was decidedly improved' (376–77).

Henry's fragile masculine identity, however, remains dangerously dependent on Fanny's judgment: "'When you give me your opinion, I always know what is right. Your judgment is my rule of right'" (383). Travelling to London without Fanny, Henry is unable to sustain his transformed masculine identity and reverts to the performative masculinity valued by his sister and polite sociability. His ensuing affair with Maria Rushworth blights any possibility of a union with Fanny, precisely at the moment when by acting 'as he intended, and as he knew he ought, by going down to Everingham after his return from Portsmouth, he might have been deciding his own happy destiny' (434). Austen is unequivocal that had Henry been capable of transforming himself, he would have succeeded:

> Her influence over him, had already given him some influence over her. Would he have deserved more, there can be no doubt that more would have been obtained; especially when that marriage had taken place, which would have given him the assistance of her conscience in subduing her first inclination, and brought them very often together. Would he have persevered, and uprightly, Fanny must have been his reward (433–34).

Henry, however, is irredeemable, and Austen divides him irretrievably from the love of his life:

> we may fairly consider a man of sense, like Henry Crawford, to be providing for himself no small portion of vexation and regret – vexation that must rise sometimes to self-reproach, and regret to wretchedness – in having so requited hospitality, so injured family peace, so forfeited his best, most estimable and endeared acquaintance, and so lost the woman whom he had rationally, as well as passionately loved (435).

Austen exposes as a dangerous fallacy the myth that a man can compensate for his deficiencies by marrying a feminine ideal to complement him. Only Mrs Norris and Mary Crawford continue to believe that Fanny should have married Henry: the former because it would have prevented the social demise of Maria Rushworth (416) and the latter because, "'She would have fixed him'" (423). Although a romantic denouement between Fanny and Henry was reportedly appealing to Austen's early readers, including Cassandra,[36] Austen defeats this narrative trajectory in *Mansfield Park*, refusing to sacrifice her heroine to atone for male weakness or to reward a man incapable of sustaining his own subjectivity.

In Henry, Austen overtly critiques and rejects the supporting role prescribed for women in Evangelical ideology. She more subtly, though no less powerfully, scrutinises this same heterosexual dynamic in the relationship between Fanny and Edmund. Indeed, Austen constructs Edmund as a greater threat even than Henry, as he represents the easy slippage between a personal commitment to the moral health and political stability of the nation and a profoundly conservative view of women defined by ideologies of sexual difference. Edmund may embody an authentic, internalised masculine identity, but he judges women through their performance of socially-prescribed roles determined by Evangelical ideology. He is displeased with Maria's choice to marry Rushworth because he does not believe that her happiness 'should centre in a large income' (38), a house in town and the agency such financial power will bring her. Edmund's love for Mary Crawford is thwarted by his concern that she will not fulfil the prescribed role of 'wife' to a rural clergyman. His views on marriage are clearly influenced by Evangelicalism as he contemplates the possibility of their union after his ordination: 'His duties would be established, but the wife who was to share, and animate, and reward those duties might yet be unattainable' (236). To Edmund, as to Henry, the feminine role is to share male responsibilities and reward male labour.

Edmund's view of marriage as a sexual exchange in which masculine identity is sustained by feminine moral and spiritual guidance is evident in his support for Henry's courtship of Fanny. Like Henry, Edmund does not see Fanny as a person but rather as the embodiment of a conservative feminine role defined by what men require:

> let him succeed at last, Fanny, let him succeed at last. You have proved yourself upright and disinterested, prove yourself grateful and tender-hearted; and then you will be the perfect model of a woman, which I have always believed you born for (322).

Austen clearly echoes Sir Thomas in Edmund's speech: the 'perfect model of a woman' must be 'grateful and tender-hearted', submit and accept. Edmund can rationalise Fanny's refusal only on the grounds that Henry has been too hasty and given her insufficient time to fall in love with him. In a letter to Fanny just days before Henry begins his affair with Maria, Edmund pleads his cause: 'I am more and more satisfied with all that I see and hear of him. There is not a shadow of wavering. He thoroughly knows his own mind, and acts up to his resolutions – an inestimable quality' (392). Edmund knows that Fanny will only accept Henry if he develops and sustains an internalised, authentic masculine identity, and remains convinced not only that Fanny can supply this deficiency, but also that it is her duty to do so.

In the closing chapters of *Mansfield Park*, Austen deftly reconciles her damning judgment of Edmund and rejection of the Evangelical masculinity he represents, with his marriage to Fanny: the inevitable conclusion of the courtship plot. Austen's judgment of Edmund is inscribed through her strategic use of silences — what is unsaid — and, echoing *Sense and Sensibility*, her satire on the generic conventions of the romantic hero.

Henry's affair with Maria and Mary's refusal to sanction it bluntly expose how flawed Edmund's judgment of the Crawfords has been. Yet in his confession to Fanny, Edmund is consumed by his disappointed love for Mary and utterly fails to reflect on his own flawed judgment, advice and behaviour. For all Edmund's self-examination he, like Henry, is incapable of personal transformation. At no point do either Edmund or Sir Thomas admit how wrong they were in pressing Fanny to marry Henry or vindicate her judgment of him. Instead, Sir Thomas, like Henry and Edmund, sees only what Fanny can do for him: his acknowledgment of paternal failure to Maria and Julia is swiftly followed by a realisation that 'Fanny was indeed the daughter that he wanted' and a reflection that in supporting her at Mansfield Park he 'had been rearing a prime comfort for himself' (438).

Describing her as 'My Fanny', Austen's narrator reminds the reader that Fanny is the heroine of a courtship romance novel and that as such, the genre dictates that she must marry someone in the final chapter. Loving Edmund since childhood despite his ample flaws and enduring years of personal trials and mortifications, Fanny deserves to be happy. Although Fanny is the heroine of a courtship romance novel, however, Edmund is far from a romantic hero. Austen resolves the courtship plot but refuses to romanticise their relationship, for which she was criticised by her early readers: Fanny Knight was 'delighted with Fanny; – but not satisfied with the end – wanting more Love between her & Edmund'.[37] Austen's glib account of Edmund falling in love denies her reader the satisfaction typical of the genre:

> I only intreat every body to believe that exactly at the time when it was quite natural that it should be so, and not a week earlier, Edmund did cease to care about Miss Crawford, and became as anxious to marry Fanny, as Fanny herself could desire (436).

As readers, we are left to take the narrator's word for it. Reminding her readers that Edmund's masculine identity is contingent on his groomed 'perfect model for a woman', Austen dwells on what Edmund perceives Fanny can offer him:

> Loving, guiding, protecting her, as he had been doing ever since her being ten years old, her mind in so great a degree formed by his care, and her comfort depending on his kindness, an object to him of such close and peculiar interest, dearer by all his own importance with her than any one else at Mansfield, what was there now to add, but that he should learn to prefer soft light eyes to sparkling dark ones (436–37).

Reducing Edmund's love for Fanny to the vanity produced by her adoration of him and his new preference for her eyes over Mary's, Austen exposes the thinness of his masculine identity and the paucity he can offer Fanny. Edmund's reflection — 'She was of course only too good for him' (437) — crystallises the central paradox of Evangelical male subjectivity. Fanny *is* too good for Edmund — 'nobody minds having what is too good for them' (437) — but the sexual hierarchy within their relationship circumscribes her agency. Indeed, Austen reveals the notion of feminine moral and spiritual guidance even over a man like Edmund to be a fallacy: Edmund may have 'formed her mind and gained her affections' (61), but in relation to the theatricals, his pursuit of Mary Crawford, and her relationship with Henry, he has consistently refused to follow her advice.

Austen's denouement in *Mansfield Park* drives a schism between romance and marriage that is unique in her work. Austen's vision of romance is defined by her heroines' marriages to men who embody a modern male subjectivity that is independent of a sexual hierarchy and who value their individuality and selfhood. The marriages that conclude Austen's novels offer the hope that her heroines will realise their best selves not because they marry, but because of who they marry; Austen's construction of the male protagonist is instrumental to the heroine's capacity for self-realisation within the institution of marriage. In *Mansfield Park*, Austen defies this typical resolution of her courtship plot. The schism between romance and marriage that concludes *Mansfield Park* results neither from Austen's narrative failure nor her inability to reconcile realism with romance. Rather, Austen refuses to romanticise Fanny's marriage to a man who does not offer her the self-realisation promised, in different ways, to Marianne, Elinor, Catherine, Elizabeth, Emma and Anne. The centrality of the male protagonist to Austen's conception of romance is starkly revealed in *Mansfield Park* by the striking absence of romance from the relationship between Fanny and Edmund.

Austen's rejoinder to the Evangelical novel concludes with her least romantic ending, because, to Austen, there is ultimately nothing to celebrate in the masculine and feminine ideals endorsed in Evangelical fiction. In *Mansfield Park*, Austen recreates Evangelical masculinity and femininity to illustrate the impossibility of romance between them, even within a courtship romance novel. Any sexual ideology in which feminine agency is circumscribed by masculine needand indeed redemption defies romance itself. In terms of her rewriting of masculinity, *Mansfield Park* is Austen's most pessimistic novel, not because of the near-destruction of the Bertram family and Mansfield Park estate and Austen's projection of this threat onto the national stage, but because no man is capable of imagining a role for women beyond the fulfilment of his own needs. In her final two novels, however, Austen returns to the celebration of authentic masculinity and feminine agency of her earlier works, with a greater awareness of the possibilities and limitations of genre and the complexity of romance and individual selfhood for both men and women.

5 'A disgrace to the name of man'

Emma, the National Tale and the Historical Novel

Emma is the only novel in which Jane Austen does not feature a male 'villain'. No man in *Emma* causes harm to others of the kind inflicted by John Willoughby, George Wickham or Henry Crawford, who leave a trail of human wreckage in their wake; no man is engaged in the brutal, mercenary games of brinkmanship in which John Thorpe, General Tilney and William Elliot indulge at the expense of those around them. Yet the behaviour of Frank Churchill — forming a secret engagement with one woman and concealing it by flirting with another — triggers the most damning criticism of a man in all of Austen's fiction. On the exposure of Frank's engagement to Jane Fairfax, Mr Knightley denounces him as an '"Abominable scoundrel!"' and, channelling the anxiety over masculinity that permeates the novel, '"a disgrace to the name of man"' (399). Emma matches Mr Knightley's gendered judgment:

> It has sunk him, I cannot say how it has sunk him in my opinion. So unlike what a man should be! – None of that upright integrity, that strict adherence to truth and principle, that disdain of trick and littleness, which a man should display in every transaction of his life (373).

Why is Frank Churchill so thoroughly damned, not only as a person, but specifically as a man? In *Emma*, the question of what a man ought to be reaches a political climax within Austen's fiction. In the world of Highbury, the stakes have become so high that the novel does not require a 'villain'. Any deviation from an authentic masculine identity — any dereliction from duty, any reliance on social performance to 'play the man', any aberration from Austen's masculine ideal — leaves a man vulnerable to the searing judgment of those around him, and his author.

Uniquely in *Emma*, as the exchange between Emma and Mr Knightley reveals, Jane Austen's rewriting of masculinity is heightened by the characters themselves repeatedly and contentiously discussing the question of what a man should be; as Claudia L. Johnson remarks, 'what "true" masculinity is like – what a "man" is, how a man speaks and behaves, what a man really wants – is the subject of continual debate'.[1] In *Emma*, Austen explores masculinity through a particularly Anglocentric, nationalist lens. Her characterisations of George Knightley and his 'rival' Frank Churchill project masculine identities into discourses of national progress and survival that reflect the ongoing conflict between Britain and France.[2] There is little that is subtle in Austen's portrayal of George Knightley. A professional estate manager, farmer and local magistrate whose home is an English agricultural idyll, Mr Knightley is personally invested in the social and moral responsibilities that come with his position. He cultivates relationships with people across the social spectrum and values individual advancement through merit and a commitment to self-improvement. His plain-spoken language, direct conversation and manners, dislike of finery and fashion, and serious disposition are hallmarks of a peculiarly English national character celebrated throughout the post-Revolutionary period.[3] The name 'George Knightley' specifically links England's patron saint with both the Hanover royal family and the chivalric masculinity popularised in the Romantic period.[4] As if this is insufficient to make her point, Austen compounds Mr Knightley's symbolism with a desirable, English masculinity by explicitly contrasting him with his foil, the Francophilic Frank, who he implicitly distrusts and relentlessly scrutinises throughout the novel.[5]

Austen's engagement with nationalist discourses in *Emma* extends well beyond her characterisation of Mr Knightley and Frank through rival national identities. Austen also intervenes in a tussle between the national tale and the historical novel, and their competing modes of national and gender representation, taking place in the Romantic literary marketplace. Having thoroughly excoriated the Evangelical novel in *Mansfield Park*, in *Emma* Austen evaluates the dual genres of history and fiction, and the merging between them, according to the same essential criteria: their capacity to rewrite masculinity through its connection to feminine agency.

As a 'voracious, and critical, reader – particularly of the novel writers who were her contemporaries',[6] Austen was well versed in the national tale and the historical novel. The national tale was established with Maria Edgeworth's *Castle Rackrent* (1800) and Sydney Owenson's *The Wild Irish Girl* (1806), and became 'one of the most important trends affecting the market for fiction' in the early decades of the nineteenth century, particularly between 1806 and 1814.[7] Following the *Acts of Union* that in 1801 merged Great Britain with Ireland to form the United Kingdom, the national tale explored the popular representation of national cultures, geographies and languages, and interrogated relationships between England, Ireland, Scotland and, to a lesser extent, Wales. Many national tales, including *The Wild Irish Girl* and Germaine de Staël's *Corinne* (1807) explore national identities and relationships through a courtship romance narrative in which an English male protagonist falls in love with a beautiful, passionate and accomplished heroine, representative of her national culture and connected to an essentialised local landscape.[8] The historical novel developed alongside the national tale and was similarly concerned with the representation of national identities by interpreting the present through the past. Although it predates the national tale, beginning with Sophia Lee's *The Recess* (1783–85), the historical novel coincided with the national tale in its popularity in the early decades of the nineteenth century, with Jane Porter's *Thaddeus of Warsaw* (1803) and *The Scottish Chiefs* (1810), Jane West's *The Loyalists* (1812) and *Alicia de Lacy* (1814), and Walter Scott's *Waverley* (1814).

When Austen was writing *Emma* in 1814, the national tale and the historical novel were both enjoying a heyday. Austen's correspondence reveals that she had read *The Wild Irish Girl* and *Corinne*. It is also probable that she had read the national tales of her favourite contemporary Maria Edgeworth, whose *Tales of Fashionable Life*, including *Ennui* (1809) and *The Absentee* (1812), are mentioned in her letters and were held in the library at Godmersham, her brother Edward's Kent estate, where she visited.[9] Austen's interest in the historical novels of 1814 is revealed in a letter to her niece Anna Austen, herself a budding novelist:

> Walter Scott has no business to write novels, especially good ones. – It is not fair. – He has Fame & Profit enough as a Poet, and should not be taking the bread out of other people's mouths. – I do not like him, & do not mean to like Waverley if I can help it – but fear I must. – I am quite determined however not to be pleased with Mrs West's Alicia de Lacy, should I ever meet with it, which I hope I may not. – I think I *can* be stout against any thing written by Mrs West. – I have made up my mind to like no Novels really, but Miss Edgeworth's, Yours & my own.[10]

The influence of both genres may be traced in *Emma*'s unique sense of England and its 'others', both local and global: Emma alludes to animosity between England and Scotland regarding the employment of a new bailiff (99); Jane Fairfax's childhood friend marries an Irish landowner; Frank Churchill is associated with French language and culture; and Mrs Elton flippantly refers to a 'fling at the slave trade' (279). Indeed, *Emma* has been described as Austen's 'riposte' to the national tale by writing England's own 'national tale'.[11]

Austen's pervading concern with masculinity in *Emma* reflects the influence of the national tale and the historical novel, genres that offered women writers new generic opportunities to interrogate masculinity in more explicitly public and political contexts. As Katie Trumpener argues, the genres were at once both interdependent and in conflict, 'almost identical in basic plot and character structures, and yet already highly polarized in their overall novelistic strategies and political implications'.[12] This volatility may stem from their very different approaches to representing gender. The national tale repeats variations on a standard courtship romance plot in which a young, jaded English male protagonist is cured from his dissolute lifestyle by falling in love with an intellectually accomplished, morally pure and essentially passive heroine who is representative of her native country. In the works of Owenson and de Staël, as Anthony Mandal argues, the heroines Glorvina and Corinne are 'objects to be gazed upon by their male counterparts' and act as 'instructress to the jaded male protagonist'.[13] A similar gender dynamic is at work in Edgeworth's *Ennui* and *The Absentee*, which abound with visions of dysfunctional and failed men: reckless and incompetent landlords; corrupt and deceptive estate managers and attorneys; and ineffectual young men of wealth and privilege.[14] Edgeworth evaluates masculine worth according to a public, professional index that focuses on relationships between estate, community and nation; Glenthorn in *Ennui* and Colambre in *The Absentee* develop or exhibit the public masculine ideals endorsed by Edgeworth and are rewarded with marriage to the passive and docile Cecilia Delamare and Grace Nugent. As a genre, the national tale was uninterested in interrogating how masculinity was constructed in relation to the feminine. Lacking the ambition to rewrite masculinity in the context of private relationships, the genre — like the Evangelical novel — relied on conservative gender hierarchies to underpin its public masculine ideals.[15]

Women writers of historical novels took a rather different approach to constructing gender through national identity. The historical novel, as Fiona Price argues, provided women writers with an opportunity 'to transform politics by rewriting the history of gender and re-imagining sexual relations'.[16] There was an urgency to the historical reappraisal of masculinity and femininity, because 'rewriting the history of gender could ... lead to a wholesale reassessment of the nation's political and moral life'.[17] This agenda is clearly at work in Jane Porter's *The Scottish Chiefs*, which was extraordinarily popular and became 'the second most reissued title of the decade'.[18] A fictionalised account of William Wallace's thirteenth-century rebellion against the English, in *The Scottish Chiefs* Porter entwines men's romantic relationships, domestic lives and public duties to celebrate a modern masculine ideal that complements a strong and empowered feminine agency.[19] As Price argues, Porter's 'emphasis on folklore, heroism and Christianity, rather than on chivalry and sexual gratification, creates a national romance in which both sexes can participate'.[20]

In *Emma*, Jane Austen dissects how each genre constructs gender ideals and the relationship between them. Austen's two central couples — Frank Churchill and Jane Fairfax, and Emma Woodhouse and Mr Knightley — reflect the masculine and feminine ideals and diverging approaches to romance, courtship and marriage represented in the national tale and the historical novel respectively. Austen specifically links Frank with Horatio and Glenthorn, heroes of *The Wild Irish Girl* and *Ennui*: wealthy, idle young men who lack responsibility and purpose, and relieve their boredom or 'ennui' through a luxurious and expensive lifestyle. Finding themselves in debt and out of favour with their parents, they travel to their families' ancestral estates in Ireland to escape metropolitan life, cure their ennui and regain financial security. Similarly rich and idle, with the exception of his demanding aunt Frank possesses complete financial independence and freedom, yet lacks purpose. Dividing his time between his family home, watering places such as Weymouth, London and, eventually, Highbury, Frank has no personal or professional responsibilities whatsoever. He falls in love with Jane Fairfax, an Anglicised version of the beautiful, modest and highly-accomplished heroine of the national tale, who holds out the promise of saving him from himself. In Frank and Jane, Austen's response to the national tale is positively vitriolic, denouncing the genre's masculine and feminine ideals and reinscription of the hierarchy between them. Like the Evangelical fiction Austen censured in *Mansfield Park*, the national tale threatened the courtship romance novel by insisting on the conservative model of gender relations she had debunked in *Sense and Sensibility*, *Northanger Abbey* and *Pride and Prejudice*.

Austen contrasts Frank and Jane with the relationship shared between Mr Knightley and Emma. Austen's characterisation of Mr Knightley through the lens of English national character and her projection of the estate into discourses of national prosperity has been interpreted as signifying a positive dialogue with the national tale.[21] Through Emma's gaze, the Donwell Abbey estate symbolises the authentic, unpolished realness at the core of Mr Knightley's persona:

> she viewed the respectable size and style of the building, its suitable, becoming characteristic situation, low and sheltered – its ample gardens stretching down to meadows washed by a stream, of which the Abbey, with all the old neglect of prospect, had scarcely a sight – and its abundance of timber in rows and avenues, which neither fashion nor extravagance had rooted up. – The house was larger than Hartfield, and totally unlike it, covering a good deal of ground, rambling and irregular, with many comfortable and one or two handsome rooms. – It was just what it ought to be, and it looked what it was (335–36).

Emma's reflection on the Knightleys as 'a family of such true gentility, untainted in blood and understanding', and praise of Isabella, who had 'connected herself unexceptionably' and 'given them neither men, nor names, nor places, that could raise a blush' (336), distinguishes the Knightley family from the reckless irresponsibility, wantonness and other mortifications of the Rackrents, Glenthorns and, to a lesser extent,

Clonbronies of Edgeworth's national tales. Instead, Mr Knightley shares the same values as Lord Colambre in *The Absentee*, viewing his estate as the centre of a thriving agricultural community:

> The considerable slope, at nearly the foot of which the Abbey stood, gradually acquired a steeper form beyond its grounds; and at half a mile distant was a bank of considerable abruptness and grandeur, well clothed with wood; – and at the bottom of this bank, favourably placed and sheltered, rose the Abbey-Mill Farm, with meadows in front, and the river making a close and handsome curve around it (337–38).

Donwell Abbey captures the integration between residence, farm and the natural environment, and the close relationship between landlord, employees and tenants, celebrated by Edgeworth.

Aligning Austen's characterisation of Mr Knightley with the public ideals of the national tale, however, persists in privileging the public over the private in Austen's rewriting of masculinity. The national tale's male protagonists may develop or express a public masculine ideal, but their understanding of male subjectivity in relation to women remains profoundly conservative. Even in *The Absentee*, Edgeworth does not require Colambre to really grapple with a woman's agency, Grace Nugent being possessed of the 'perfect simplicity and innocence' reflected in Isabella Knightley and Harriet Smith.[22] For all Mr Knightley's laudable qualities — his progressive approach to land ownership and class mobility, his strong sense of social and community responsibility and his symbolism in terms of English national culture — his transformative power lies not in what he can offer the community or the nation, but in what he can offer Emma.

Emma Woodhouse is, and knows herself to be, fundamentally incompatible with prescribed feminine roles within romance, courtship and marriage. Emma contemplates this conventional mode of 'romance' when she tells Harriet, '"I never have been in love; it is not my way, or my nature; and I do not think I ever shall"' (82). Emma declares early in the novel that she will never marry because she is unwilling to surrender the power and freedom she enjoys at Hartfield and in Highbury. Highly individualistic and determined to retain her agency, Emma refuses to be subordinated within a sexual hierarchy of any kind. She explicitly renounces the deferential wifely role typified in her sister Isabella when she refuses to humour John Knightley's complaints about dining out on a snowy evening: 'Emma did not find herself equal to give the pleased assent, which no doubt he was in the habit of receiving, to emulate the "Very true, my love," which must have been usually administered by his travelling companion' (108). Emma's real maturation throughout the novel is not to curb her individualism or to cement her social integration, but to accurately identify the desirable man and recognise the opportunity that has been before her all along. Emma's marriage is not enabled by any personal development within her, but instead by the model of masculinity Mr Knightley represents.

In *Emma*, Austen turns to history writing not to draw on the past to explain the present, or to locate her courtship romance within a historical narrative of progress or continuity, but for the rewriting of gender that was taking place within the genre.[23] Although Johnson claims that Mr Knightley has few if any literary predecessors — 'there is nothing in Scott, Burney, More, Burke, Radcliffe, or Edgeworth remotely like him'[24] — there may perhaps be in Jane Porter. There is no surviving evidence to establish with certainty that Austen read *The Scottish Chiefs*, although the novel's extraordinary popularity, combined with Austen's avid consumption of contemporary fiction and her references to the work of Porter's sister Anna Maria, make it unlikely that Austen would not have opened its pages. As Mandal argues, 'the peripatetic historical romances of the Porters' may be traced in Austen's 'Plan of a Novel', written shortly after the publication of *Emma* in December 1815.[25] Accounts of the connections between Austen and Porter typically focus on the latter due to her longevity (she lived until 1850), her admiration of Austen's work and connections between the Porter and Austen families that postdate Austen's death.[26] There are clear parallels, however, between the rewriting of masculinity and its enabling of feminine agency in *Emma* and *The Scottish Chiefs*, revealing dialogic textual connections between Austen and Porter that are worthy of investigation.

Porter's invention of a heroine, Lady Helen Mar, offers a feminine perspective on historical events in *The Scottish Chiefs* and enables a courtship romance to take place within her historical narrative. Helen Mar embodies an agency grounded in her responsibilities as a social leader, a Christian woman and her patriotic duty, which she pursues despite the social expectations and limitations placed upon her as a single woman in the context of a military conflict. Helen orchestrates the retrieval of Marion Wallace's body and its Christian burial while the rebellion is unfolding. She walks alone through the night to convey to Wallace a letter dropped by an enemy messenger, feeling 'her soul awake to all its antient patriotic enthusiasm' and hoping he '"will excuse the, perhaps, unsexual action of this night?"'[27] Helen uses violence to defend herself from the predations of English and Scottish men, whose patriotic duty is compromised by their compulsion to possess her. Twice saved by Wallace, Helen in turn acts as his saviour from an assassin when they are praying together in her family chapel. She repeatedly expresses her wish to fight alongside him: '"Ah, what would I give to be my cousin Murray, to bear this pennon at his side!"' and later, '"Ah, that I could be in Edwin's place, and wait upon his smiles, and with my bosom shield his breast! But that may not be: I am a woman, and formed to suffer in silence and seclusion"'.[28]

More powerful than Porter's characterisation of Helen Mar is her construction of William Wallace as embodying a masculine identity that is drawn to rather than repelled by her agency and autonomy. In contrast to the men who seek to limit and control Helen, Wallace represents a male subjectivity that exists independently of the ideologies of sexual difference that underpin conventional gender hierarchies. He allows women to speak for him publicly: first Marion in her confrontation with his English attackers and later Helen in her conference with King Edward. He despises the model of femininity typified by courtly love and the women who perform it. It is Helen's mental strength — she claims '"my frame is weaker than my mind"' — that ignites his love for her: '"If aught on earth ever resembled the beloved of my soul, it is Helen Mar!"'[29] Learning of Wallace's imprisonment in the Tower of London and probable execution, Helen dresses as a page, rides a horse alone to a port, boards a ship and sails for ten days to London, then bribes a guard to join Wallace in his cell. Fearful that he will reproach her for her conduct, 'she wondered how she could ever have so trampled on the retreating modesty of her nature, as to have brought herself thus into his presence', asking Wallace, '"will you not abhor me for this act of madness? But I was not myself ... you pardon me this apparent forgetfulness of my sex?"'[30] Far from deploring her conduct, Wallace declares his love and marries her. Unwilling to confine women like Helen to their prescribed roles within chivalric discourse, Wallace's challenge throughout *The Scottish Chiefs* is to balance Helen's determined individualism and autonomy with the very real need to protect her.

Porter's courtship narrative is ultimately subservient to historical events; Wallace's execution denies the realisation of the alternative approach to gender relationships she forecasts. In *Emma*, Austen domesticates, modernises and Anglicises the masculine and feminine gender identities Porter creates in *The Scottish Chiefs* and the dynamic relationship between them. In her preface to the 1840 edition, Porter described *The Scottish Chiefs* as 'a tale ... of men true to themselves, to the laws and rightful independence of their country'[31]; for both Mr Knightley and Wallace, the measure of masculine authenticity lies not only in national affiliation and service, but also in the realisation of feminine agency. Austen's dialogue with *The Scottish Chiefs* anchors her futuristic vision of romance and marriage in a historical foundation,[32] privileging women's history and its focus on the private over the public within a contentious political climate. Walter Scott, who commented privately on *The Scottish Chiefs* and reviewed *Emma*, appears not to have noticed the revolutionary sexual politics at the heart of both novels. He lambasted Porter for her characterisation of Wallace:

> Lord help her! Her Wallace is no more our Wallace than Lord Peter is, or King Henry's messenger to Peter Hotspur. It is not safe

meddling with the hero of a country; and of all other, I cannot bear to see the character of Wallace frittered away to that of a fine gentleman.[33]

In his review of *Emma*, Scott described Mr Knightley, Austen's revolutionary male paragon, as 'the sturdy, advice-giving bachelor'.[34]

Mr Knightley possesses the most stable, assured and authentic masculine identity in all of Austen's fiction. In a marked distinction from Henry Tilney, Fitzwilliam Darcy and Frederick Wentworth, he does not develop or change at all in the course of the courtship romance plot. Instead, Austen presents the worth and security of Mr Knightley's masculine identity and its inherent desirability as a *fait accompli*. Austen repeatedly contrasts him with the other men of the novel, particularly Frank and Mr Elton, for whom masculinity is essentially a matter of social performance rather than internalised subjectivity. Shaped by the context of polite sociability and its insistence on a sexual hierarchy to maintain masculine status, these men are unable to extricate themselves from traditional roles within romance, courtship and marriage. They are, therefore, wholly unable to meet the needs of a woman like Emma. These men are judged and found wanting not because of the threat they present to the community and the nation, but because their adherence to performative masculinity renders them incapable of enabling feminine agency. Even among men less focused on social performance — his brother John Knightley and his tenant Robert Martin — Mr Knightley seems unaware of his exceptionalism when he proclaims to Emma: '"Men of sense, whatever you may chuse to say, do not want silly wives"' (63).[35] John Knightley and Robert Martin may be men of sense, but they still desire women who are charming and sociable but are ultimately vapid and weak-willed. John Knightley may share frank conversations with Isabella, Emma and Jane, but it is difficult to imagine this preview of the Victorian *paterfamilias*, 'rising in his profession, domestic, and respectable in his private character' (89), desiring as his wife a woman with even half Emma's sense of agency.

If the heroines of national tales and Evangelical fiction mirrored popular taste in feminine characterisation, Austen's remark that Emma Woodhouse would be 'a heroine whom no one but myself will much like' is an acerbic reflection on the Romantic literary marketplace.[36] Emma's agency and individualism, combined with her fallibility, blindness and propensity to interfere in the affairs of others, are critical to Austen's interventions in genre to rewrite masculinity in *Emma*. Austen dramatises Emma's development through her growing understanding and appreciation of the masculine ideal she champions. The heroine's narrative perspective drives a dual critique of masculinities. Her declaration that she will never marry displaces her scrutiny of men from herself onto others; her work as a matchmaker, community observer and social leader frames her evaluations of the men around her. As Emma surveys Highbury's eligible bachelors on behalf of other women, she refines her ideas about desirable masculinity through the language of conventional attitudes to romance and courtship. Simultaneously, she unconsciously develops a conception of her own masculine ideal who is far from conventional and increasingly resembles the model of masculinity embodied in Mr Knightley. This duality anchors Austen's critique of masculinities at the centre of *Emma*, as the reader receives both Emma's cognitive analysis of the men she encounters and, on another level, observes her unconsciously emerging vision of the desirable man.

From the novel's beginning, it is apparent that once Emma has established a man's marital status and socio-economic eligibility, her index of his desirability is constituted wholly by his capacity for social performance. Emma's identification of Mr Weston as a suitable match for Miss Taylor is grounded in his 'unexceptionable character, easy fortune, suitable age and pleasant manners' (8). Apart from his social position, Emma's chief objection to Robert Martin as a husband for Harriet relates to his '"entire want of gentility"' (32). She tells Harriet, '"I had no idea he could be so very clownish, so entirely without air"', describes him as '"awkward and abrupt"' and forecasts that with age he will become '"a completely gross, vulgar farmer – totally inattentive to appearances, and thinking of nothing but profit and loss"' (33). The match Emma proposes for Harriet, Mr Elton, is by contrast a man whose 'gallantry was always on the alert' (47) and whose manners are so good, Emma informs her, that he might be '"held up as a pattern"' (33). As the reader suspects and John Knightley divulges, Mr Elton's manners change drastically in female company:

> I never in my life saw a man more intent on being agreeable than Mr. Elton. It is downright labour to him where ladies are concerned. With men he can be rational and unaffected, but when he has ladies to please every feature works (106).

Despite remarking to herself that '"he does sigh and languish, and study for compliments rather more than I could endure as a principal"' (48), Emma perversely approves such a performative masculinity, assuming it represents what other women want.

Emma's resolute belief in male social performance is only temporarily rocked by her entanglement with Mr Elton, whose marriage proposal exposes him as 'proud, assuming, conceited; very full of his own claims, and little concerned about the feelings of others' (128). The charm of manners is evident in her hopes for Frank Churchill, the only man she is prepared to contemplate as a potential suitor: 'She had frequently thought – especially since his father's marriage with Miss Taylor – that if she *were* to marry, he was the very person to suit her in age, character and condition' (112). Emma's quarrel with Mr Knightley reveals her vision of Frank as a polite ideal:

> My idea of him is, that he can adapt his conversation to the taste of every body, and has the power as well as the wish of being universally agreeable ... having that general information on all subjects which will enable him to follow the lead, or take the lead, just as propriety may require, and to speak extremely well on each (141).

Mr Knightley counters:

> your amiable young man can be amiable only in French, not in English. He may be very 'aimable,' have very good manners, and be very agreeable; but he can have no English delicacy towards the feelings of other people: nothing really amiable about him (141).[37]

Mr Knightley's criticism of Frank, before he has even arrived in Highbury, is triggered by his absence on his father's marriage, in which Austen matches Edgeworth's critique of absentee English landlords in *Castle Rackrent*, *Ennui* and *The Absentee*. To both Emma and Mr Knightley, Frank's absence is not only a failure of duty, but also a failure of gender. Emma explicitly connects Frank's capacity to perform his duty to his father with the freedom that comes from being male:

> If he could stay only a couple of days, he ought to come; and one can hardly conceive a young man's not having it in his power to do as much as that ... one cannot comprehend a young *man*'s being under such restraint, as not to be able to spend a week with his father, if he likes it (116).

Frank's flourishing letters of apology do not convince Mr Knightley: "'It is Frank Churchill's duty to pay this attention to his father. He knows it to be so, by his promises and messages; but if he wished to do it, it might be done"' (138). His language clearly links Frank with the idle pleasure-seeking of Horatio and Glenthorn: "'He cannot want money – he cannot want leisure. We know, on the contrary, that he has so much of both, that he is glad to get rid of them at the idlest haunts in the kingdom"' (138). Refusing to allow Emma to advocate for Frank and his responsibilities to the Churchills, Mr Knightley claims fulfilment of duty as critical to a stable, authentic masculine identity: "'There is one thing, Emma, which a man can always do, if he chuses, and that is, his duty; not by manoeuvring and finessing, but by vigour and resolution ... A man who felt rightly would"' (138).

Emma remains captivated by form over substance, and on Frank's arrival he more than answers her wishes:

> he was a *very* good looking young man; height, air, address, all were unexceptionable, and his countenance had a great deal of the spirit and liveliness of his father's; he looked quick and sensible. She felt immediately that she should like him (179).

In his description of Highbury as 'home' and his professions that he had 'always felt the sort of interest in the country which none but one's *own* country gives, and the greatest curiosity to visit it' (179), Frank performs the role played by English travellers to their ancestral origins in the national tale. Frank's desire to '"prove myself to belong to the place, to be a true citizen of Highbury"' (187) — making a purchase at Ford's — both mirrors and satirises the process by which Horatio, Glenthorn and Colambre learn to appreciate Irish culture and nationhood. Emma is charmed — '"I do admire your patriotism"' (187) — and praising his pleasant manners and desire to please, her chief regret on Frank's abrupt departure is the loss of his 'indescribable spirit; the idea, the expectation of seeing him which every morning had brought, the assurance of his attentions, his liveliness, his manners!' (243). Emma's approbation begins and remains solely with Frank's social performance; she fancies herself in love, albeit temporarily, despite their relationship having acquired no depth beyond the predictable, formulaic interactions of polite sociability.

Austen's critique of Frank through the national tale intensifies in volume three, when he returns to Highbury and relationships between him, Jane, Emma and Mr Knightley become increasingly fraught. Austen's critique of the national tale reaches its zenith in the strawberry-picking outing to Donwell Abbey, as she aligns Frank and Mr Knightley with diverging masculine types drawn from the genre. To Emma, Donwell Abbey is a specifically English idyll: 'English verdure, English culture, English comfort, seen under a sun bright, without being oppressive' (338). The Englishness of Mr Knightley's estate establishes a platform from which Austen refutes the masculinity symbolised in the national tale's jaded, indulged male protagonist. Arriving late and distressed by his meeting with Jane, Frank declares '"I am sick of England – and would leave it to-morrow, if I could"', directly echoing Glenthorn's statement that he is 'tired of England' in *Ennui*.[38] Like Horatio and Glenthorn, Frank proposes travel as his cure: a tour to 'Swisserland', from which Emma will receive '"my sketches ... or my tour to read – or my poem"' (342). Exploiting the language of ennui that afflicts these 'heroes', Emma refuses to humour or indulge him: '"You are sick of prosperity and indulgence. Cannot you invent a few hardships for yourself, and be contented to stay?"' Persisting in his discontent, Frank claims that he is '"not at all a fortunate person"' and, like Horatio and Glenthorn, seeks solace and redemption in the heroine: "'I shall sit by you. You are my best cure"'. It is a role Emma explicitly renounces, and Mr Knightley would never ask a woman to play.

It is not Emma, however, but Jane Fairfax who will be Frank's 'cure'. The 'heroes' of national tales, including Horatio and Glenthorn, must learn both an appreciation of Irish culture, and the value of work, enterprise and independence, before they are rewarded with marriage to Glorvina and Cecilia. Unlike his counterparts, however, Frank effects no personal reform whatsoever. Content to play the urbane, agreeable, flirtatious young man, Frank's concealment of his private engagement to Jane is but another kind of performance that provides ample material for his mock flirtation with Emma. Unlike Henry Tilney and Edward Ferrars, who find themselves in similarly compromised positions with the women they love and who also bear the yoke of parental oppression, for most of the novel Frank is untroubled by this state of affairs. It is only when Jane can bear his histrionics no longer and all but severs their engagement that he is forced to act, and even his aunt's timely death means that, unlike Henry and Edward, he is not required to make difficult choices or mature in any way to be united with the woman he loves. Unlike Glorvina and Cecilia, Jane is less a reward for masculine reform than the lynchpin on which it depends; as Mr Knightley concedes, "'he may yet turn out well. – With such a woman he has a chance"' (400).

With Frank's highly sexualised view of Jane, however, Austen throws into doubt the possibility of any real reform. Like Glorvina, Cecilia and Grace, Jane is unequivocally objectified within the male gaze, as Frank reveals in his platitudes to Emma on her body and beauty:

> She is a complete angel. Look at her. Is not she an angel in every gesture? Observe the turn of her throat. Observe her eyes ... my uncle means to give her all my aunt's jewels. They are to be new set. I am resolved to have some ornament for the head. Will not it be beautiful in her dark hair? (448).

Impatient with his vacuous praise, Emma can only respond, "'Very beautiful, indeed"'. As Mr Knightley had prophesied, Emma's "'own good sense could not endure such a puppy when it came to the point"' (142). Frank's identity begins and remains essentially a social construct underpinned by ideologies of sexual difference, the shallowness of which prevents him from forging the authentic masculine identity demanded by a woman such as Emma.

Austen's construction of the relationship between Frank Churchill and Jane Fairfax illuminates the spectacular failure of the national tale to reform masculinity and the perverse sexual hierarchy at the heart of the genre. The national tale offers only a model of masculinity that, in *Emma*, Austen labels '"a disgrace to the name of man"' (399). Her contrasting couple, Mr Knightley and Emma, represent a wholly different approach to heterosexual romance, reflecting the gender identities rewritten through the historical novel. Mr Knightley, like Porter's William Wallace, rejects chivalric discourse and, with it, all forms of social performance that are founded on ideologies of sexual difference. More than any of Austen's other male protagonists, he embodies Mary Wollstonecraft's 'wish to see the distinction of sex confounded in society'.[39] His (vain) attempts to influence Emma are intended to make her a better person, not a better woman to be judged by any standard or model of femininity. Austen's diversions from Emma's narrative perspective reveal Mr Knightley's conversations with Mrs Weston, Miss Bates, Mrs Elton and Jane Fairfax, in which he reflects Wollstonecraft's vision of a man whose communication with women reflects 'that reciprocation of civility which the dictates of humanity and the politeness of civilization authorise between man and man'.[40] He argues with Mrs Weston about Emma's friendship with Harriet Smith, refuses to humour Mrs Elton, and despite his openly expressed admiration for her, declines to flatter Jane Fairfax on her accomplishments, preferring instead rational conversation.

Emma's mistaken value for male social performance prevents her, almost until the end of the novel, from really understanding Mr Knightley or appreciating what he alone can offer her. Her praise focuses on his '"downright, decided, commanding sort of manner"' (33) and she tells Harriet, '"Mr Knightley's air is so remarkably good, that it is not fair to compare Mr. Martin with *him*. You might not see one in a hundred, with *gentleman* so plainly written as in Mr Knightley"' (32). Blinded by her own obsession with manners and enticed by Mr Elton and Frank to participate in their brand of gallant sociability, Emma does not see that for Mr Knightley, social performance is wholly irrelevant to either his gender identity or his relationships with others. Emma's confusion is evident on his arrival at the Coles' dinner party: 'Mr Knightley ... was too apt, in Emma's opinion, to get about as he could, and not use his carriage so often as became the owner of Donwell Abbey' (199). She praises him for using his carriage, unaware that it is on Jane Fairfax's account:

> There is always a look of consciousness or bustle when people come in a way which they know to be beneath them. You think you carry it off very well, I dare say, but with you it is a sort of bravado, an air of affected unconcern; I always observe it whenever I meet you under those circumstances. *Now* you have nothing to try for. You are not afraid of being supposed ashamed. You are not striving to look taller than any body else (199).

Still ignorant that Mr Knightley is the last man who would behave with such 'bravado' or 'affected unconcern' — merely alternative forms of social performance — Emma fails to recognise his genuine disregard for people whose opinion would be influenced by displays of wealth or social position. Her later comment to Mrs Weston on discovering his kindness to Jane that Mr Knightley is '"not a gallant man, but he is a very humane one"' (208) reveals both her value for his benevolence and her regret that he is unsuited to the social performance that she values.

While Emma obsesses over the manners of her male acquaintance and laments Mr Knightley's unwillingness to perform a prescribed social role, she unconsciously develops her own vision of what a man ought to be that increasingly resembles the masculine identity he embodies. Her remarks on Robert Martin's letter of proposal to Harriet could be made of Mr Knightley:

> No doubt he is a sensible man, and I suppose may have a natural talent for – thinks strongly and clearly – and when he takes a pen in hand, his thoughts naturally find their proper words. It is so with some men. Yes, I understand the sort of mind. Vigorous, decided, with sentiments to a certain point, not coarse (50).

When she reflects on John Knightley's dislike of socialising away from home, she could be thinking of his brother:

> There was something honourable and valuable in the strong domestic habits, the all-sufficiency of home to himself, whence resulted her brother's disposition to look down on the common rate of social intercourse, and those to whom it was important. – It had a high claim to forbearance (93).

Contemplating Mr Weston's lack of discernment in social company, she thinks to herself, 'General benevolence, but not general friendship, made a man what he ought to be. – She could fancy such a man' (300), reflecting her appreciation of Mr Knightley's intelligent liberality within his community.

Like William Wallace, George Knightley falls in love with a strong, determined and independent woman and, also like Wallace, he is torn between doing nothing so that her agency can flourish and protecting her from threats presented by other men: Mr Elton, Frank Churchill and, in a different though equally dangerous way, Mr Woodhouse. When Mr Knightley suspects a relationship between Frank and Jane, he tries in vain to warn Emma and emotionally shield her from Frank's duplicity and faithlessness. His anxiety over Emma peaks during the excursion to Box Hill, when her offensive rudeness to Miss Bates signifies Frank's increasing influence and the misuse of her autonomy. Unable to bear it any longer, he retreats to the Knightleys in London. Austen emphasises his heightened emotional state on his departure:

> he took her hand, pressed it, and certainly was on the point of carrying it to his lips – when, from some fancy or other, he suddenly let it go. – Why he should feel such a scruple, why he should change his mind when it was all but done, she could not perceive. – He would have judged better, she thought, if he had not stopped. – The intention, however, was indubitable; and whether it was that his manners had in general so little gallantry, or however else it happened, but she thought nothing became him more. – It was with him, of so simple, yet so dignified a nature (362).

Even when this act triggers Emma's realisation of her love for Mr Knightley — when she sees 'her own heart … with a clearness which had never blessed her before' (382) — still she misunderstands him and fears that he will ultimately prefer a woman who will play a deferential feminine role. While Mr Knightley's refuge in London fails because Isabella is 'too much like Emma – differing only in those striking inferiorities, which always brought the other in brilliancy before him' (405), Emma agonises over the possibility that he may, after all, prefer a conventional, submissive wife. Her earlier teasing that Harriet '"is the very woman for you"' (62) shadows her later contemplation of the possibility that he may return her love: 'Was it a new circumstance for a man of first-rate abilities to be captivated by very inferior powers? Was it new for one, perhaps too busy to seek, to be the prize of a girl who would seek him?' (387).

In the denouement of *Emma*, Austen draws Porter's masculine and feminine ideals and the relationship between them into the domestic courtship romance genre and England's modernising future. Mr Knightley's declaration of his love for Emma is preceded by the '"How d'ye do's"' with which, earlier in the novel, he had greeted his brother (87, 397). Persistent in his refusal to compliment and flatter — '"I cannot make speeches, Emma"' — Austen contrasts his plain-spoken approach with the romantic verbosity of Frank Churchill, which Mr Knightley equates with shallowness of feeling: '"if I loved you less I might be able to talk about it more"' (403). His authenticity is revealed in the simple statement: '"you know what I am – You hear nothing but truth from me"' (403). He may be '"a very indifferent lover"' (403) according to conventional modes of courtship replicated in the relationships of Mr and Mrs Elton and Frank and Jane, but neither he nor Emma is interested in a conventional marriage.

Austen's determination to modernise romance, courtship and marriage in the relationship between Emma and Mr Knightley has been interpreted as signifying a fraternal or fratriarchal, rather than erotic, heterosexual relationship.[41] The need to label their relationship as anything other than erotic reflects the persistence in the twenty-first century of the prescriptive notions of masculinity and femininity and their proper roles in romance and courtship that, in the 1810s, Austen sought to debunk. Emma clearly views Mr Knightley with an eroticism reminiscent of Catherine Morland and Elizabeth Bennet before her, as Austen focalises through her gaze at the ball:

> There he was, among the standers-by, where he ought not to be; he ought to be dancing, – not classing himself with the husbands, and fathers, and whist-players, who were pretending to feel an interest in the dance till their rubbers were made up, – so young as he looked! – He could not have appeared to greater advantage perhaps any where, than where he had placed himself. His tall, firm, upright figure, among the bulky forms and stooping shoulders of the elderly men, was such as Emma felt must draw every body's eyes; and, excepting her own partner, there was not one among the whole row of young men who could be compared with him. – He moved a few steps nearer, and those few steps were enough to prove how gentlemanlike a manner, with what natural grace, he must have danced, would he but take the trouble (305).

Mr Knightley, with characteristic sincerity, openly declares to Mrs Weston: "'I confess that I have seldom seen a face or figure more pleasing to me than her's ... I love to look at her'" (38). Far from advocating marriage based on friendship or the necessary elision of sexuality to achieve marital equality, in *Emma* Austen reveals the essential compatibility of eroticism with an equal relationship.

Even after their mutual love is declared, Emma's thinking about the possibility of their marriage remains framed by convention. Emma 'the imaginist' cannot imagine a way she can fulfil her responsibilities to her father and also marry Mr Knightley; she cannot imagine a change to gender relationships and to marriage itself as radical as the one Mr Knightley represents. He, by contrast, approaches the issue in the 'plain, unaffected, gentleman-like English, such as Mr Knightley used even to the woman he was in love with' (419). Determined to leave Donwell Abbey and move to Hartfield, a plan that 'had not occurred to her' (419), Mr Knightley is 'fully convinced, that no reflection could alter his wishes or his opinion on the subject' (420). In his move to Hartfield, Austen creates a male protagonist who is truly exceptional in the history of literary masculinities.[42] His disruptive potential is illustrated in the responses of his neighbours. Mrs Elton's exclamation, "'Poor Knightley! poor fellow! – sad business for him. – She was extremely concerned; for, though very eccentric, he had a thousand good qualities. – How could he be so taken in? ... Shocking plan, living together. It would never do'" (438–39), reveals his power to challenge the values of the fashionable world and the gender hierarchies on which it insists. Mrs Weston's quiet reflection, by contrast, highlights the uniqueness of the arrangement — 'it was in every respect so proper, so suitable and unexceptionable a connexion, so peculiarly eligible, so singularly fortunate' (437) — and acknowledges that it is wholly due to Mr Knightley and his embodiment of an unconventional masculine identity: 'How very few of those men in a rank of life to address Emma would have renounced their own home for Hartfield!' (437). Mrs Weston, so often the repository of wisdom in *Emma*, acknowledges Mr Knightley as the way forward for independent, individualistic women like Emma: 'It was all right, all open, all equal' (437).

In *Emma*, Austen draws the rewriting of gender taking place in women's historical fiction into the courtship romance genre. Her creative borrowing from a historical genre that was urgently rewriting masculinity confounds the polarities that have been ascribed to her connection with history.[43] *Emma* exposes the fallacy of an opposition between fiction and history, which, as Devoney Looser argues, were 'presented as competitors more often than coconspirators'.[44] The influence of Jane Porter's *The Scottish Chiefs* — an arguably feminist historical novel that rewrites the history of masculinity, femininity and the interaction between them — on *Emma* complicates the binary between the gendering of fiction as domestic and feminine, and history as epic and masculine, with which Austen has been associated.[45] In April 1816, just a few months after the publication of *Emma*, Austen declined James Stanier Clarke's suggestion that she write 'an Historical Romance, founded on the House of Saxe Cobourg', claiming that she 'could no more write a Romance than an Epic Poem'. In gendering such literary forms as masculine and contrasting them to her own feminised 'pictures of domestic Life in Country Villages',[46] Austen does no more than pander to Clarke's ego; she had already collapsed such binaries in *Emma*. Austen and Porter both kept to their 'own style' and went on in their 'own Way'.[47] Austen was already underway with *Persuasion*, and it was Porter who wrote the history of the House of Saxe-Coburg, *Duke Christian of Luneberg, or, Tradition from the Hartz* (1824), ostensibly at the invitation of Clarke, but also in a vain attempt to curry royal favour for her family and secure a pension for herself and her sister.[48]

In *Emma*, Austen's rewriting of masculinity echoes transformations in sexual politics taking place in the historical novel, particularly in Jane Porter's *The Scottish Chiefs*. Austen's frustration with other Romantic fictional genres and their persistence in perpetuating conservative myths of masculinity and femininity, however, is evident in *Mansfield Park*, *Emma*, and finally in her 'Plan of a Novel, according to hints from various quarters'.[49] The 'Hero' of this work is 'all perfection of course' and, revealing Austen's enduring distaste for performative rather than authentic masculinities, 'only prevented from paying his addresses' to the heroine 'by some excess of refinement'.[50] In her footnotes to the

Plan, Austen attributes the 'hint' regarding the necessary perfection of the hero to her niece Fanny Knight, which may have sprung from her praise of Mr Knightley, arguably Austen's male paragon, recorded in 'Opinions of Emma'.[51] Austen's sharply satiric 'Plan of a Novel' and its notions of ideal literary heroism appears to have functioned as a kind of cathartic release of the anxiety over masculine identity and its shaping through genre that pervade *Mansfield Park* and *Emma*. In her final, post-war novel, Austen returns to her earlier rewriting of masculinity through the transformative power of romantic love, and through the wild and erratic passions of a thoroughly imperfect male protagonist.

6 'Feelings glad to burst their usual restraints'

Persuasion

Where *Emma* is a novel about what men ought to be, *Persuasion* (1818) is a novel about how men ought to feel. Or rather, how they do feel, for better and for worse. For instance: 'He walked to the window to recollect himself, and feel how he ought to behave' (73); 'There had been just that degree of feeling and curiosity about her in his manner which must give her extreme agitation' (82); 'he could not be unfeeling' (84); 'he sat near a table, leaning over it with folded arms and face concealed, as if overpowered by the various feelings of his soul' (104); 'as our bodies are the strongest, so are our feelings"' (219); 'Tell me not that I am too late, that such precious feelings are gone for ever' (222); 'he had seized a sheet of paper, and poured out his feelings' (226).

Persuasion represents a post-war emotional release of feeling from the anxiety that had gripped the nation for so long, as Jane Austen demonstrates in *Emma* and *Mansfield Park*. Now, in her final completed novel, she rewrites masculinity by exploring the range, depth and intensity of men's feelings. In *Persuasion*, feelings matter as much to Austen as other aspects of masculine identity, including her celebration of the navy, her projection into popular cults of national heroism, and her championing of the meritocracy of the professional classes.[1] Captain Frederick Wentworth is Austen's most expressive and emotionally volatile male protagonist, and Austen's task in *Persuasion* — unique within her fiction — is to expose the effects of such depth and contradiction of feeling on the masculine self. By uniting highly politicised aspects of masculine identity with an emotional and all-consuming interiority, Wentworth becomes Austen's most complex male protagonist.

To Anne Elliot, the grieving Captain Benwick is not reserved, as he appears to other characters in the novel, for his feelings appear 'glad to burst their usual restraints' (93–94). In describing Benwick's emotional release, Austen could be writing about her final novel as a whole. The experienced, expressed, and unexpressed feelings of her central characters drive *Persuasion* physically, intellectually and emotionally. In dialogue with Austen's earlier work, *Persuasion* is an explosion in the textual representation of feeling, as though the courtship romance itself is bursting its generic restraints. Austen's exploration of feeling, together with her focus on masculine emotions and their implications for gender identities, shares more with *Pride and Prejudice* than with either *Mansfield Park* or *Emma*. In the earlier novel, Austen stakes a claim for the courtship romance as a key genre of Romanticism by celebrating the transformative effects of romantic love on masculine identity. In *Persuasion*, Austen dramatically expands her investigation by exploring in greater complexity the experience of love, rejection, jealousy and endurance. Romantic love triggers not only passion and devotion but also grief, anger, bitterness, resentment and envy. Exploring the effects of these powerful feelings on Wentworth's sense of self, Austen creates a fresh approach to masculine identity in her last male protagonist.

Austen rewrites masculinity through an ongoing engagement with her chosen genre, the courtship romance novel. In *Sense and Sensibility* and *Northanger Abbey*, she satirises its generic conventions and literary clichés to offer a new model of desirable masculinity; in *Pride and Prejudice*, she arguably perfects it; and in *Mansfield Park* and *Emma*, she defends it and its possibilities for rewriting masculinity from the ideological threats presented by the emergence of Evangelical fiction and the national tale. In *Persuasion*, Austen's task is not to satirise, perfect, or defend the genre, but rather to rewrite it to permit greater scope for the exploration of men's emotional lives. Austen disrupts the usual trajectory of the courtship plot to create a narrative that enables her to investigate a wider range of male experience of romantic love. She imbues *Persuasion* with a sense of longevity in the relationship between Wentworth and Anne that forecasts the more complex investigation of the realities of romantic love in both courtship and marriage that would be taken up by her nineteenth-century inheritors. When Austen began *Persuasion* on 8 August 1815, the day after Napoleon's exile to St Helena, she anticipated the romance novels of the future, pioneering a new approach to the courtship romance to match what must, at the time, have felt like a new and modern chapter in European history.

Unlike her earlier novels, *Persuasion* is less in dialogue with Austen's fictional predecessors and contemporaries than with her poetic counterparts, particularly in her preoccupation with feelings — not only Wentworth, but also in other male characters and most revealingly, in the heroine herself. The same is true of her representations of nature and in her exploration of the effects of feeling and nature on the body and the mind. In *Persuasion*, Austen clearly responds to contemporary Romantic poets, two of whom — Lord Byron and Walter Scott — she mentions throughout the novel, including in an explicit discussion between Anne and Benwick.[2] Locating her novel within this poetic moment, Austen offers an alternative vision of Romantic masculinity to the autonomous, socially-detached vision of the male self, lauded in the poetry of Byron and Scott and also Wordsworth and Coleridge. The intensity of Wentworth's feelings — and indeed, of the feelings of his fellow naval officers Admiral Croft and Captains Harville and Benwick — arise not from solitary contemplation and fulfilment through nature, nor from the fervour of patriotic service celebrated in popular cults of national heroism,[3] but instead from the experience of romantic love. Poetry, written by men who '"have had every advantage of us in telling their own story"' and for whom '"the pen has been in their hands"' (220), extolled a solitary, individual and isolated vision of the male self; but in *Persuasion* Austen demonstrates that '"a larger allowance of prose"' (94), in the form of courtship romance novels written by women, can offer an alternative model of Romantic masculinity.

In *Persuasion*, then, Austen recreates Romantic masculinity by merging the authentic, internalised sense of self she celebrates throughout her novels with a new emphasis on the experience and expression of emotions. Drawing on focalisation and free indirect discourse to destabilise the narrator from the central characters — a technique Olivia Murphy describes as 'the most sophisticated narrative technique yet developed'[4] — Austen provides the reader with greater access to Wentworth's consciousness and hence to his emotional state. Austen also draws on Anne's prior knowledge of Wentworth and her interpretation of his looks, facial expressions, and tone of voice to expose a state of feeling that is concealed from the other characters. The effect of these narrative techniques is impressive, including on her early readers, for Maria Edgeworth commented that *Persuasion*:

> appears to me, especially in all that relates to poor Anne and her lover, to be exceedingly interesting and natural. The love and the lover admirably well drawn; don't you see Captain Wentworth, or rather don't you in her place feel him taking the boisterous child off her back as she kneels by the sick boy on the sofa? And is not the first meeting after their long separation admirably well done? And the overheard conversation about the nut?[5]

Through these textual innovations, Austen projects the nascent Romantic ideal of *Pride and Prejudice* into an explicit dialogue with her poetic contemporaries, rewriting the courtship romance as an essentially Romantic genre.

A troubling paradox lies at the heart of Austen's rewriting of masculinity in *Persuasion*, however. Even as Austen celebrates this new model of Romantic masculinity, fulfilled through romantic love, she problematises the vision of ideal heterosexual romance that has dominated her novels. Austen concludes *Northanger Abbey*, *Pride and Prejudice* and *Emma* with the satisfying marriage of a male protagonist whose authentic, internalised masculine identity enables the free expression of the heroine's agency, and laments the absence of such a possibility in *Mansfield Park*. In *Persuasion*, Austen rejects such an uncomplicated resolution of the complexity inherent in the textual reconstruction of gender. Instead, she exposes the potentially dark underside of this vision: the reality that courtship and marriage involve tension, resistance and conflict, even between two people passionately committed to each other. As Murphy claims, *Persuasion* 'more explicitly than any other of Austen's works, grapples with concepts that today may confidently be labelled feminist',[6] an agenda signalled by Austen's identification and struggle with the reality that masculine authenticity and feminine agency will not always be complementary. In *Persuasion*, they clash. Despite the neat resolution of the navy's 'national importance' with its 'domestic virtues' promised in her final sentence, Austen does not offer in the relationship between Anne and Wentworth the 'perfect happiness of the union' that she foresaw in *Emma* between the fiercely independent gentleman's daughter and the man possessed of the most authentic, assured and secure sense of self of all her male protagonists. Austen commented of her own work that 'pictures of perfection as you know make me sick & wicked',[7] seeing perhaps something too seamless, too harmonious — perhaps too implausible — in the marriage of Emma Woodhouse and George Knightley. *Persuasion* is Austen's necessary corrective to *Emma*, and the result is her richest, most complex exploration of masculine identity and its relationship to feminine agency.

Austen rewrites the courtship romance plot in *Persuasion* to tackle her new model of Romantic masculinity, to offer a more nuanced exploration of feminine agency through an enhanced capacity for women to act, and to unpack the potential for disharmony between the two. From the novel's beginning, Austen overturns the usual trajectory of the courtship romance plot and opens with a vision of romantic love between heroine and male protagonist such as she achieves only at the end of her earlier works, as is typical of the genre. The imminent arrival of Admiral and Mrs Croft as tenants of Kellynch Hall prompts Anne Elliot's recollection of the 'exquisite felicity' of her brief engagement to Captain Frederick Wentworth, a couple 'rapidly and deeply in love': 'It would be difficult to say which had seen the highest perfection in the other, or which had been the happiest; she, in receiving his declarations and proposals, or he in having them accepted' (26). As Anne later reflects:

> There *had* been a time, when of all the large party now filling the drawing-room at Uppercross, they would have found it difficult to cease speaking to one another ... there could have been no two hearts so open, no tastes so similar, no feelings so in unison, no countenances so beloved (59–60).

Anne's decision to sever her engagement to Wentworth shatters not only the 'happily ever after' conclusion of the generic narrative, but also the harmonious balance between feminine agency and the internalised masculine self that underpins her idealised romantic relationships.

When Wentworth first meets Anne in 1806, he already possesses the authentic masculine subjectivity Austen champions. Rather than gradually cultivating Wentworth's essential realness as she had done for her earlier male protagonists Henry Tilney, Edward Ferrars and Fitzwilliam Darcy, Austen deploys symbolism associated with particular masculine ideals circulating in the 1810s as a shorthand to establish his masculine credentials. Wentworth's professional identity projects him into the popular celebration of England's naval prowess and cults of national heroism associated with Nelson and Cook, and guarantees his value for national service, social mobility and advancement through work and merit. Austen recasts her masculine ideal away from the ownership and control of land that enabled its fulfilment in *Pride and Prejudice* and *Emma* and relocates it to the professional working classes. The democratising effect highlights both the availability and desirability of a masculinity to complement feminine agency to a wider range of men and women. Through her vocabulary, she dwells on the link between Wentworth's professional success, talent and endeavour: he 'got employ', 'distinguished himself', 'gained' his promotion and 'made' his fortune (29). Emphasising his authenticity by baring not only his virtues, but also his faults, she writes: 'Captain Wentworth had no fortune. He had been lucky in his profession, but spending freely, what had come freely, had realized nothing' (27).

As with Darcy before him, Wentworth's authentic masculinity is revealed at its best through the experience and expression of romantic love. Turned onshore after the Battle of San Domingo,[8] this naval embodiment of English national pride falls deeply and passionately in love: 'He had been most warmly attached to her, and had never seen a woman since whom he thought her equal' (57). Anne's reflections on seeing him again reveal the depth of their intimacy: 'Anne felt the utter impossibility, from her knowledge of his mind, that he could be unvisited by remembrance any more than herself' (59); 'she heard the same voice, and discerned the same mind' (60). Wentworth is uniquely emotionally expressive among Austen's male protagonists. Critics accuse Austen of a distrust of men who externalise their feelings, such as John Willoughby, George Wickham and Henry Crawford, but Anne loves that quality most. Whereas she implicitly distrusts her cousin William Elliot because there 'was never any burst of feeling, any warmth of indignation or delight' (151), she loves Wentworth for that very capacity: 'She prized the frank, the openhearted, the eager character beyond all others. Warmth and enthusiasm did captivate her still' (151). Wentworth's openness in fact contributes to his authenticity, signalling confidence in himself and a willingness to express thoughts and feelings in defiance of social forms and practices.

Anne and Wentworth's relationship seems, then, to include all the necessary ingredients within Austen's taxonomy for a successful romantic partnership: a passionate yet deep emotional and intellectual connection, and a man possessing the authentic realness that alone enables feminine agency. In *Persuasion*, however, Austen rewrites the courtship romance plot and in the process destroys this image of ideal romantic love. She must destroy it if she is to achieve her dual objectives of bringing a new emotional depth to her male protagonist and enabling an enhanced role for feminine agency within the courtship plot. The two are inextricably linked, for it is Anne's agency that severs their engagement for reasons explicitly connected to the model of masculinity Wentworth embodies. The authenticity that captures Anne's heart — the qualities that to Anne are 'intelligence, spirit and brilliancy' (26) and a 'sanguine temper, and fearlessness of mind' — are to Lady Russell 'a dangerous character', 'brilliant ... headstrong' (27). In Lady Russell's eyes, Wentworth is 'a stranger without alliance or fortune' and 'a young man, who had nothing but himself to recommend him, and no hopes of attaining affluence, but in the chances of a most uncertain profession, and no connexions to secure even his farther rise in that profession' (26–27). As Anne comes to view their engagement 'a wrong thing – indiscreet, improper, hardly capable of success, and not deserving it' (27), she ends it under the 'belief of being prudent, and self-denying principally for *his* advantage' (27–28).

Anne's Romantic feminine agency fuses an autonomous with a relational self. In refusing Wentworth, she disregards her own desires and elevates the claims of others, but also insists on the integrity of her decision in her own interests:

> I must believe that I was right, much as I suffered from it, that I was perfectly right in being guided by the friend whom you will love better than you do now [...] I was right in submitting to her, and that if I had done otherwise, I should have suffered more in continuing the engagement than I did in giving it up, because I should have suffered in my conscience (230–31).

Questions concerning the balance between strength and malleability of character, the ethics of giving and receiving advice, and the comparative constancy of men and women all recur throughout *Persuasion*. They represent facets of Austen's nuanced investigation of feminine agency as composite, complex and fundamentally misunderstood. No one misunderstands that agency more than Wentworth himself, whose response to Anne's decision is to express 'opinions totally unconvinced and unbending', to feel 'himself ill-used by so forced a relinquishment' (28), and to leave his beloved. Both Wentworth's predecessors in romantic rejection — Darcy and Crawford — offer a more empathic response to the women they love, even in circumstances where their love is unrequited. When Wentworth returns to England two years later, having proved himself as Captain of the Laconia and the possessor of '"a few thousand pounds"', he was '"proud, too proud to ask again"' (231). Even on his return to Somerset he can still think of her "'only as one who had once yielded, who had given me up, who had been influenced by any one rather than by me"' (229).

Anne's rejection of Wentworth is only the beginning of Austen's re-writing of the courtship romance plot. When the novel opens, the heroine has already met, fallen in love with, and rejected the male protagonist. Further, she is still in love with him, despite his anger:

> No one had ever come within the Kellynch circle, who could bear a comparison with Frederick Wentworth, as he stood in her memory. No second attachment, the only thoroughly natural, happy, and suf-ficient cure, at her time of life, had been possible to the nice tone of her mind, the fastidiousness of her taste, in the small limits of the society around them (28).

Experienced readers of the genre should expect no parade of eligible young men to pass under the heroine's scrutinising gaze in the manner of Catherine Morland and Elizabeth Bennet, for they know from the opening pages that Anne Elliott is going to marry only one man: Cap-tain Frederick Wentworth. Although briefly attracted to the fantasy of becoming Lady Elliot and returning to Kellynch Hall, Anne swiftly re-nounces the idea of marriage to Mr Elliot because of her enduring love for Wentworth: 'it was not only that her feelings were still adverse to any man save one; her judgment, on a serious consideration of the possibil-ities of such a case, was against Mr Elliot' (150). After Mr Elliot's per-nicious attentions to her at the concert, Anne resolves to remain faithful to Wentworth for life, regardless of the outcome:

> How she might have felt, had there been no Captain Wentworth in the case, was not worth enquiry; for there was a Captain Wentworth: and be the conclusion of the present suspense good or bad, her af-fection would be his for ever. Their union, she believed, could not divide her more from other men, than their final separation (181).

As a courtship romance heroine, Anne's emotional unavailability to any-one but the male protagonist — a man she has already rejected — is singular within the genre, a phenomenon William Galperin describes as 'Anne's resistance to imagining herself in a courtship narrative'.[9] Yet Anne *is* the heroine of a courtship novel and the question becomes, then, how will Austen unite her two central characters and maintain the read-er's interest given the novel's inevitable conclusion?

Austen creates narrative suspense in *Persuasion* by her subtle and empathic exploration of the consequences of rejection on the authentic male self. Despite Wentworth's churlish departure and prolonged bit-terness towards Anne, Austen spares him the merciless judgment she rains down on Crawford, and to a lesser extent on Darcy. Far from securing his everlasting happiness, Captain Wentworth's authenticity and its momentary fulfilment through romantic love cause him lasting pain and suffering. Indeed, Wentworth symbolises the more tormenting aspect of John Tosh's description of modern masculine subjectivity as 'an expression of the self ... tormenting and liberating as the case may be'.[10] Uniquely, in Captain Wentworth Austen concerns herself with the damaging rather than liberating effects of such a male subjectivity when it is grounded in an authentic but rejected sense of self.

Wentworth's immediate response is to escape through a long period of exile enabled by Napoleon's desire for conquest throughout Europe, especially England; as he later says, '"It was a great object with me, at that time, to be at sea, – a very great object. I wanted to be doing something"' (61). By setting the novel in the summer of 1814, shortly after Napoleon's exile to Elba,[11] Austen represents Wentworth's return to England as an involuntary act necessitated by the peace. Thanks to an 'arrangement of Providence' (99), his sister leases his former fiancée's ancestral family home. Now, Wentworth is forced to confront the emotional reality of his thwarted love for Anne and its consequences, all of which he has managed to avoid for eight years. Although her reunion with Wentworth prompts Anne to wonder, 'how were his sentiments to be read?' (56), Austen leaves the reader with no such sense of mystery. For only the second time in her writing career, she focalises through her male protagonist; where her focalisation through Darcy reveals his increasing attraction to Elizabeth, her focalisation through Wentworth exposes the depth of his anger and bitterness towards Anne:

> He had not forgiven Anne Elliot. She had used him ill; deserted and disappointed him; and worse, she had shewn a feebleness of character in doing so, which his own decided, confident temper could not endure. She had given him up to oblige others. It had been the effect of over-persuasion. It had been weakness and timidity (57).

Wentworth's reflection confirms that even at a distance of eight years, he remains unable to recognise Anne's renunciation of the engagement as a legitimate act of feminine agency.

Paradoxically, Austen also reveals Wentworth's enduring love through this same technique. He tries to convince himself that 'he had no desire of meeting her again' and that her 'power with him was gone forever' (57). His strategy for coping with the emotional toll of the reunion is to close down any possibility of a relationship with her, despite his mission to actively seek a wife:

> It was now his object to marry. He was rich, and being turned on shore, fully intended to settle as soon as he could be properly tempted; actually looking around, ready to fall in love with all the speed which a clear head and quick taste could allow. He had a heart

for either of the Miss Musgroves, if they could catch it; a heart, in short, for any pleasing young woman who came in his way, excepting Anne Elliot. This was his only secret exception (58).

In spite of himself, Wentworth cannot suppress a vision of his first love when he describes his ideal woman to his sister: 'Anne Elliot was not out of his thoughts, when he more seriously described the woman he should wish to meet with' (58). His prescription — '"A strong mind, with sweetness of manner"' (58) — exposes his ongoing inability either to recognise the form such a strong mind might take or its consequences for himself.

Austen dramatically deepens the psychological darkness surrounding Captain Wentworth by explicitly associating him with the figure of the Byronic hero popularised throughout the 1810s in *Childe Harold's Pilgrimage* (1812), *The Giaour* (1813), *The Corsair*, and *Lara* (both 1814). As an extreme incarnation of the detached, autonomous and socially-alienated male self located within Romantic culture, the Byronic hero was characterised by ambition, desire and aggressive individualism, as well as being associated with travel, conflict and violence.[12] In September 1813, Austen's comment to Cassandra on seeing a pantomime of Don Juan, whose central character Byron would later satirise in *Don Juan* (1819), reveals her fascination with this icon of morally dubious, seductive and dangerous masculinity: 'I must say that I have seen nobody on the stage who has been a more interesting Character than that compound of Cruelty & Lust'.[13] Several critics find clear parallels between the Byronic hero and Wentworth, including their shared history of exile, voyages and conflict; their emotionally volatile personalities, including their ambition and self-reliance as well as their capacity for anger and resentment; and their physical appearance — the post-war Wentworth possesses 'a more glowing, manly, open look, in no respect lessening his personal advantages' (57).[14]

Austen especially associates Captain Wentworth with Conrad, hero of the immensely popular and influential *The Corsair*. Within weeks of its publication on 1 February 1814, she wrote to Cassandra: 'I have read the Corsair, mended my petticoat, & have nothing else to do'.[15] Wentworth and Conrad represent two sides of the same coin: one a naval captain whose 'cruises' around the Mediterranean have enabled him to capture enemy vessels and amass a fortune; the other a pirate or privateer whose search for glory, plunder and riches is also enabled by violence. Their shared facial features expose the dissonance between their externalised social performance and the darker, tormented and inscrutable self within. The turn of Conrad's mouth reveals the conflict between his outer and inner worlds, his torment arising from a painful yet unknown history:

And oft perforce his rising lip reveals
The haughtier thought it curbs, but scarce conceals.

Though smooth his voice, and clam his general mien,
Still seems there something he would not have seen:
His features' deepening lines and varying hue
At times attracted, yet perplex'd the view,
As if within that murkiness of mind
Work'd feelings fearful, and yet undefined;
Such might it be – that none could truly tell –
Too close enquiry his stern glance would quell (I, 205–212).[16]

Byron's representation of Conrad's 'rising lip' emphasises his emotional depth as well as the range of emotions triggered by romantic love:

Love shows all changes – Hate, Ambition, Guile,
Betray no further than the bitter smile;
The lip's least curl, the lightest paleness thrown
Along the govern'd aspect, speak alone
Of deeper passions (I, 229–33).

Austen similarly reveals Captain Wentworth's 'haughtier thoughts', 'murkiness of mind' and 'deeper passions' through his lips. As Mrs Musgrove speaks of her deceased son, Wentworth's mouth betrays the dissonance between his outward behaviour and his true feelings:

There was a momentary expression in Captain Wentworth's face at this speech, a certain glance of his bright eye, and curl of his handsome mouth, which convinced Anne, that instead of sharing in Mrs Musgrove's kind wishes, as to her son, he had probably been at some pains to get rid of him (63).

In a similar fashion, Captain Wentworth's mouth reveals his contempt for Mary Musgrove's class snobbery during the walk to the Hayters: 'She received no other answer, than an artificial, assenting smile, followed by a contemptuous glance, as he turned away, which Anne perfectly knew the meaning of' (80). This contemptuous smirk reappears in response to Elizabeth Elliot's invitation to her card party in Bath, exposing his disdain for her social pretensions, given his history of rejection by the Elliot family and their social circle: 'Anne caught his eye, saw his cheeks glow, and his mouth form itself into a momentary expression of contempt' (212).[17]

Austen's choice of Conrad as the Byronic hero to frame her male protagonist links Wentworth's 'murkiness of mind' with his painful romantic history. Keen readers of the 'first-rate poets' (94) like Anne and Captain Benwick — and tens of thousands read *The Corsair* — may have drawn their own conclusions about *Persuasion*'s courtship romance narrative from Austen's parallels between Wentworth and Conrad.

According to Caroline Franklin, Conrad is the first of Byron's heroes to maintain a monogamous relationship.[18] Byron extols the constancy of Conrad's love for his wife Medora, his single enduring virtue:

> love – unchangeable – unchanged,
> Felt but for one from whom he never ranged;
> Though fairest captives daily met his eye,
> He shunn'd, nor sought, but boldly passed them by (I, 287–89).

Even after Medora's death during his absence, Conrad refuses to marry Gulnare, who has released him from captivity. As Mary Waldron argues, Conrad is 'an icon of male constancy to a single love'.[19] The central drama of Captain Wentworth's return to Somerset is the tension between his simmering love for Anne, which threatens to explode at any moment, and his ongoing resentment towards her.

Austen dramatises this tension through Wentworth's ostensible desire for a new romance. His strategy for coping with his thwarted love for Anne when circumstances throw them back together again does not augur well for their romantic resolution. Reluctant to expose the authentic self already rejected, Wentworth retreats into stylised, performative codes of masculine behaviour. Thus, he can participate in the conventional forms and practices of social life while attempting to conceal his inner torment and confusion.[20] Austen reveals the performative nature of Wentworth's publicly-enacted self during his visits to Uppercross through his treatment of Anne. Polite sociability offers a refuge from his incapacity to confront and address his confused feelings. It provides a conventional language for civilised behaviour between them that Anne finds loathsome, describing it as 'cold politeness' and 'ceremonious grace' (67). Austen exposes his civility in the presence of others as a veneer that is unsustainable when they are alone: 'The surprise of finding himself almost alone with Anne Elliot, deprived his manners of their usual composure: he started … he walked to the window to recollect himself, and feel how he ought to behave' (73). His interventions to release her from her clamorous nephew, and to secure her a place in the Crofts' carriage, reveal an ongoing tenderness that he can neither acknowledge nor express. But Anne understands:

> Yes, – he had done it. She was in the carriage, and felt that he had placed her there, that his will and his hands had done it, that she owed it to his perception of her fatigue, and his resolution to give her rest … She understood him. He could not forgive her, – but he could not be unfeeling (84).

Wentworth turns to polite sociability, with its established structure of courtship rituals, to attempt to forge a new romantic relationship. His tongue-in-cheek conversation with his sister reveals that he is actively looking for a wife:

> Yes, here I am, Sophia, quite ready to make a foolish match. Any body between fifteen and thirty may have me for asking. A little beauty, and a few smiles, and a few compliments to the navy, and I am a lost man. Should not this be enough for a sailor, who has had no society among women to make him nice? (58).

His introduction to the Musgrove sisters, both of whom 'seemed so entirely occupied by him', triggers his performance of courtship rituals: 'no one seemed in higher spirits than Captain Wentworth. She felt that he had every thing to elevate him, which general attention and deference, and especially the attention of all the young women could do' (66–67). He is persuaded to delay visiting his brother in Shropshire in preference for Uppercross. Because there 'was so much of friendliness, and of flattery, and of every thing most bewitching in his reception there' (68), Anne readily perceives both the performative nature of Wentworth's flirtation with the Musgrove sisters and its potentially damaging consequences. Unlike Mary and Charles Musgrove, who squabble over whether he prefers one sister or the other based on their different views for the aggrandisement of the Musgrove family, Anne cares only that he understands himself: 'As to Captain Wentworth's views, she deemed it of more consequence that he should know his mind, early enough not to be endangering the happiness of either sister, or impeaching his own honour, than that he should prefer Henrietta to Louisa, or Louisa to Henrietta' (72). Increasingly confident that his courtship is performative rather than authentic:

> Anne had soon been in company with all the four together often enough to have an opinion ... while she considered Louisa to be rather the favourite, she could not but think, as far as she might dare to judge from memory and experience, that Captain Wentworth was not in love with either (76).

She only censures him for 'accepting the attentions – (for accepting must be the word) of two young women at once' (76).

The confirmation of Henrietta's courtship with her cousin Charles Hayter shifts his focus to Louisa, whose commitment to a '"character of decision and firmness"' (81) he is particularly disposed to approve. In their shared conversations, Austen draws out Wentworth's ongoing confusion about both the complexity of feminine agency and his misunderstanding of Anne's decision to end their engagement:

> It is the worst evil of too yielding and indecisive a character, that no influence over it can be depended on. – You are never sure of a good

impression being durable. Every body may sway it; let those who would be happy be firm (81).

Wentworth seems to confirm his romantic interest in Louisa by declaring: '"My first wish for all, whom I am interested in, is that they should be firm. If Louisa Musgrove would be beautiful and happy in her November of life, she will cherish all her present powers of mind"' (81–82). Anne herself begins to be convinced by the performance that Wentworth himself later acknowledges it to be: 'In his preceding attempts to attach himself to Louisa Musgrove (the attempts of angry pride), he protested that he had for ever felt it to be impossible; that he had not cared, could not care for Louisa' (226–27). He admits he was grossly mistaken: '"I had no right to be trying whether I could attach myself to either of the girls, at the risk of raising even an unpleasant report, were there no other consequences"' (227).

Despite the harm to himself and others that could flow from flirting with Louisa Musgrove, the most insidious aspect of Captain Wentworth's refuge into stylised masculinities lies in his performance of the chivalrous and gallant male, for it relates directly to his ongoing confusion about femininity agency. In response to Admiral Croft accusing him of his 'want of gallantry' for his dislike of transporting women on board ship, Wentworth defends himself by projecting on to women the fragile, coddled, passive model of femininity extolled within chivalric discourse revived in wartime:

> if I know myself … this is from no want of gallantry towards them. It is rather from feeling how impossible it is, with all one's efforts, and all one's sacrifices, to make the accommodation on board, such as women ought to have. There can be no want of gallantry, admiral, in rating the claims of women to every personal comfort *high* – and this is what I do (64).[21]

Wentworth's expressed view of women and his responsibilities towards them openly conflicts with both his previous willingness to transport the Harville family and the evidence of his own sister's naval career. Indeed, Mrs Croft immediately sees through his '"superfine, extraordinary sort of gallantry"', calling it out for what it is: '"Oh Frederick! – But I cannot believe it of you. – All idle refinement! – Women may be as comfortable on board, as in the best house in England"' (65). Mrs Croft — like Anne — knows that she is not hearing the real Frederick Wentworth: '"I hate to hear you talking so, like a fine gentleman, and as if women were all fine ladies, instead of rational creatures. We none of us expect to be in smooth waters all our days"' (65).

Austen's phrase 'rational creatures' specifically recalls Mary Wollstonecraft, for whom women's rationality formed the philosophical basis for a new conceptualisation of femininity in *A Vindication of the Rights of Woman* (1792). Mrs Croft, Mrs Harville and Anne Elliot embody Wollstonecraft's vision of the educated, active, competent and rational woman, equipped for a life of domestic, social and national service, more compellingly than any other women in Austen's fiction. In an apparent homage to her brothers Francis and Charles, whose own naval careers provide a factual basis for Austen's composite naval characters,[22] Austen represents the navy as capable of enabling Wollstonecraft's vision of feminine agency by offering a complementary model of authentic masculinity on a mass scale. She does not present the realisation of feminine agency through a new model of masculinity that is exceptional or isolated — or, as in *Pride and Prejudice* and *Emma*, as unique to one man among several of his class — but as endemic to a culture that recognises its inherent desirability. The 'domestic virtues' extolled by Austen in the final sentence of *Persuasion* inhere not in the physical space of the home, which is transitory for all naval couples and families, but instead in the model of companionate marriage represented by the navy.[23]

By travelling with, and occasionally without, their husbands Mrs Croft and Mrs Harville have, in effect, enjoyed their own naval careers, become versant in various aspects of public life, gained skills and developed as individuals through experiences otherwise unavailable to them. Austen's characterisation of Mrs Croft falls little short of representing her as a naval officer in addition to her husband: Anne observes her in Bath 'looking as intelligent and keen as any of the officers around her' (158). Mary Musgrove's fashionable education, by contrast, has equipped her only for the life of privileged confinement deplored by both Wollstonecraft and Mrs Croft, rendering her incapable of assisting Louisa Musgrove after her injury at Lyme. It is Mrs Harville, 'a degree less polished than her husband' (91), who has the expertise to act.[24] Both Admiral Croft and Captain Harville recognise and value these qualities in their wives, and are willing to express their love for and emotional dependence upon them in a manner unmatched in Austen's fiction. Admiral Croft's prediction that Captain Wentworth will change his mind regarding carrying women on ships when he is married reflects his own attitude:

> When he is married, if we have the good luck to live to another war, we shall see him do as you and I, and a great many others, have done. We shall see him very thankful to any body that will bring him his wife (65).

Captain Harville is even more expressive during his conversation with Anne at the White Hart in Bath:

> if I could but make you comprehend what a man suffers when he takes a last look at his wife and children, and watches the boat that he has sent them off in, as long as it is in sight, and then

turns away and says, 'God knows when we meet again!' And
then, if I could convey to you the glow of his soul when he does
see them again [...] I speak, you know, only of such men as have
hearts! (220).

For these men, romantic love is deeply experienced and powerfully expressed, in a manner that would be inconceivable for men such as Sir
Walter, William Elliot or Charles Musgrove, and only imaginary in relation to Austen's earlier male protagonists.

The result for the Croft and Harville marriages, as Anne repeatedly
notes, is an overwhelming sense of 'happiness'. Observing the Crofts in
Bath, she reflects:

Knowing their feelings as she did, it was a most attractive picture
of happiness to her. She always watched them as long as she could;
delighted to fancy she understood what they might be talking of, as
they walked along in happy independence (158).

On meeting the Harvilles at Lyme, and despite their transient lifestyle,
their financial want and his physical disability, 'Anne thought she left
great happiness behind her when they quitted the house' (92). Their
warmth is clear from their kind welcome to the visitors despite the
size of their home, which contains 'rooms so small as none but those
who invite from the heart could think capable of accommodating so
many' (92). Anne cannot but be impressed by the strong emotions she
witnesses between the Harville family, Captain Benwick and Captain
Wentworth at Lyme:

There was so much attachment to Captain Wentworth in all this,
and such a bewitching charm in a degree of hospitality so un-
common, so unlike the usual style of give-and-take invitations,
and dinners of formality and display, that Anne felt her spirits
not likely to be benefited by an increasing acquaintance among
his brother-officers. 'These would have been all my friends,' was
her thought; and she had to struggle against a great tendency to
lowness (91–92).

Thus, Anne's visit to Lyme performs a similar function as Catherine
Morland's visit to Woodston, Elizabeth Bennet's visit to Pemberley and
Emma's visit to Donwell Abbey. It provides a glimpse into the married
life that awaits her, or, more accurately for Anne, the opportunity for a
happiness that she has lost.

The events at Lyme wrench Captain Wentworth from his emotional
retreat into performative, ritualised codes of masculinity, raise the consciousness of his enduring love for Anne, and awaken him to the second

opportunity to achieve self-realisation through the romantic love that his own misdeeds have all but destroyed. Neither his polite civility, nor his thin courtship rituals, nor his 'superfine gallantry' can assist him in the near tragedy of Louisa's fall from the Cobb. The veneer lifts to expose the rawness of his emotion in his cry, "'Is there no one to help me?" ... in a tone of despair, and as if all his own strength were gone' (102). Overwhelmed by the gravity of Louisa's condition and the part he has played in her injury, 'he sat near a table, leaning over it with folded arms, and face concealed, as if overpowered by the various feelings of his soul and trying by prayer and reflection to calm them' (104). Unable to control his anguish during his subsequent drive to Uppercross with Anne and Henrietta, 'he burst forth, as if wholly overcome ... "Oh God! That I had not given way to her at the fatal moment! Had I done as I ought! But so eager and so resolute! Dear, sweet Louisa!"' (108). Adding to Wentworth's heightened emotional state is the contrast between Louisa's stubborn determination and Anne's collected response in the face of catastrophe. On the edge of 'Lord Byron's "dark blue seas"' (101), a further reference to *The Corsair*,[25] Wentworth acknowledges his love for Anne and begins 'to understand himself' (226).

Whether and how he will fulfil that self through realising his love for Anne forms the focus of Austen's narrative in the second volume of *Persuasion*. The fact that she drafted, revised, and then abandoned the concluding chapters suggests that Austen herself grappled repeatedly with this question. After completing a first draft of the original chapters ten and eleven of volume two on 16 July 1816, she revised and extended it two days later. In the subsequent ten days, she rewrote the ending, cancelling almost all of the original chapter ten and writing two new chapters (chapters ten and eleven in the final print version), and shifting the original chapter eleven to the final chapter twelve. As Jocelyn Harris observes, 'Austen's hesitations and reworkings in chapter 10 show her struggling to resolve her tale' (39). Although Harris and Kathryn Sutherland reveal that Austen incorporated and revised significant material from the original draft,[26] she completely rewrote the denouement of her disrupted courtship romance plot, to foreground her reformation of masculine and feminine gender identities. In the splendid scene at the White Hart Inn, and in Captain Wentworth's letter to Anne, Austen's revisions and new material foreground the feminine agency necessary to unite them, and celebrate the model of emotionally expressive masculinity represented in Captain Wentworth.

As soon as news of Louisa Musgrove's engagement to Captain Benwick reaches Captain Wentworth in Shropshire, he sets out for Bath in pursuit of his beloved. The 'white glare' (32) of this Regency spa and the ostentatious display of Anne's family and social circle throw the rawness of Wentworth's extreme emotional state into sharp relief. Within this epicentre of polite sociability that Anne so despises, Wentworth can no longer take refuge in the stylised performance of masculinity, a performance antithetical to both his authentic self and his love for Anne. Wentworth is a desperate man, torn between his passionate love for Anne, his fear of another rejection, his jealousy of William Elliot, and his self-blame for his own wilful blindness. Austen turns to dialogue to dramatise his interactions with Anne, enhancing his emotional intensity and volatility in the closing chapters. Her preference for dialogue represents a significant departure from her established practice in her earlier novels, in which she relied on free indirect speech to communicate her male protagonists' love for the heroines, including their marriage proposals. She calls on dialogue only after their engagements, if at all. Indeed, in both *Pride and Prejudice* and *Emma*, Austen specifically draws attention to the inadequacy of male speech to convey the depth of their emotions: when Elizabeth remarks, '"You might have talked to me more when you came to dinner"', Darcy responds, '"A man who had felt less, might"' (360). Likewise, Mr Knightley tells Emma, '"If I loved you less, I might be able to talk about it more"' (403). In *Persuasion*, Austen both remarks upon and dramatises this same inadequacy, in passages of direct speech that reveal the depth and anxiety of Wentworth's emotional volatility.

Wentworth's emotional fragility is evident in his first chance meeting with Anne:

> He was more obviously struck and confused by the sight of her, than she had observed before; he looked quite red. For the first time, since their renewed acquaintance, she felt that she was betraying the least sensibility of the two (165).

Austen emphasises that the polite civility that has framed their interactions is both performative and no longer acceptable to him:

> They had, by dint of being so very much together, got to speak to each other with a considerable portion of apparent indifference and calmness; but he could not do it now. Time had changed him, or Louisa had changed him. There was consciousness of some sort or other (166).

This Captain Wentworth is 'not comfortable, not easy, not able to feign that he was' (166).

Wentworth flounders again when he sees Anne at the concert. She draws him into a conversation about James Benwick's engagement to Louisa Musgrove, and as he reflects on his friend's swift recovery from grief, he finds himself with neither the language nor the self-control to continue: '"Fanny Harville was a very superior creature; and his attachment to her was indeed attachment. A man does not recover from such a devotion of the heart to such a woman! – He ought not – he does not"' (173). In her subsequent reflections, Anne perceives his fragmented language and behaviour — 'sentences begun which he could not finish – his half averted eyes, and more than half expressive glance' — which she can interpret in only one way:

> all, all declared that he had a heart returning to her at least; that anger, resentment, avoidance were no more; and that they were succeeded, not merely by friendship and regard, but by the tenderness of the past; yes, some share of the tenderness of the past. She could not contemplate the change as implying less. – He must love her (175).

His perception of William Elliot as a rival triggers a darker emotional shift: 'he looked grave, and seemed irresolute, and only by slow degrees came at last near enough to speak to her' (179). Austen shows the extremity of Wentworth's reaction: 'The change was indubitable. The difference between his present air and what it had been in the octagon room was strikingly great' (179). His outburst, '"there is nothing worth my staying for"' (180), reveals his enduring emotional volatility despite acknowledging his love for Anne.

Anne correctly attributes Wentworth's abrupt change to jealousy of Mr Elliot. Paralysed by envy of his apparent rival and the ubiquitous presence of the Elliot family — 'the formidable father and sister in the back ground' (171) and 'those who could not be my well-wishers' (228–29) — Wentworth is forced to endure the false politeness of Sir Walter and Elizabeth Elliot. Anne interprets his resignation as 'polite acknowledgment rather than acceptance': 'She knew him; she saw disdain in his eye, and could not venture to believe that he had determined to accept such an offering, as atonement for all the insolence of the past' (212). Unlike Conrad and other Byronic heroes who escape similar class snobbery and the conformism of polite society, Wentworth's love for Anne compels him to remain, unable to reveal the depth of his contempt for her family.

In Austen's most radical rewriting of the courtship romance plot in *Persuasion*, it is the heroine's agency rather than the male protagonist's declaration of love that unites them.[27] In her abandoned draft chapters, Wentworth stumbles through a commission for Admiral Croft, and is united with Anne almost by a series of fluke events; in the print version, Austen heightens Wentworth's emotional turmoil to an excruciating level and endows Anne with what Harris describes as a 'deliberate plan of action'.[28] Anne initially intends to 'leave things to take their course' (207), but witnessing Wentworth's paralysis in the face of her family, she realises that if they are to be reconciled, it is she who must act. In the scene at the White Hart, Anne reaches out to Wentworth through her conversation with Captain Harville, implicitly revealing her enduring love for him: '"We certainly do not forget you, so soon as you forget us. It is, perhaps, our fate rather than our merit. We cannot help ourselves. We live at home, quiet, confined, and our feelings prey upon us"' (218). As she declares, '"All the privilege I claim for my own sex ... is that of loving longest, when existence or when hope is gone"' (221), Anne is obviously speaking for and of herself: 'She could not immediately have uttered another sentence; her heart was too full, her breath too much oppressed' (221).

Wentworth abandons the dialogue that has failed him and seizes a different form of direct speech — his letter to Anne. His feelings finally 'burst their usual restraints' in the most emotive marriage proposal in all of Austen's fiction:

> Tell me not that I am too late, that such precious feelings are gone for ever. I offer myself to you with a heart even more your own, than when you almost broke it eight years and a half ago. Dare not say that man forgets sooner than woman, that his love has an earlier death. I have loved none but you. Unjust I may have been, weak and resentful I have been, but never inconstant (222).

Wentworth not only reveals the depth of his passion for Anne but openly admits his weakness and resentment. Through the letter, Austen reinforces Wentworth's emotionally fraught state, as he both experiences and explains his changing feelings as he hears her speech: 'You pierce my soul. I am half agony, half hope ... I can hardly write. I am every instant hearing something which overpowers me' (222).

In the highly-charged conversation that follows, Wentworth confirms that it was Anne's agency that overcame his jealousy of Mr Elliot:

> It had been gradually yielding to the better hopes which her looks, or words, or actions occasionally encouraged; it had been vanquished at last by those sentiments and those tones which had reached him while she talked with Captain Harville (226).

Their reunion is possible because Anne possesses 'the loveliest medium of fortitude and gentleness' (226). That realisation dawned on Wentworth only at Lyme: 'There, he had learnt to distinguish between the steadiness of principle and the obstinacy of self-will, between the darings of heedlessness and the resolution of a collected mind' (227). Wentworth is unable to remain wilfully blind to his enduring love for Anne, despite the emotional turmoil it has cost him, his desire to suppress it, and his half-hearted attempts to fall in love with another:

> he had seen every thing to exalt in his estimation the woman he had lost, and there begun to deplore the pride, the folly, the madness of resentment, which had kept him from trying to regain her when thrown in his way (227).

As Sarah Raff puts it, 'Wentworth at last recognizes that his susceptibility to error might justify a difference of opinion even in one who loves him'.[29]

Although Austen neatly resolves Captain Wentworth's mistaken understanding of Anne's agency, she insists on his Byronic 'murkiness of mind'. Wentworth acknowledges to Anne his faults and mistakes, his capacity for anger, resentment and bitterness — even his desire to forget her — and the fact that these feelings have protracted their estrangement:

> He persisted in having loved none but her. She had never been supplanted. He never even believed himself to see her equal. Thus much indeed he was obliged to acknowledge – that he had been constant unconsciously, nay unintentionally; that he had meant to forget her, and believed it to be done. He had imagined himself indifferent, when he had only been angry; and he had been unjust to her merits, because he had been a sufferer of them (226).

Wentworth recognises that his '"own self"' (231) has kept them apart, and in his new understanding of Anne's agency, absolves her of all responsibility. And yet, despite his gracelessness in the face of rejection, Austen steadfastly refuses to judge him. She gives no indication whatsoever in the final chapters that he has undergone a moral or emotional growth to subdue or control his feelings. On the contrary, she normalises — even celebrates — Wentworth's extreme emotional responses as natural incidents of passionate romantic love within a volatile personality. To do otherwise would be to erase the qualities Anne most loves about him. Harris remarks that Austen's 'numerous false starts expose her struggle to extenuate Captain Wentworth',[30] but her refusal to soften his fraught emotional life may be interpreted less a struggle and more a strategy, for she highlights the complexity and even the inscrutability of her male protagonist to the very end.

Marriage ultimately fulfils the romantic love that has simmered through an agonising wait. Unlike the marriages that typically conclude the courtship romance, this marriage, though happy, will not necessarily be always harmonious. Austen may write that Anne and Wentworth are 'more tried, more fixed in a knowledge of each other's character, truth, and attachment' (225), but that knowledge includes both her determined agency and his volatile temperament, neither of which, Austen suggests, have been subdued. Indeed, as Raff argues, Wentworth has only recently discovered 'that he may not in fact have any title to persuade those who love him'.[31] Austen's final assertion that 'Anne was tenderness itself, and she had the full worth of it in Captain Wentworth's affection' (236) gestures thinly toward marital harmony in comparison with the emotional upheaval over the course of the summer. Austen compounds both that upheaval and the potential for future conflict through the timing of

Wentworth and Anne's reconciliation. Early readers would know that Anne's 'dread of a future war' would be realised, at the very least, in Napoleon's escape from Elba, the Hundred Days and the Battle of Waterloo. By rewriting the courtship romance in *Persuasion*, Austen goes beyond championing feminine agency and masculine emotion and envisages companionate marriage as a passionate commitment that carries with it volatility, responsibility and the potential for conflict. This profoundly modern vision of heterosexual romance would be revisited, teased out, adapted and celebrated by her literary inheritors throughout the nineteenth and twentieth centuries. It still resonates in the modern era.

Conclusion
Sanditon, Unfinished Work and New Directions

On 27 January 1817, Jane Austen began her final work: a new novel now known as *Sanditon*, but which Austen referred to as 'The Brothers'.[1] The twelve chapters Austen completed before her death in July that year is the only work since her juvenilia that she named with an explicit and exclusive masculine focus. Austen's title alone suggests a new if unfinished direction in rewriting masculinity. In *Sanditon*, Austen expands her characterisation of men into as yet unchartered territory, with a new focus on the commercialisation of leisure and print culture. How Austen's critique of masculinity would have developed had she completed the novel remains, however, obscure. The men of *Sanditon*, the environmental, social and economic settings in which Austen places them, and the relationships she draws between them and the women of the novel, are so different from the patterns of plot and characterisation of her previous work that it is risky to speculate on the new direction she was taking.

In his unsigned review of *Emma*, Walter Scott distinguishes Austen's novels from both the sentimental novel and 'the ephemeral productions which supply the regular demand of watering-places and circulating libraries'.[2] In *Sanditon*, Austen dramatises Scott's distinction between her novels of modern realism, the sentimental novel, and stock popular fiction.[3] Austen embeds the action of her novel in an aspirational Regency spa, the social hub of which is Whitby's circulating library, and portrays her characters through their relationships to print culture. Austen's heroine, Charlotte Heywood, is 'a very sober-minded young lady, sufficiently well-read in novels to supply her imagination with amusement, but not at all unreasonably influenced by them' (140). Charlotte's knowledge of Frances Burney's *Camilla*, which she notices at Whitby's, links her to a more cultivated and complex class of fiction than the usual fare of the circulating library. Charlotte mirrors Austen's own ideal reader: an eager yet discriminating and judicious consumer of fiction. She may perceive the genteel but impoverished Clara Brereton as 'the most perfect representation of whatever heroine might be most beautiful and bewitching, in all the numerous volumes they had left behind them on Mrs Whitby's shelves' (139), but she moderates her speculation about

Clara's dependent state on Lady Denham when she perceives that 'they appeared to be on very comfortable terms' (140). Akin to Charlotte, Austen's reader may rely on the heroine's judgment in scrutinising the new people and places she encounters; a judgment which, in the court-ship romance genre, is central to Austen's rewriting of masculinity.

In the chapters Austen completed, Charlotte's scrutiny of men is dom-inated by Sir Edward Denham, a handsome but impecunious baronet. Austen expands Scott's critique of the sentimental novel by ridiculing the genre's stereotyping of seductive villainy and satirising the literary critics, public commentators and moralists who persisted in castigat-ing the novel as a dangerous influence on the unformed female mind. A devotee of Samuel Richardson's Lovelace and the literary villains who followed him, Sir Edward fancies himself a seductive and dangerous lover.[4] His ambition is to fulfil Clara's destiny as a sentimental heroine, a recognisable feminine type described by Scott as 'regularly exposed to being forcibly carried off like a Sabine virgin by some frantic ad-mirer' and subject to 'the terrors of masked ruffians, an insidious rav-isher, a cloak wrapped forcibly around her head, and a coach with the blinds up driving she could not conjecture whither'.[5] Sir Edward views such novels and their representations of male violence against women as works that:

> display human nature with grandeur – such as show her in the sub-limities of intense feeling – such as exhibit the progress of strong passion from the first germ of incipient susceptibility to the utmost energies of reason half-dethroned, – where we see the strong spark of woman's captivations elicit such fire in the soul of man as leads him – (though at the risk of some aberration from the strict line of primitive obligations) – to hazard all, dare all, achieve all, to obtain her (150).

To Sir Edward, the sentimental novel and its glamorisation of male vio-lence are not only entertaining but morally instructive:

> Such are the works which I peruse with delight, and I hope I may say, with amelioration [....] These are the novels which enlarge the primitive capability of the heart, and which it cannot impugn the sense or be any dereliction of the character, of the most anti-puerile man, to be conversant with (150).

In Sir Edward Denham, then, Austen transposes the endemic public concern with the morality of novels and their influence on youth from young women to young men. Austen attributes the influence of senti-mental novels and their seductive villains on Sir Edward to qualities typ-ically associated with poorly educated middle- and gentry-class young women: he 'had not a very clear brain ... and talked a good deal by rote'

(146) and a 'perversity of judgement, which must be attributed to his not having by nature a strong head' (151).

Like young women of his class, Sir Edward possesses a social rank that prevents him engaging in productive employment despite his impoverished financial situation. Too poor to travel in the manner enjoyed by other gentry young men, Sir Edward — like women — has been 'confined very much to one spot' and, endowed with so much leisure, has 'read more sentimental novels than agreed with him' (151). Consequently, the novels that 'occupied the greater part of his literary hours' have 'formed his character' (151). Austen illuminates the absurdity of the moral panic over women's reading by refracting it through a masculine lens: Sir Edward may be influenced by sentimental fiction, but he is a ridiculous character who deludes only himself. Neither Clara nor Lady Denham perceive him as a threat, and to Charlotte he is 'downright silly' (145). Sir Edward Denham is Austen's riposte to a commentariat bent on policing women's reading.

In contrast to Sir Edward, Austen presents three brothers — Thomas, Arthur and Sidney Parker — in the more complex, realist mode familiar to her published novels. The Parker brothers are, to use Scott's phrase, men drawn 'from nature as she really exists in the common walks of life, and presenting to the reader, instead of splendid scenes of an imaginary world, a correct and striking representation of that which is daily taking place around him'.[6] Austen's realism targets the commercialisation of leisure and health among the landowning Regency gentry, superficial values she sardonically critiques in Thomas and Arthur Parker. The former is a financial speculator and chief champion of Sanditon, whose association with print culture is channelled entirely through advertising and news, and the latter a lazy, gluttonous hypochondriac, whose manufactured illnesses allow him to indulge his love of food and drink and shield him from productive employment. Sidney Parker, 'very good-looking, with a decided air of ease and fashion, and a lively countenance' (170), is the only brother who resembles the men of Austen's completed novels, and then only through a brief glimpse at an introductory meeting with Charlotte. All other information about Sidney is derived from unreliable characters whose skewed view of reality and questionable values renders them untrustworthy sources.

In terms of Austen's rewriting of masculinity, the new direction she appears to be taking in *Sanditon* is revealed more in the absence of narrative strategies for portraying men she established in her earlier work, than in the presence of a coherent new approach. It is impossible to identify either Austen's male protagonist or even, with a degree of certainty, her heroine.[7] In none of the characters — neither Charlotte nor any of the men around her — does Austen invest the interiority and psychological depth typical of her completed work. Although Austen may have added such depth through focalisation and shifting narrative perspectives in the editing process,[8] it is possible that she was embarking on a wholly new approach to both characterisation and plot. Austen's title 'The Brothers' suggests a narrative focus on the men of the Parker family rather than on the courtship romance. Although Brian Southam claims that 'it is difficult to imagine' that Thomas, Sidney and Arthur 'are really to dominate the story, or to provide structural centres for the plotting',[9] Austen had already worked with a split narrative focus across several male characters in *Sense and Sensibility* and *Mansfield Park*, the two novels in which her characterisation of men is mostly clearly driven by refuting conventional literary masculinities on one hand, and by her political, social and economic commentary on the other. These dual agendas are also clearly at work in the men of *Sanditon*.

It is probable that, had Austen completed the novel, her critique of masculinity would have extended into new areas of Romantic debate concerned with financial speculation, the commercialisation of leisure and health, and the commodification of literary culture.[10] Yet, as George Justice comments, 'we don't know and cannot prove the author's aim in these manuscript pages'.[11] So different is each of the men of this fragment from either the male protagonists or the peripheral men of Austen's complete works that speculating on how she may have developed them individually is fruitless. However we can be certain that in her final work, Austen's rewriting of masculinity remained invested in her engagement with genre and her ambition for the novel as a literary form.

*****

Just as *Sanditon* remains unfinished, so too is our understanding of men and masculinity in Jane Austen's novels. In this book, I have explored Austen's rewriting of masculinity through the courtship romance genre in the cultural context of the Romantic era. Austen pioneered a new vision of masculinity as a way of understanding the self that could match emerging conceptions of feminine individualism, agency and selfhood, and liberate men from a social and economic order that enforced a performative definition of manhood. Recreating masculinity as an internalised male subjectivity rather than an identity defined by social performance, Austen developed innovative narrative techniques for the representation of more nuanced, composite and psychologically complex male characters in the courtship romance genre. Exploring Austen's men in dialogue with the 'common Novel', Evangelical fiction, the national tale and the historical novel illuminates in new ways relationships of influence between Austen and a group of contemporary Romantic women writers equally committed to interrogating masculinity through the novel. Despite their evident differences, Jane Austen, Maria Edgeworth, Jane Porter, Hannah More, Mary Brunton, Sydney Owenson and Jane West, among others, were connected by a shared ambition for the advancement of the novel, a literary project that demanded greater complexity in writing masculinity.

My focus on masculinity in the courtship romance genre has necessarily excluded other available approaches to interpreting Austen's men and her representation of masculinity that I hope will be taken up by other scholars. My concentration on Austen's construction of the male protagonist through his relationship to the heroine privileges a heterosexual perspective on Austen's work that aligns masculine gender identities with the male and interprets men chiefly through their relationships with women. In choosing this focus, I am not denying the availability of other rich interpretive possibilities regarding masculinity in Austen's fiction; rather, such approaches were beyond the scope of my book. New directions in exploring Austen, men and masculinity could fruitfully investigate her alignment of masculinity (or, at the very least, qualities typically gendered as masculine) with women, as has been suggested, for example, in relation to Elinor Dashwood and Emma Woodhouse,[12] and its consequences for Austen's construction of masculine and feminine gender identities.

My concentration on Austen's male protagonists and their rivals has left her peripheral characters largely unaddressed in this book. I have not investigated Austen's fathers, brothers and sons beyond their influence on the heroine, the male protagonist and the courtship plot. Her representation of relationships between men is particularly worthy of greater analysis.[13] Austen presents complex relationships between fathers, sons and brothers in *Sense and Sensibility*, *Northanger Abbey* and *Mansfield Park*, which I have explored only to the extent that they affect masculine identity in the context of socio-economic status and heterosexual love. Similarly, I have only glanced at the male friendships Austen constructs in *Pride and Prejudice* and *Persuasion*, which are potentially richer than the male rivalries of these novels and may arguably have a greater bearing on her construction of masculine identity itself. Revisiting Austen's interrogation of masculinity through the lens of professional responsibilities, particularly the obligations of estate stewardship, beyond her evaluation of the responsible landlord or clergyman, could also yield further insights into the implications of public duties for male selfhood and subjectivity.

I have also confined my investigation to Austen's professional career: the six complete novels that were published in the 1810s, together with the unfinished *Sanditon*. Austen's rewriting of masculinity commenced well before *Sense and Sensibility*, however, in the juvenilia that constitutes her apprenticeship as a novelist.[14] Investigating Austen's juvenilia may not only shed new light on her responses to her eighteenth-century forbears, but also reveal the origins of the authentic male self she celebrates in her published work and its dynamic, dialogic relationship to feminine agency.

The most compelling new scholarly direction in Austen and masculinity, however, could be to chart the influence of Austen's pioneering vision of masculine identity on her Romantic contemporaries and Victorian inheritors, and on her legacy in the twentieth- and twenty-first centuries. To fully understand the cultural power of Austen's men — to properly account for Fitzwilliam Darcy's recreation as a fibreglass statue two hundred years after *Pride and Prejudice* was published — we need to investigate the effects of Austen's rewriting of masculinity through the courtship romance genre. Although I have explored Austen's replication, reworking and rejection of the literary masculinities of contemporaries including Jane West, Maria Edgeworth and Jane Porter, the influence of Austen's rewriting of masculinity on them and other novelists of the Romantic era remains largely unaddressed. Austen's influence on her Victorian inheritors promises to be a similarly rich area for exploration. In *Jane Austen and the Victorian Heroine*, Cheryl A. Wilson makes a compelling argument for Austen's influence on Victorian readers, writers and literary heroines, as the novel rose to dominate the literary field throughout the nineteenth century.[15] Austen's pioneering representation of masculinity as a psychologically complex gender identity and its dialogic relationship with feminine agency clearly resonates in novels by Charlotte Brontë, Emily Brontë, Anne Brontë, George Eliot, and Elizabeth Gaskell.

A richer understanding of how Austen's vision of male subjectivity was scrutinised, adopted, challenged and rewritten by Victorian novelists will provide a platform for understanding the reach and diversity of her influence in the twentieth century. Theatre, film and screen adaptations of Austen's novels are instrumental to her legacy, but what threads of continuity and change link the visualisation of Austen's men to her rewriting of masculinity and how do such selections influence the reception not only of her men but of Austen herself? How has Austen's conception of desirable masculinity and its relationship to her vision of romantic love been deployed in biopics about the novelist? Can a focus on Austen rewriting masculinity illuminate relationships between contemporary mash-ups of Austen with genre fiction and her own engagement with fictional genres and their construction of gender? Exploring these and other questions will drive new approaches to appreciating the cultural import of Austen's rewriting of masculinity through the courtship romance novel in the Romantic era.

Exploring Jane Austen's representations of masculinity, femininity and the complex relationship between them reveals the striking modernity of her Romantic novels in the twenty-first century. We are still grappling with many of the critical questions of gender, romantic love and individual selfhood Austen explored through the courtship romance genre more than two hundred years ago. To read a Jane Austen novel is to hold up a mirror and see many of the challenges that continue to confront men and women in the modern era. Her celebration of a dynamic, if complex and potentially conflicting, relationship between male selfhood and feminine agency, offers contemporary readers a compelling vision of heterosexual complementarity, a resolution in literature, if not in life.

Notes

Introduction

1 'Recent additions to the circulating library, Corio', *Geelong Advertiser*, Saturday 26 June 1841, 3.

2 Devoney Looser, *The Making of Jane Austen* (Baltimore: Johns Hopkins University Press, 2017).

3 On this feature of screen adaptations, see Lisa Hopkins, 'Mr Darcy's Body: Privileging the Female Gaze', *Jane Austen in Hollywood*, ed. Linda Troost and Sayre Greenfield (Lexington: University of Kentucky Press, 2001), 111–21; Gayle Magee, 'Performing to Strangers: Masculinity, Adaptation, and Music in *Pride and Prejudice* (1995)', *Jane Austen and Masculinity*, ed. Michael Kramp (Lewisburg: Bucknell University Press, 2017), 233–51; Cheryl L. Nixon, 'Balancing the Courtship Hero: Masculine Emotional Display in Film Adaptations of Austen's Novels', *Jane Austen in Hollywood*, ed. Troost and Greenfield, 22–43; Kathryn Sutherland, *Jane Austen's Textual Lives: From Aeschylus to Bollywood* (Oxford: Oxford University Press, 2005).

4 See Deborah Cartmell, '*Pride and Prejudice* and the Adaptation Genre', *Journal of Adaptation in Film & Performance*, 3(3) (2010), 227–43; Marion Gymnich and Kathrin Ruhl, 'Revisiting the Classical Romance: *Pride and Prejudice, Bridget Jones's Diary* and *Bride and Prejudice*', *Gendered (Re) Visions: Constructions of Gender in Audiovisual Media*, ed. Marion Gymnich, Kathrin Ruhl and Klaus Scheunemann (Goettingen: Bonn University Press, 2010), 23–44; Lisa Hopkins, 'Waltzing with Wellington, Biting with Byron: Heroes in Austen Tribute Texts', *Jane Austen and Masculinity*, ed. Kramp, 173–89; Rebecca White, '"What a Man Should Be": (Re)-imagining Austenian Masculinity in Film and YouTube Fanvids', *Jane Austen and Masculinity*, ed. Kramp, 191–209.

5 Anne K. Mellor, *Romanticism and Gender* (New York: Routledge, 1993), 52; Anne K. Mellor, *Mothers of the Nation: Women's Political Writing in England, 1780–1830* (Bloomington: Indiana University Press, 2000), 105–06; Enit Karafili Steiner, *Jane Austen's Civilised Women: Morality, Gender and the Civilizing Process* (London: Pickering & Chatto, 2012), 9.

6 Ashley Tauchert, *Romancing Jane Austen: Narrative, Realism and the Possibility of a Happy Ending* (Houndmills: Palgrave Macmillan, 2005), xiii.

7 Ibid.

8 Mary Poovey, *The Proper Lady and the Woman Writer: Ideology as Style in the Works of Mary Wollstonecraft, Mary Shelley, and Jane Austen* (Chicago: University of Chicago Press, 1984), 203.

9 Devoney Looser, 'Jane Austen "Responds" to the Men's Movement', *Persuasions*, 18 (1996), 159–70, 164.

10 See, for example, Irene Collins, *Jane Austen and the Clergy* (London & New York: Hambledon and London, 2003); Audrey Hawkridge, *Jane and*

Her Gentlemen: Jane Austen and the Men in Her Life and Novels (London & Chester Springs: Peter Owen Publishers, 2000); Brian Southam, *Jane Austen and the Navy*, 2nd ed. (Hambledon & London: National Maritime Museum Publishing, 2005).

11   Claudia L. Johnson, *Jane Austen: Women, Politics and the Novel* (Chicago: Chicago University Press, 1988); Claudia L. Johnson, *Equivocal Beings. Politics, Gender, and Sentimentality in the 1790s: Wollstonecraft, Radcliffe, Burney, Austen* (Chicago: University of Chicago Press, 1995); Joseph Kestner, 'Jane Austen: Revolutionizing Masculinities', *Persuasions: The Jane Austen Journal*, 16 (1994) 147–60; Looser, 'Jane Austen "Responds" to the Men's Movement'; E. J. Clery, 'Austen and Masculinity', *A Companion to Jane Austen*, ed. Claudia L. Johnson and Clara Tuite (Chichester: Wiley-Blackwell, 2009), 332–42.

12   For historical accounts of masculinities in the eighteenth century and the Romantic period, see Philip Carter, *Men and the Emergence of Polite Society, Britain 1660–1800* (Harlow: Longman, 2001); Philip Carter, 'Polite "Persons": Character, Biography and the Gentleman', *Transactions of the Royal Historical Society*, 12 (2002), 333–54; Michèle Cohen, *Fashioning Masculinity: National Identity and Language in the Eighteenth Century* (London: Routledge, 1996); Michèle Cohen, '"Manners" Make the Man: Politeness, Chivalry, and the Construction of Masculinity, 1750–1830', *Journal of British Studies*, 44(2) (April 2005), 312–29; Tim Fulford, *Romanticism and Masculinity: Gender, Politics and Poetics in the Writings of Burke, Coleridge, Cobbett, Wordsworth, De Quincey and Hazlitt* (Houndmills: Macmillan Press, 1999); Tim Fulford, 'Romanticizing the Empire: The Naval Heroes of Southey, Coleridge, Austen and Marryat', *Modern Language Quarterly*, 60(1) (March 1999), 161–96; Tim Hitchcock and Michèle Cohen (eds.), *English Masculinities, 1660–1800* (London: Longman, 1999); Paul Langford, *A Polite and Commercial People: England 1727–1783* (Oxford: Clarendon Press, 1989); Paul Langford, *Englishness Identified: Manners and Character, 1650–1850* (Oxford: Oxford University Press, 2000); Paul Langford, 'The Uses of Eighteenth-Century Politeness', *Transactions of the Royal Historical Society*, 12 (2002), 311–31.

13   Cohen, '"Manners" Make the Man'; Sarah S. G. Frantz, 'Jane Austen's Heroes and the Great Masculine Renunciation', *Persuasions*, 25 (2003), 165–75; Fulford, 'Romanticizing the Empire', 171; John Peck, *Maritime Fiction: Sailors and the Sea in British and American Novels, 1719–1917* (Houndmills: Palgrave Macmillan, 2001); Jason D. Solinger, *Becoming the Gentleman: British Literature and the Invention of Modern Masculinity, 1660–1815* (New York: Palgrave Macmillan, 2012); Brian C. Southam, 'Jane Austen's Englishness: *Emma* as National Tale', *Persuasions*, 30 (2008), 187–201; Megan A. Woodworth, *Eighteenth-Century Women Writers and the Gentleman's Liberation Movement: Independence, War, Masculinity and the Novel, 1778–1818* (Farnham & Burlington: Ashgate, 2011).

14   Michael Kramp, *Disciplining Love: Austen and the Modern Man* (Columbus: Ohio State University Press, 2007), 3.

15   Michael Kramp (ed.), *Jane Austen and Masculinity* (Lewisburg: Bucknell University Press, 2017), 1.

16   Woodworth, *Eighteenth-Century Women Writers*; Solinger, *Becoming the Gentleman*, 91–110.

17   Patricia Menon, *Austen, Eliot, Charlotte Brontë and the Mentor-Lover* (Houndmills: Palgrave Macmillan, 2003) addresses the figure of the 'mentor-lover' in Austen's work, but does not explore her rewriting of masculinity itself through the courtship romance genre.

18 Catharine Macaulay, *Letters on Education* (London, 1790); Mary Wollstonecraft, *A Vindication of the Rights of Woman* (1792), ed. Anne K. Mellor and Noelle Chai (Pearson Longman, 2007); Mary Hays, *Appeal to the Men of Great Britain in Behalf of Women* (London, 1798); Mary Robinson, *A Letter to the Women of England* (London, 1799); Priscilla Wakefield, *Reflections on the Present Condition of the Female Sex, with Suggestions for Its Improvement* (London, 1798); Lucy Aikin, *Epistles on Women, Exemplifying their Character and Condition in Various Ages and Nations, with Miscellaneous Poems* (London, 1810).

19 Macaulay, *Letters on Education*, Letter XXII, 207.

20 The relationship between Macaulay and Wollstonecraft is explored in Bridget Hill, 'The Links between Mary Wollstonecraft and Catharine Macaulay: New Evidence', *Women's History Review*, 4(2) (1995), 177–92; Elizabeth Frazer, 'Mary Wollstonecraft and Catharine Macaulay on education', *Oxford Review of Education*, 37(5) (2011), 603–17; Devoney Looser, '"Those Historical Laurels which Once Graced My Brow and Now in Their Wane": Catharine Macaulay's Last Years and Legacy', *Studies in Romanticism*, 42(2) (2003), 203–25.

21 See Steiner, *Jane Austen's Civilised Women*, 13.

22 Wollstonecraft, *Rights of Woman*, 182. For a discussion of Wollstonecraft's strategy in appealing to a male readership, see Mellor, *Romanticism and Gender*, 33–34, and Woodworth, *Eighteenth-Century Women Writers*, 88.

23 Hays, *Appeal to the Men of Great Britain*, iv.

24 On Wollstonecraft, see Mellor, *Mothers of the Nation*, 104, and Katharina Rennhak, 'Hailing a New Man: The Rights of Women, Constructions of Masculinity and Solidarity', *Called to Civil Existence: Mary Wollstonecraft's* A Vindication of the Rights of Woman, ed. Enit Karafili Steiner (Amsterdam & New York: Rodopi, 2014), 181–202, 182–183.

25 Macaulay, *Letters on Education*, Letter XXIV, 216.

26 John Tosh, *A Man's Place: Masculinity and the Middle-Class Home in Victorian England* (New Haven: Yale University Press, 1999), 2.

27 Ibid. 2–3.

28 John Tosh, *Manliness and Masculinities in Nineteenth-Century Britain: Essays on Gender, Family, and Empire* (Harlow: Pearson Longman, 2005), 71.

29 Leonore Davidoff and Catherine Hall, *Family Fortunes: Men and Women of the English Middle Class 1780–1850* (London: Routledge, 1992), 110.

30 Carter, *Men and the Emergence of Polite Society*, 209.

31 John Tosh, 'The Old Adam and the New Man: Emerging Themes in the History of English Masculinities, 1750–1850', *English Masculinities, 1660–1800*, ed. Tim Hitchcock and Michèle Cohen (London: Longman, 1999), 217–38, 229; Tosh, *Manliness and Masculinities*, 2, 5.

32 See, for example, Robin Gilmour, *The Idea of the Gentleman in the Victorian Novel* (London: George Allen & Unwin, 1981); Gerard A. Baker, *Grandison's Heirs. The Paragon's Progress in the Late Eighteenth-Century English Novel* (Newark: University of Delaware Press, 1985); Brian Southam, 'Sir Charles Grandison and Jane Austen's Men', *Persuasions*, 18 (1996), 74–87.

33 In making this argument, I am cognisant of Judith Butler's theory of the performativity of gender. I am not arguing for a distinction between performative and authentic, internalised masculine identities within the scope of Butler's theory. Rather, I am exploring constructions of masculinity in the Romantic era, and a detailed analysis of Butler's theory in relation to either Romantic masculinities or Austen is beyond the scope of my book. See Judith Butler, *Gender Trouble* (1999) (New York: Routledge, 2006).

34 Tosh, 'The Old Adam', 231, 219.
35 Ibid., 232.
36 Ibid.
37 April London, *The Cambridge Introduction to the Eighteenth-Century Novel* (Cambridge & New York: Cambridge University Press, 2012), 5.
38 Dror Wahrman, *The Making of the Modern Self: Identity and Culture in Eighteenth Century England* (New Haven: Yale University Press, 2004), 276.
39 Deidre Lynch, *The Economy of Character: Novels, Market Culture and the Business of Inner Meaning* (Chicago: Chicago University Press, 1998), 129, 151.
40 Gillian Russell and Clara Tuite, 'Introducing Romantic Sociability', *Romantic Sociability: Social Networks and Literary Culture in Britain, 1770–1840*, ed. Gillian Russell and Clara Tuite (Cambridge: Cambridge University Press, 2006), 1–23, 5.
41 Austen's connection to Romanticism more broadly has been explored in William Christie, *The Two Romanticisms, and Other Essays* (Sydney: Sydney University Press, 2016); William Deresiewicz, *Jane Austen and the Romantic Poets* (New York: Columbia University Press, 2004); Clara Tuite, *Romantic Austen: Sexual Politics and the Literary Canon* (Cambridge: Cambridge University Press, 2004); Beth Lau, 'Placing Jane Austen in the Romantic Period: Self and Solitude in the Works of Austen and the Male Romantic Poets', *European Romantic Review*, 15(2) (June 2004), 255–67; Beth Lau (ed.), *Fellow Romantics: Male and Female British Writers, 1790–1835* (Aldershot: Ashgate, 2009).
42 See Anthony Mandal, *Jane Austen and the Popular Novel: The Determined Author* (Houndmills: Palgrave Macmillan, 2007); Olivia Murphy, *Jane Austen the Reader: The Artist as Critic* (Houndmills: Palgrave Macmillan, 2013).
43 Murphy, *Jane Austen the Reader*, 29. See also Jocelyn Harris, *Jane Austen's Art of Memory* (Cambridge & New York: Cambridge University Press, 1989).
44 On women writing men, see George Haggerty, *Unnatural Affections: Women and Fiction in the Later Eighteenth Century* (Bloomington: Indiana University Press, 1998); Katharine M. Rogers, 'Dreams and Nightmares: Male Characters in the Feminine Novel of the Eighteenth Century', *Men by Women*, ed. Janet Todd (New York & London: Holmes & Meier Publishers, 1981), 9–24; Sarah S. G. Frantz and Katharina Rennhak (eds.), *Women Constructing Men: Female Novelists and their Male Characters, 1750–2000* (Lanham: Lexington Books, 2010); Woodworth, *Eighteenth-Century Women Writers*, 4.
45 Sarah Wootton, *Byronic Heroes in Nineteenth Century Women's Writing and Screen Adaptation* (Houndmills: Palgrave Macmillan, 2016).
46 Nancy Armstrong, *Desire and Domestic Fiction: A Political History of the Novel* (New York & Oxford: Oxford University Press, 1987), 29; Harriet Guest, *Small Change. Women, Learning, Patriotism 1750–1810* (Chicago & London: University of Chicago Press, 2000); Mellor, *Mothers of the Nation*, 9, 104; Lisa Wood, *Modes of Discipline: Women, Conservatism, and the Novel after the French Revolution* (Lewisburg: Bucknell University Press, 2003), 26.
47 Jane West, *Letters to a Young Man* (London, 1803), Vol 1, xx.
48 West, *Letters to a Young Man*, Vol 1, xx.
49 Austen to Cassandra, 8–9 September 1816, *Letters*, 321.
50 West, *Letters to a Young Man*, Vol 1, xx.
51 Fiona Price, '"A Great Deal of History": Romantic Women Writers and Historical Fiction', *Women's Writing*, 19(3) (2012), 259–72, 259.
52 Devoney Looser, 'The Great Man and Women's Historical Fiction: Jane Porter and Sir Sidney Smith', *Women's Writing*, 19(3) (2012), 293–314, 294.

53 Devoney Looser, 'The Porter Sisters, Women's Writing, and Historical Fiction', *The History of British Women's Writing*, ed. Jacqueline Labbe (Houndmills: Palgrave Macmillan, 2010), 233–52, 234.

54 Mandal, *Jane Austen*, 25. *Thaddeus of Warsaw* was well reviewed in the *Critical Review* (September 1803, 120), the *Monthly Review* (February 1804, 214–15), the *Imperial Review* (February 1804, 309–14), and the *Annual Review and History of Literature* (1803, Vol. 2, 604–05).

55 Looser, 'The Great Man', 302–04.

56 *The Scots Magazine* (1810, pp. 278–83), quoted in Jane Porter, *The Scottish Chiefs*, ed. Fiona Price (Peterborough: Broadview Editions, 2007), 751.

57 Irene Basey Beesemyer, '"I Thought I Never Set My Eyes on a Finer Figure of a Man": Maria Edgeworth Scrutinizes Masculinity in *Castle Rackrent, Ennui,* and *The Absentee*', *New Essays on Maria Edgeworth*, ed. Julie Nash (Aldershot: Ashgate, 2006), 109–29. *Ennui* was reviewed in the *Edinburgh Review* (July 1809, 375–88), *Monthly Review* (February 1810, 96–97), *Critical Review* (October 1809, 181–91), and the *Quarterly Review* (August 1809, 146–54). *The Absentee* was reviewed in the *Quarterly Review* (June 1812, 329–42), *British Review* (vol. iv, 64–90), and the *Edinburgh Review* (July 1812, 100–26).

58 Connor Carville and Marilyn Butler have also identified 'the widespread view that she was trespassing in a masculine public world' and noted that *Patronage* also sparked a furore in London professional circles, ('Introductory Note', *Patronage, The Novels and Selected Works of Maria Edgeworth*, vol. 6 (London: Pickering & Chatto, 1999), vii–xxx).

59 *Quarterly Review*, January 1814, 301–23, 311.

60 *British Critic*, January 1814, 159–73, 166, 165.

61 Ibid., 171.

62 Carville and Butler, 'Introductory Note', xxii.

63 James Stanier Clarke to Austen, 16 November 1815, *Letters*, 296–97; Clarke to Austen, 21 December 1815, *Letters*, 307.

64 Austen to Clarke, 11 December 1815, *Letters*, 306.

65 Jane Austen, 'Plan of a Novel, According to Hints from Various Quarters', *The Works of Jane Austen. Vol. VI Minor Works*, ed. R. W. Chapman (Oxford: Oxford University Press, 1954), 428–30; Murphy, *Jane Austen the Reader*, 123.

66 Clery, 'Austen and Masculinity', 334.

67 Ibid., 332.

68 Ibid., 333.

69 Austen to Clarke, 1 April 1816, *Letters*, 312.

70 On the courtship romance genre, see Katherine Sobba Green, *The Courtship Novel 1740–1820: A Feminized Genre* (Lexington: University of Kentucky Press, 1991); Lynne Pearce, *Romance Writing* (Cambridge: Polity Press, 2007); Jane Spencer, *The Rise of the Woman Novelist: From Aphra Behn to Jane Austen* (Oxford: Basil Blackwell, 1986).

71 Tauchert, *Romancing Jane Austen*, 7.

72 Austen to Crosby & Co, 5 April 1809, and Richard Crosby to Austen, 8 April 1809, *Letters*, 174–75.

73 Austen to Cassandra, 24 May 1813, *Letters*, 213.

74 Murphy, *Jane Austen the Reader*, 123–24.

75 Austen to Cassandra, 24 January 1809, *Letters*, 170.

Chapter 1

1 Austen to Anna Lefroy, 28 September 1814, *Letters*, 277.

2 J. M. S. Tompkins, 'Elinor and Marianne: A Note on Jane Austen', *The Review of English Studies* 16(6) (1940), 33–43, 33. On Minerva Press writers and

literary formula, see Elizabeth A. Neiman, 'A New Perspective on the Minerva Press's "Derivative" Novels: Authorizing Borrowed Material', *European Romantic Review* 26(5) (2015), 633–58 <DOI:10.1080/10509585.2015.1070344>

3 Peter Gardside, 'Authorship', *The Oxford History of the Novel in English Vol. 2, English and British Fiction 1750–1820*, ed. Peter Garside and Karen O'Brien (Oxford: Oxford University Press, 2015), 29–52, 32. See also Stephen C. Behrendt, 'Publishing and the Provinces in Romantic-era Britain', *The Cambridge Companion to British Romanticism*, ed. Stuart Curran (Cambridge: Cambridge University Press, 2010), 153–68.

4 On the development of the courtship romance novel, see Katharine Sobba Green, *The Courtship Novel, 1740–1820: A Feminized Genre* (Lexington: University Press of Kentucky, 1991).

5 See Anthony Mandal, *Jane Austen and the Popular Novel: The Determined Author* (Houndmills: Palgrave Macmillan, 2007) for an account of shifting trends in the publication of fiction between the 1790s and 1810s.

6 J. M. S. Tompkins, *The Popular Novel in England 1770–1800* (Lincoln: University of Nebraska Press, 1961), 130.

7 Ibid., 128–33.

8 Deidre Lynch, *The Economy of Character: Novels, Market Culture and the Business of Inner Meaning* (Chicago: Chicago University Press, 1998), 129, 151.

9 Unsigned review, *Critical Review*, February 1812, *Jane Austen: The Critical Heritage*, ed. B. C. Southam (London: Routledge & Kegan Paul, 1968), 35–39.

10 E. J. Clery, 'Austen and Masculinity', *A Companion to Jane Austen*, ed. Claudia L. Johnson and Clara Tuite (Chichester: Wiley-Blackwell, 2009), 332–42, 332–33.

11 Jane Austen, 'Opinions of *Mansfield Park*', *The Works of Jane Austen. Vol. VI Minor Works*, ed. R. W. Chapman (Oxford: Oxford University Press, 1954), 431–35, 431, and 'Opinions of *Emma*', *The Works of Jane Austen. Vol. VI Minor Works*, ed. Chapman, 436–39, 438.

12 Letter from Lady Bessborough to Granville Leveson Gower, 24 November 1811, *Lord Granville Leveson Gower: Private Correspondence 1781–1821*, ed. Castalia Countess Granville (London: John Murray, 1817), Vol. 2, 418; Isabelle Bour, 'The Reception of Jane Austen's Novels in France and Switzerland: The Early Years, 1813–1828', *The Reception of Jane Austen in Europe*, ed. Anthony Mandal and Brian Southam (London: Bloomsbury, 2014), 12–33, 22.

13 See, for example Claudia L. Johnson, *Jane Austen: Women, Politics and the Novel* (Chicago: Chicago University Press, 1988), 58; Laura G. Mooneyham, *Romance, Language and Education in Jane Austen's Novels* (Houndmills: Macmillan, 1988), 30–31; Mary Poovey, *The Proper Lady and the Woman Writer. Ideology as Style in the Works of Mary Wollstonecraft, Mary Shelley, and Jane Austen* (Chicago: University of Chicago Press, 1984), 185. Rachel Brownstein, 'Northanger Abbey, Sense and Sensibility and Pride and Prejudice', *The Cambridge Companion to Jane Austen*, ed. Edward Copeland and Juliet McMaster (Cambridge: Cambridge University Press, 1997), 32–57; and Clara Tuite, *Romantic Austen: Sexual Politics and the Literary Canon* (Cambridge: Cambridge University Press, 2004), 92, have also noted this phenomenon.

14 Tompkins, 'Elinor and Marianne'; Mary Waldron, *Jane Austen and the Fiction of Her Time* (Cambridge: Cambridge University Press, 1999), 68–70. For a discussion of the men of *A Gossip's Story* in relation to West's conservative politics, see Megan A. Woodworth, *Eighteenth-Century Women Writers and the Gentleman's Liberation Movement. Independence, War, Masculinity and the Novel, 1778–1818* (Ashgate: Farnham, 2011), 111–15.

15 For an alternative view on primogeniture in *Sense and Sensibility*, see Joyce Kerr Tarpley, 'Playing with Genesis: Sonship, Liberty, and Primogeniture in *Sense and Sensibility*', *Persuasions*, 33 (2011), 89–102.

16 Matthew McCormack, *The Independent Man: Citizenship and Gender Politics in Georgian England* (Manchester: Manchester University Press, 2005), 1–2.

17 Miranda Burgess, 'Sentiment and Sensibility: Austen, Feeling and Print Culture', *A Companion to Jane Austen*, ed. Claudia L. Johnson and Clara Tuite (Oxford: Blackwell, 2009), 226–36, 230–31.

18 Philip Carter, *Men and the Emergence of Polite Society, Britain 1660–1800* (Harlow: Longman, 2001), 92.

19 Carole Berger, 'The Rake and the Reader in Jane Austen's Novels', *Studies in English Literature, 1500–1900*, 15(4) (1975), 533; Emily Auerbach, *Searching for Jane Austen* (Madison: University of Wisconsin Press, 2004), 123.

20 Peter Knox-Shaw, *Jane Austen and the Enlightenment* (Cambridge: Cambridge University Press, 2004), 149.

21 Carter, *Men and the Emergence of Polite Society*, 104, 96.

22 Ibid., 111.

23 Tuite, *Romantic Austen*, 67.

24 Tony Tanner, *Jane Austen* (London: Macmillan, 1986), 100; Darryl Jones, *Jane Austen* (Houndmills: Palgrave Macmillan, 2004), 63.

25 On Colonel Brandon's duel with Willoughby, see also Megan A. Woodworth, '"I could meet him in no other way": Dueling, the Culture of Honor, and Modern Masculinity in *Sense and Sensibility*', *Jane Austen and Masculinity*, ed. Michael Kramp (Lewisburg: Bucknell University Press, 2017), 81–96.

26 John Tosh, *A Man's Place: Masculinity and the Middle-Class Home in Victorian England* (New Haven: Yale University Press, 1999), 2.

Chapter 2

1 Enit Karafili Steiner, *Jane Austen's Civilised Women: Morality, Gender and the Civilizing Process* (London: Pickering & Chatto, 2012), 65; Claudia L. Johnson, *Jane Austen: Women, Politics and the Novel* (Chicago: Chicago University Press, 1988), 37; Stephanie M. Eddleman, 'Henry Tilney: Austen's Feminized Hero?', *Persuasions*, 32 (2010), 68–77, 68; Emily Auerbach, *Searching for Jane Austen* (Madison: University of Wisconsin Press, 2004), 83.

2 Jillian Heydt-Stevenson, '*Northanger Abbey*, *Desmond*, and History', *Wordsworth Circle*, 44(2–3) (Spring–Summer 2013), 140–48, 142.

3 Jan Fergus, *Jane Austen and the Didactic Novel: Northanger Abbey, Sense and Sensibility and Pride and Prejudice* (London: Macmillan, 1983), 15.

4 Nancy Armstrong and Leonard Tennenhouse (eds.), *The Ideology of Conduct: Essays on Literature and the History of Sexuality* (New York: Methuen, 1987), 2–3; Nancy Armstrong, *Desire and Domestic Fiction: A Political History of the Novel* (New York: Oxford University Press, 1987).

5 Lawrence Stone, *The Family, Sex and Marriage in England 1500–1800* (London: Weidenfeld and Nicolson, 1977), 390–99; Robert B. Shoemaker, *Gender in English Society, 1650–1850: The Emergence of Separate Spheres?* (London: Longman, 1998), 90–101.

6 Sarah S. G. Frantz and Katharina Rennhak, 'Female Novelists and Their Male Characters, 1750–2000: An Introduction', *Women Constructing Men: Female Novelists and Their Male Characters 1750–2000*, ed. Sarah S. G. Frantz and Katharina Rennhak (Lexington: Rowman and Littlefield, 2009); Katharine Sobba Green, Introduction. *The Courtship Novel, 1740–1820: A Feminized Genre* (Lexington: University Press of Kentucky, 1991); George Haggerty, *Unnatural Affections: Women and Fiction in the later Eighteenth Century* (Bloomington: Indiana University Press, 1998), 4; Lisa

Wood, *Modes of Discipline: Women, Conservatism and the Novel after the French Revolution* (Lewisburg: Bucknell University Press, 2003), 125.

7 Kathy Justice Gentile, '"A Forward, Bragging, Scheming Race": Comic Masculinity in *Northanger Abbey*', *Persuasions* 32 (2010), 78–89.

8 Marilyn Butler, 'Notes to *Northanger Abbey*' (London: Penguin Classics, 1995), 249; Susan Allen Ford, 'Ingenious Torments, or Reading Instructive Texts in *Northanger Abbey: The Mirror, The Rambler*, and Conduct Books', *Persuasions On-Line* 31(1) (Winter 2010), < http://www.jasna.org/persuasions/on-line/vol31no1/ford.html>; Mary Waldron, *Jane Austen and the Fiction of her Time* (Cambridge: Cambridge University Press, 1999), 18–19.

9 JoEllen M. DeLucia, 'A Delicate Debate: Mary Wollstonecraft, the Bluestockings, and the Progress of Women', *Called to Civil Existence. Mary Wollstonecraft's* A Vindication of the Rights of Woman, ed. Enit Karafili Steiner (Amsterdam & New York: Rodopi, 2014), 113–30, 124.

10 Diane Hoeveler, 'Vindicating *Northanger Abbey*: Mary Wollstonecraft, Jane Austen, and Gothic Feminism', *Jane Austen and Discourses of Feminism*, ed. Devoney Looser (New York: St. Martin's Press, 1995), 117–36, 120.

11 Michael Kramp, *Disciplining Love: Austen and the Modern Man* (Columbus: Ohio State University Press, 2007), 47.

12 Jane Austen, *Northanger Abbey*, ed. Marilyn Butler (London: Penguin, 1995), 249, n5.

13 Judith Mitchell, *The Stone and the Scorpion: The Female Subject of Desire in the Novels of Charlotte Brontë, George Eliot and Thomas Hardy* (London: Greenwood Press, 1994), 9–10.

14 Leroy Smith, *Jane Austen and the Drama of Woman* (New York: St. Martin's Press, 1983), 61; Alison G. Sulloway, *Jane Austen and the Province of Womanhood* (Philadelphia: University of Pennsylvania Press, 1989), 124; Steiner, *Jane Austen's Civilised Women*, 65–66.

15 John Gregory, *Legacy to His Daughters* (London, 1774), 15.

16 Philip Carter, *Men and the Emergence of Polite Society, Britain 1660–1800* (Harlow: Longman, 2001).

17 Gillian Williamson, *British Masculinity in the* 'Gentleman's Magazine', *1731–1815* (Houndmills: Palgrave Macmillan, 2016).

18 John Harris, *Essay on Politeness* (London, 1775), 18.

19 Carter, *Men and the Emergence of Polite Society*, 38.

20 James Forrester, *The Polite Philosopher* (London, 1734), 71.

21 Williamson, *British Masculinity*; Markman Ellis, *The Coffee-House, A Cultural History* (London: Phoenix, 2004).

22 On Austen's construction of fatherhood in General Tilney, see Kit Kincade, 'Failures of the Patriarchy: Fathers as Role Models in Jane Austen', *Jane Austen and Masculinity*, ed. Michael Kramp (Lewisburg: Bucknell University Press, 2017), 41–44.

23 Johnson, *Jane Austen*, 35; Auerbach, *Searching for Jane Austen*, 91.

24 John Tosh, *A Man's Place: Masculinity and the Middle-Class Home in Victorian England* (New Haven, London: Yale University Press, 1999), 4.

25 Eddleman, 'Henry Tilney', 73.

26 Tosh, *A Man's Place*, 2–3.

27 Matthew McCormack, *The Independent Man: Citizenship and Gender Politics in Georgian England* (Manchester: Manchester University Press, 2005), 1–2.

28 Kramp, *Disciplining Love*, 50–51.

29 Gregory, *Legacy to His Daughters*, 82.

Chapter 3

1 Austen to Cassandra, 29 January 1813, *Letters*, 201.
2 Austen to Cassandra, 4 February 1813, *Letters*, 203.
3 Ibid.
4 Ibid; Austen to Cassandra, 9 February 1813, *Letters*, 205.
5 Austen to Frank Austen, 25 September 1813, *Letters*, 231.
6 Austen to Cassandra, 29 January 1813, *Letters*, 201.
7 Austen to Cassandra, 24 May 1813, *Letters*, 213.
8 Marion Gymnich and Kathrin Ruhl, 'Revisiting the Classical Romance: *Pride and Prejudice, Bridget Jones's Diary* and *Bride and Prejudice*', *Gendered (Re)Visions: Constructions of Gender in Audiovisual Media*, ed. Marion Gymnich, Kathrin Ruhl and Klaud Scheunemann (Gottingen: V & R Unipress; Bonn: Bonn University Press, 2010), 23–44; Meaghan Malone, '"You Have Bewitched Me Body and Soul": Masculinity and the Female Gaze in Jane Austen's *Pride and Prejudice*', *At the Edge* 1 (2010) <http://journals.library.mun.ca/ojs/index.php/ate/article/view/91/46>; Sarah Raff, *Jane Austen's Erotic Advice* (Oxford: Oxford University Press, 2014), 40–41.
9 Janet Todd, 'The Romantic Hero', *The Cambridge Companion to Pride and Prejudice*, ed. Janet Todd (Cambridge: Cambridge University Press, 2013), 150–61; Deborah Lutz, *The Dangerous Lover: Gothic Villains, Byronism and the Nineteenth-Century Seduction Narrative* (Columbus: Ohio State University Press, 2006), 43; Sarah Wootton, *Byronic Heroes in Nineteenth-Century Women's Writing and Screen Adaptation* (Houndmills: Palgrave Macmillan, 2016).
10 Austen to Cassandra, 4 February 1813, *Letters*, 203.
11 Accounts of Austen's Romanticism tend to focus on *Sense and Sensibility, Mansfield Park*, and *Persuasion* rather than *Pride and Prejudice*. See, for example Clara Tuite, *Romantic Austen: Sexual Politics and the Literary Canon* (Cambridge: Cambridge University Press, 2004); Beth Lau, 'Placing Jane Austen in the Romantic Period: Self and Solitude in the Works of Austen and the Male Romantic Poets', *European Romantic Review*, 15(2) (June 2004), 255–67; Beth Lau (ed.), *Fellow Romantics: Male and Female British Writers, 1790–1835* (Aldershot: Ashgate, 2009).
12 E. J. Clery, 'Austen and Masculinity', *A Companion to Jane Austen*, ed. Claudia L. Johnson and Clara Tuite (Chichester: Wiley-Blackwell, 2009), 332–42, 335.
13 Austen to Cassandra, 29 January 1813, *Letters*, 202.
14 Olivia Murphy, 'Rethinking Influence by Reading with Austen', *Women's Writing*, 20(1) (2013), 100–14, 103.
15 Katherine Binhammer, 'Thinking Gender with Sexuality in 1790s' Feminist Thought', *Feminist Studies*, 28(3) (2002), 667–90; Anne K. Mellor, *Mothers of the Nation: Women's Political Writing in England, 1780–1830* (Bloomington: Indiana University Press, 2000), 104–06; Mitzi Myers, 'Reform or Ruin: "A Revolution in Female Manners"', *Studies in Eighteenth-Century Culture*, 11 (1982), 199–216, 201.
16 Binhammer, 'Thinking Gender with Sexuality', 677.
17 See Gillian Dooley, 'A Most Luxurious State: Men and Music in Jane Austen's Novels', *English Studies*, 98(6) (2017), 598–607.
18 For alternative readings of Darcy's development in *Pride and Prejudice*, see Sarah S. G. Frantz, 'Jane Austen and the Great Masculine Renunciation', *Persuasions*, 25 (2003), 165–75; Claudia L. Johnson, *Jane Austen: Women, Politics, and the Novel* (Chicago: Chicago University Press, 1988), 81–82,

84; Jennifer Preston Wilson, '"One Has Got All the Goodness, and the Other All the Appearance of It": The Development of Darcy in *Pride and Prejudice*', *Persuasions On-Line*, 25(1) (2004): no pag. <http://www.jasna.org/persuasions/on-line/vol25no1/wilson.html>; Megan A. Woodworth, *Eighteenth-Century Women Writers and the Gentleman's Liberation Movement: Independence, War, Masculinity and the Novel, 1778–1818* (Farnham & Burlington: Ashgate, 2011), 152; Wootton, *Byronic Heroes*, 39.

19 Sonjeong Cho, *An Ethics of Becoming: Configurations of Feminine Subjectivity in Jane Austen, Charlotte Brontë, and George Eliot* (New York & London: Routledge, 2005), 47–49; Malone, 'You Have Bewitched Me'; Douglas Murray, 'Gazing and Avoiding the Gaze', *Jane Austen's Business*, ed. Juliet McMaster and Bruce Stovel (Houndmills: Macmillan Press, 1996), 42–53.

20 See also Elaine Bander, 'Neither Sex, Money, nor Power: Why Elizabeth Finally Says "Yes!"', *Persuasions*, 35 (2012), 25–41.

21 Wootton, *Byronic Heroes*, 12.

22 Alternative readings of Elizabeth's visit to Pemberley emphasise her eroticism and empowerment in landscape. See Barbara Britton Wenner, *Prospect and Refuge in the Landscape of Jane Austen* (Aldershot: Ashgate, 2006), 56–59; Peter de Bolla, 'The Charm'd Eye', *Body and Text in the Eighteenth Century*, ed. Veronica Kelly and Dorothea von Mucke (Stanford: Stanford University Press, 1994), 89–111; H. Elisabeth Ellington, '"A Correct Taste in Landscape": Pemberley as Fetish and Commodity', *Jane Austen in Hollywood*, ed. Linda Troost and Sayre Greenfield (Lexington: University of Kentucky Press, 2001), 90–110; Daryl Ogden, *The Language of the Eyes: Science, Sexuality, and Female Vision in English Literature and Culture, 1690–1927* (New York: State University of New York Press, 2005), 58–59; Roger Sales, *Closer to Home: Writers and Places in England, 1780–1830* (Cambridge: Harvard University Press, 1986), 41; Todd, 'The Romantic Hero', 152–53.

23 Enit Karafili Steiner, *Jane Austen's Civilised Women: Morality, Gender and the Civilizing Process* (London: Pickering & Chatto, 2012), 9.

24 Clery, 'Austen and Masculinity', 339.

Chapter 4

1 Lisa Wood, *Modes of Discipline: Women, Conservatism, and the Novel after the French Revolution* (Lewisburg: Bucknell University Press, 2003), 15.

2 Anthony Mandal, 'Fiction', *The Cambridge Companion to Women's Writing in the Romantic Period*, ed. Devoney Looser (Cambridge: Cambridge University Press, 2015), 16–31, 23; Anthony Mandal, 'Introduction', Mary Brunton, *Self-Control*, ed. Anthony Mandal (Routledge: London & New York, 2016), xx, xxi.

3 Anthony Mandal, 'Evangelical Fiction', *The Oxford History of the Novel in English. Volume 2: English and British Fiction 1750–1820*, ed. Peter Garside and Karen O'Brien (Oxford: Oxford University Press, 2015), 255–72, 271.

4 Lisa Wood, 'The Evangelical Novel', *The Oxford Handbook of the Eighteenth-Century Novel*, ed. Alan Downie (Oxford: Oxford University Press, 2016), 528.

5 Anthony Mandal, *Jane Austen and the Popular Novel: The Determined Author* (Houndmills: Palgrave Macmillan, 2007), 92.

6 Ibid., 169.

7 See, for example Claudia L. Johnson, *Jane Austen: Women, Politics and the Novel* (Chicago: Chicago University Press, 1988); Michael Kramp, *Disciplining Love: Austen and the Modern Man* (Columbus: Ohio State University Press, 2007); Roger Sales, *Jane Austen and Representations of Regency England* (London: Routledge, 1994); Megan A. Woodworth, *Eighteenth-Century Women Writers and the Gentleman's Liberation Movement: Independence, War, Masculinity and the Novel, 1778–1818* (Farnham & Burlington: Ashgate, 2011).

8 On *Mansfield Park*'s Regency contexts, see Sheryl Craig, *Jane Austen and the State of the Nation* (Houndmills: Palgrave Macmillan, 2015), 88–117, and Susan Allen Ford, 'Working Out a Happy Conclusion: *Mansfield Park* and the Revision of *King Lear*', *Sensibilities*, 27 (2003), 95–110. Gabrielle White, *Jane Austen in the Context of Abolition: 'A Fling at the Slave Trade'* (Houndmills: Palgrave Macmillan, 2006) provides a comprehensive account of the novel's abolitionist context, which has also been explored by Edward Said, *Culture and Imperialism* (New York: Vintage, 1994); Susan Fraiman, 'Jane Austen and Edward Said: Gender, Culture, and Imperialism', *Janeites: Austen's Disciples and Devotees*, ed. Deidre Lynch (Princeton: Princeton University Press, 2000), 206–23; Moira Ferguson, *Colonialism and Gender Relations from Mary Wollstonecraft to Jamaica Kincaid: East Caribbean Connections* (New York: Columbia University Press, 1993).

9 Wood, *Modes of Discipline*, 117. See also Elizabeth Kowalski-Wallace, *Their Fathers' Daughters: Hannah More, Maria Edgeworth and Patriarchal Complicity* (New York & Oxford: Oxford University Press, 1991).

10 Peter Knox-Shaw, *Jane Austen and the Enlightenment* (Cambridge: Cambridge University Press, 2004), 171.

11 Austen to Cassandra, 24 January 1809, *Letters*, 169–70.

12 Austen to Cassandra, 30 January 1809, *Letters*, 172.

13 Wood, *Modes of Discipline*, 28.

14 Austen to Cassandra, 30 April 1811, *Letters*, 186.

15 Austen to Cassandra, 11 October 1813, *Letters*, 234.

16 Austen to Anna Lefroy, 24 November 1814, *Letters*, 283.

17 Austen to Fanny Knight, 18 November 1814, *Letters*, 280.

18 Austen's relationship to Evangelicalism is discussed by Knox-Shaw, *Jane Austen*, 167–73; Mandal, *Jane Austen*, 91–130; Laura Mooneyham White, *Jane Austen's Anglicanism* (Farnham: Ashgate, 2011), 25–27.

19 Graham Dawson, 'The Imaginative Geography of Masculine Adventure', *Renaissance and Modern Studies*, 39 (1996), 27–45, 42.

20 Wood, *Modes of Discipline*, 85.

21 Knox-Shaw, *Jane Austen*, 167; Leonore Davidoff and Catherine Hall, *Family Fortunes: Men and Women of the English Middle Class 1780–1850* (London: Routledge, 1992), 113.

22 Wood, *Modes of Discipline*, 41–42.

23 Mandal, 'Evangelical Fiction', 266–67.

24 Wood, *Modes of Discipline*, 75.

25 Ashley Tauchert, *Romancing Jane Austen: Narrative, Realism and the Possibility of a Happy Ending* (Houndmills: Palgrave Macmillan, 2005), 104.

26 On professionalism in *Mansfield Park*, see Jason D. Solinger, *Becoming the Gentleman: British Literature and the Invention of Modern Masculinity, 1660–1815* (New York: Palgrave Macmillan, 2012), and Woodworth, *Eighteenth-Century Women Writers*, 181–89.

27 White, *Jane Austen*, 23.

28 Stephen Daniels and Charles Watkins, 'Picturesque Landscaping and Estate Management: Uvedale Price and Nathaniel Kent at Foxley', *The Politics*

of the Picturesque: Literature, Landscape, and Aesthetics since 1770, ed. Stephen Copley and Peter Garside (Cambridge: Cambridge University Press, 1994), 13–41; Jillian Heydt-Stevenson, 'Liberty, Connection, and Tyranny: The Novels of Jane Austen and the Aesthetic Movement of the Picturesque', *Lessons of Romanticism: A Critical Companion*, ed. Thomas Pfau and Robert F. Gleckner (Durham: Duke University Press, 1998), 261–79, 263.

29 White, *Jane Austen*, 39–40 explores the broader context of Rushworth's political ambitions.

30 John Tosh, 'The Old Adam and the New Man: Emerging Themes in the History of English Masculinities, 1750–1850', *English Masculinities, 1660–1800,* ed. Tim Hitchcock and Michèle Cohen (London: Longman, 1999), 217–38, 233.

31 Ibid., 233.

32 Ibid.

33 See Penny Gay, *Jane Austen and the Theatre* (Cambridge: Cambridge University Press, 2002) and Paula Byrne, *Jane Austen and the Theatre* (London: Hambledon Continuum, 2002) for a detailed discussion of the home theatricals and Austen's choice of *Lovers' Vows*.

34 William H. Galperin, *The Historical Austen* (Philadelphia: University of Pennsylvania Press, 2003), 172. See also Kathleen E. Urda, 'Why the Show Must Not Go On: "Real Character" and the Absence of Theatrical Performances in *Mansfield Park*', *Eighteenth-Century Fiction*, 26(2) (Winter 2013–2014), 281–302.

35 Ruth Bernard Yeazell, *Fictions of Modesty: Women and Courtship in the English Novel* (Chicago: University of Chicago Press, 1991), 33.

36 Ibid., 143.

37 Jane Austen, 'Opinions of *Mansfield Park*', *The Works of Jane Austen. Vol. VI Minor Works*, ed. R. W. Chapman (Oxford: Oxford University Press, 1954), 431–35.

Chapter 5

1 Claudia L. Johnson, *Equivocal Beings. Politics, Gender, and Sentimentality in the 1790s: Wollstonecraft, Radcliffe, Burney, Austen* (Chicago: University of Chicago Press, 1995), 196. Emily Auerbach, *Searching for Jane Austen* (Madison: University of Wisconsin Press, 2004), 221, and Jan Fergus, 'Sketches of Men's Kvetches: Domestic Masculinities in *Emma* and *Persuasion*', *Jane Austen and Masculinity*, ed. Michael Kramp (Lewisburg: Bucknell University Press, 2017), 25–39 also note Austen's peculiar interest in masculinity in *Emma*.

2 Joseph A. Kestner, 'Jane Austen: Revolutionizing Masculinities', *Persuasions* 16 (1994) 147–60; Michèle Cohen, '"Manners" Make the Man: Politeness, Chivalry, and the Construction of Masculinity, 1750–1830', *Journal of British Studies,* 44(2) (2005), 312–29; Brian C. Southam, 'Jane Austen's Englishness: *Emma* as National Tale', *Persuasions*, 30 (2008), 187–201.

3 Paul Langford, *Englishness Identified: Manners and Character, 1650–1850* (Oxford: Oxford University Press, 2000), 85–92.

4 Southam, 'Jane Austen's Englishness', 196; Anthony Mandal, *Jane Austen and the Popular Novel: The Determined Author* (Houndmills: Palgrave Macmillan, 2007), 164.

5 For further discussion of the political significance of Austen's characterisations of George Knightley and Frank Churchill, see Marilyn Butler, *Jane Austen and the War of Ideas* (Oxford: Clarendon Press, 1975), 272–73; Johnson, *Equivocal Beings*, 198–200; Michael Kramp, *Disciplining Love: Austen and the Modern Man* (Columbus: Ohio State University Press, 2007),

109–10; Mandal, *Jane Austen*, 166; Janet Todd, *The Cambridge Introduction to Jane Austen*, 2nd ed. (Cambridge: Cambridge University Press, 2015), 114–18; Megan A. Woodworth, *Eighteenth-Century Women Writers and the Gentleman's Liberation Movement: Independence, War, Masculinity and the Novel, 1778–1818* (Farnham & Burlington: Ashgate, 2011), 194.

6 Gillian Dow, 'Reading at Godmersham: Edward's Library and Marianne's books', *Persuasions*, 37 (2015), 152–62, 154–55.

7 Mandal, *Jane Austen*, 132. On the national tale, see Miranda Burgess, 'The National Tale and Allied Genres, 1770s–1840s', *The Cambridge Companion to the Irish Novel*, ed. John Wilson Foster (Cambridge: Cambridge University Press, 2006), 39–59; Claire Connolly, 'The National Tale', *The Oxford History of the Novel in English. Vol. 2: English and British Fiction, 1750–1820*, ed. Peter Garside and Karen O'Brien (Oxford: Oxford University Press, 2015), 216–33, 224; Ina Ferris, 'The Irish Novel 1800–1829', *The Cambridge Companion to Fiction in the Romantic Period*, ed. Richard Maxwell and Katie Trumpener (Cambridge: Cambridge University Press, 2008), 235–49; Gary Kelly, 'Fiction: Britain', *Encyclopedia of the Romantic Era, 1760–1850*, ed. Christopher John Murry (New York & London: Fitzroy Dearborn, 2004), 349–50.

8 Connolly, 'The National Tale', 217; Mandal, *Jane Austen*, 131–67; Southam, 'Jane Austen's Englishness', 187–201.

9 'Library Catalogue, Godmersham Park, 1818', available through Chawton House Library, < https://chawtonhouse.org/the-library/library-collections/the-knight-collection/>, accessed 2 November 2018.

10 Austen to Anna Austen, 28 September 1814, *Letters*, 277–78.

11 Southam, 'Jane Austen's Englishness', 191; Mandal, *Jane Austen*, 133.

12 Katie Trumpener, 'National Character, Nationalist Plots: National Tale and Historical Novel in the Age of Waverley, 1806–1830', *English Literary History*, 60(3) (1993), 685–731, 688.

13 Mandal, *Jane Austen*, 166–67, 44.

14 Irene Basey Beesemyer, 'I Thought I Never Set My Eyes on a Finer Figure of a Man': Maria Edgeworth Scrutinizes Masculinity in *Castle Rackrent, Ennui,* and *The Absentee*', *New Essays on Maria Edgeworth*, ed. Julie Nash (Aldershot: Ashgate, 2006), 109–29, 109; Woodworth, *Eighteenth-Century Women Writers*, 141.

15 See also Julia Anne Miller, 'Acts of Union: Family Violence and National Courtship in Maria Edgeworth's *The Absentee*, and Sydney Owenson's *The Wild Irish Girl*', *Border Crossings: Irish Women Writers and National Identities* (Tuscaloosa & London: University of Alabama Press, 2000), 13–37.

16 Fiona Price, '"A Great Deal of History": Romantic Women Writers and Historical Fiction', *Women's Writing*, 19(3) (2012), 259–72, 266.

17 Ibid., 266.

18 Mandal, *Jane Austen*, 25.

19 Recent work on the Porter sisters has illuminated this aspect of their fiction. See Devoney Looser, 'The Porter Sisters, Women's Writing, and Historical Fiction', *The History of British Women's Writing*, ed. Jacqueline Labbe (Houndmills: Palgrave Macmillan, 2010), 233–52; Devoney Looser, 'The Great Man and Women's Historical Fiction: Jane Porter and Sir Sidney Smith', *Women's Writing*, 19(3) (2012), 293–314; Thomas McLean, 'Nobody's Argument: Jane Porter and the Historical Novel', *Journal for Early Modern Cultural Studies*, 7(2) (2007), 88–103; Diana Wallace, 'Difficulties, Discontinuities and Differences: Reading Women's Historical Fiction', *The Female Figure in Contemporary Historical Fiction*, ed. Katherine Cooper and Emma Short (Houndmills: Palgrave Macmillan, 2012), 206–22.

20 Fiona Price, 'Introduction', Jane Porter, *The Scottish Chiefs: A Romance*, ed. Fiona Price (Peterborough: Broadview, 2007), 25.

21 Mandal, *Jane Austen*, 163–66; Southam, 'Jane Austen's Englishness', 195–97.

22 Maria Edgeworth, *The Absentee*, ed. Heidi Van de Veire & Kim Walker with Marilyn Butler, *The Novels and Selected Works of Maria Edgeworth*, Vol. 5 (London: Pickering & Chatto, 1999), 157.

23 See Fiona Price, 'Resisting "The Spirit of Innovation": The Other Historical Novel and Jane Porter', *Modern Language Review*, 101 (2006), 638–51.

24 Johnson, *Equivocal Beings*, 201.

25 Mandal, *Jane Austen*, 181; Olivia Murphy, *Jane Austen the Reader: The Artist as Critic* (Houndmills: Palgrave Macmillan, 2013), 123.

26 Ruth Knezevich and Devoney Looser, 'Jane Austen's Afterlife, West Indian Madams, and the Literary Porter Family: Two New Letters from Charles Austen', *Modern Philology*, 112(3) (2015), 554–68.

27 Porter, *Scottish Chiefs*, 450.

28 Ibid., 100, 347.

29 Ibid., 452.

30 Ibid., 680.

31 Porter, 'Recollective Preface, 1840', Porter, *Scottish Chiefs*, 738.

32 Devoney Looser, 'Dealing in Notions and Facts: Jane Austen and History Writing', *A Companion to Jane Austen*, ed. Claudia Johnson and Clara Tuite (Blackwell, 2009), 216–25.

33 James Hogg, *The Domestic Manners and Private Life of Sir Walter Scott* (Glasgow: John Reid & Co; Edinburgh: Oliver & Boyd; London: Whittaker & Co, 1834), 128.

34 Walter Scott, 'Unsigned Review of *Emma*', *The Quarterly Review* (October 1815), 188–201, 196.

35 On 'men of sense' see Woodworth, *Eighteenth-Century Women Writers*, 194, 197.

36 James Edward Austen-Leigh, *A Memoir of Jane Austen* (London: Richard Bentley, 1871), 148.

37 Roger Sales, *Jane Austen and Representations of Regency England* (London and New York: Routledge, 1994), 145.

38 Maria Edgeworth, *Ennui*, ed. Jane Desmarais, Tim McLoughlin and Marilyn Butler, *The Novels and Selected Works of Maria Edgeworth*, Vol. 1 (London: Pickering & Chatto, 1999), 182.

39 Mary Wollstonecraft, *A Vindication of the Rights of Woman*, ed. Anne K. Mellor and Noelle Chai (Pearson Longman, 2007), 79.

40 Wollstonecraft, *Rights of Woman*, 77.

41 Johnson, *Equivocal Beings*, 201; Woodworth, *Eighteenth-Century Women Writers*, 197–98.

42 See Auerbach, *Searching for Jane Austen*, 230; Murphy, *Jane Austen the Reader*, 148; Enit Karafili Steiner, *Jane Austen's Civilised Women: Morality, Gender and the Civilizing Process* (London: Pickering & Chatto, 2012), 132; Woodworth, *Eighteenth-Century Women Writers*, 198.

43 Clara Tuite, 'Jane Austen', *Companion to Women's Historical Writing*, ed. Mary Spongberg, Ann Curthoys and Barbara Caine (Houndmills: Palgrave Macmillan, 2005), 40.

44 Devoney Looser, *British Women Writers and the Writing of History, 1670–1820* (Baltimore: Johns Hopkins University Press, 2000), 203.

45 Lisa Kasmer, *Novel Histories: British Women Writing History, 1760–1830* (Lanham: Fairleigh Dickinson University Press, 2012), 2–3.

46 Austen to James Stanier Clarke, 1 April 1816, *Letters*, 312.

47 Ibid.

48 Devoney Looser, *Women Writers and Old Age in Great Britain, 1750–1850* (Baltimore: Johns Hopkins University Press, 2008), 142–55.
49 Jane Austen, 'Plan of a Novel, According to Hints from Various Quarters', *The Works of Jane Austen. Vol. VI Minor Works*, ed. R. W. Chapman (Oxford: Oxford University Press, 1954), 428–30.
50 Ibid., 429–30.
51 Jane Austen, 'Opinions of *Emma*', *The Works of Jane Austen. Vol. VI Minor Works*, ed. Chapman, 436–39, 436.

Chapter 6

1 On Austen's celebration of the navy, see Tim Fulford, 'Romanticizing the Empire: The Naval Heroes of Southey, Coleridge, Austen and Marryat', *Modern Language Quarterly*, 60 (1) (1999); Jocelyn Harris, 'Domestic Virtues and National Importance: Lord Nelson, Captain Wentworth, and the English Napoleonic War Hero', *Eighteenth-Century Fiction*, 19 (1–2) (2006–07), 181–205; Fulford, 'Romanticizing the Empire', 147–60; John Peck, *Maritime Fiction: Sailors and the Sea in British and American Novels, 1719–1917* (Houndmills: Palgrave, 2001); Brian Southam, *Jane Austen and the Navy*, 2nd ed. (Hambledon & London: National Maritime Museum Publishing, 2005). On Wentworth's association with professional masculinity, see Jason D. Solinger, *Becoming the Gentleman: British Literature and the Invention of Modern Masculinity, 1660–1815* (New York: Palgrave Macmillan, 2012); Megan A. Woodworth, *Eighteenth-Century Women Writers and the Gentleman's Liberation Movement: Independence, War, Masculinity and the Novel, 1778–1818* (Farnham & Burlington: Ashgate, 2011).
2 On Austen's engagement with Scott, Byron, and literary Romanticism more broadly, see William Deresiewicz, *Jane Austen and the Romantic Poets* (New York: Columbia University Press, 2004); Jocelyn Harris, *A Revolution Almost Beyond Expression: Jane Austen's Persuasion* (Newark: University of Delaware Press, 2008); Peter Knox-Shaw, *Jane Austen and the Enlightenment* (Cambridge: Cambridge University Press, 2004); Anthony Mandal, *Jane Austen and the Popular Novel: The Determined Author* (Houndmills: Palgrave Macmillan, 2007).
3 For a detailed discussion of Austen's engagement with popular cults of heroism associated with both Admiral Lord Nelson and Captain James Cook, see Harris, *Revolution*.
4 Olivia Murphy, *Jane Austen the Reader: The Artist as Critic* (Houndmills: Palgrave Macmillan, 2013), 170.
5 Maria Edgeworth to Mrs Ruxton, 21 February 1818, Maria Edgeworth, *Chosen Letters*, ed. F. V. Barry (London: Jonathan Cape, 1931), 232.
6 Murphy, *Jane Austen the Reader*, 166.
7 Austen to Fanny Knight, 23 March 1817, *Letters*, 335.
8 Susan Morgan, 'Captain Wentworth, British Imperialism and Personal Romance', *Persuasions*, 18 (1996), 88–97.
9 William H. Galperin, *The Historical Austen* (Philadelphia: University of Pennsylvania Press, 2003), 25.
10 John Tosh, 'The Old Adam and the New Man: Emerging Themes in the History of English Masculinities, 1750–1850', *English Masculinities, 1660–1800*, ed. Tim Hitchcock and Michèle Cohen (London: Longman, 1999), 217–38, 232.
11 Harris, *Revolution*, 63. Deresiewicz, *Jane Austen*, 146 and Knox-Shaw, *Jane Austen*, 220, also discuss the timing of the novel's composition and setting.

12 Atara Stein, *The Byronic Hero in Fiction, Film and Television* (Carbondale: Southern Illinois University Press, 2004), 102. See also Sarah S. G. Frantz, 'Jane Austen's Heroes and the Great Masculine Renunciation', *Persuasions*, 25 (2003), 165–75.

13 Austen to Cassandra, 15–16 September 1813, *Letters*, 221.

14 On Wentworth's Byronism, see Sarah Wootton, *Byronic Heroes in Nineteenth-Century Women's Writing and Screen Adaptation* (Houndmills: Palgrave Macmillan, 2016), 71–73; Harris, *Revolution*, 201–203.

15 Austen to Cassandra, 5–8 March 1813, *Letters*, 257.

16 Lord Byron, 'The Corsair', *Selected Poems*, ed. Susan J. Wolfson and Peter J. Manning (London: Penguin, 2005), 248–307.

17 On parallels between Captain Wentworth and Conrad, see Knox-Shaw, *Jane Austen*, and Mary Waldron, *Jane Austen and the Fiction of her Time* (Cambridge: Cambridge University Press, 1999).

18 Caroline Franklin, *Byron's Heroines* (Oxford: Clarendon Press, 1992), 64.

19 Waldron, *Jane Austen*, 147.

20 Michael Kramp, *Disciplining Love: Austen and the Modern Man* (Columbus: Ogio State University Press, 2007) also explores Wentworth's retreat into performative masculinity.

21 On the revival of chivalry in the Romantic era, see Michèle Cohen, *Fashioning Masculinity: Natioal Identity and Language in the Eighteenth Century* (London: Routledge, 1996); Michèle Cohen, '"Manners" Make the Man: Politeness, Chivalry, and the Construction of Masculinity, 1750–1830', *Journal of British Studies*, 44(2) (April 2005), 312–29; Tim Fulford, *Romanticism and Masculinity: Gender, Politics and Poetics in the Writings of Burke, Coleridge, Cobbett, Wordsworth, De Quincey and Hazlitt* (Houndmills: Macmillan Press, 1999); and Roger Sales, *Jane Austen and Representations of Regency England* (London: Routledge, 1996).

22 Harris, *Revolution*; Southam, *Jane Austen*.

23 Emily Auerbach, *Searching for Jane Austen* (Madison: University of Wisconsin Press, 2004), 242–44.

24 On women's involvement with the navy, see Southam, *Jane Austen*, 277, and Mary Favret, 'Everyday War', *English Literary History*, 72(3) (2005), 605–33.

25 Byron, 'Corsair', Canto 1, st. 1, lines 1–6.

26 For a detailed account of Austen's editing and redrafting of the concluding chapters of *Persuasion*, see Kathryn Sutherland, *Jane Austen's Textual Lives: From Aeschylus to Bollywood* (Oxford: Oxford University Press, 2005); Harris, *Revolution*.

27 Harris, *Revolution*, 47–49.

28 Ibid., 49.

29 Sarah Raff, *Jane Austen's Erotic Advice* (Oxford: Oxford University Press, 2013), 143.

30 Harris, *Revolution*, 56.

31 Raff, *Jane Austen*, 142.

Conclusion

1 B. C. Southam, *Jane Austen's Literary Manuscripts: A Study of the Novelist's Development through the Surviving Papers* (London: Oxford University Press, 1964), 112.

2 Walter Scott, 'Unsigned Review of *Emma*', *The Quarterly Review* (October 1815), 188–201, 189.

3 For an extended discussion of print culture in *Sanditon*, see George Justice, '*Sanditon* and the Book', *A Companion to Jane Austen*, ed. Claudia L. Johnson and Clara Tuite (Chichester: John Wiley & Sons, 2009), 153–62, and Enit K. Steiner, '"Till He Began to Stagger Her": Literary Men and Melancholia', *Jane Austen and Masculinity*, ed. Michael Kramp (Lewisburg: Bucknell University Press, 2017), 113–28.

4 Southam, *Jane Austen's Literary Manuscripts*, 102.

5 Scott, 'Unsigned Review', 190.

6 Ibid., 193.

7 Justice, '*Sanditon* and the Book', 160.

8 Southam, *Jane Austen*; Kathryn Sutherland, *Jane Austen's Textual Lives: From Aeschylus to Bollywood* (Oxford: Oxford University Press, 2005), 168–97; and John Wiltshire, *Jane Austen and the Body: 'The Picture of Health'* (Cambridge: Cambridge University Press, 1992), 197–221, discuss the manuscript of *Sanditon*.

9 Southam, *Jane Austen*, 112.

10 See Anthony Mandal, *Jane Austen and the Popular Novel: The Determined Author* (Houndmills: Palgrave Macmillan, 2007); and Clara Tuite, *Romantic Austen: Sexual Politics and the Literary Canon* (Cambridge: Cambridge University Press, 2004), for discussion of *Sanditon*'s Regency and Romantic contexts.

11 Justice, '*Sanditon* and the Book', 162.

12 Moreland Perkins, *Reshaping the Sexes in Sense and Sensibility* (Charlottesville & London: University of West Virginia Press, 1998); Claudia L. Johnson, *Equivocal Beings. Politics, Gender, and Sentimentality in the 1790s: Wollstonecraft, Radcliffe, Burney, Austen* (Chicago: University of Chicago Press, 1995).

13 Jan Fergus, 'Sketches of Men's Kvetches: Domestic Masculinities in *Emma* and *Persuasion*' *Jane Austen and Masculinity*, ed. Michael Kramp (Lewisburg: Bucknell University Press, 2017), 25–39, and Kit Kincade, 'Failures of the Patriarchy: Fathers as Role Models in Jane Austen', *Jane Austen and Masculinity*, ed. Michael Kramp (Lewisburg: Bucknell University Press, 2017), 41–44, address Austen's peripheral male characters.

14 On Austen's socio-economic critique of masculinity in the juvenilia, see Joanne Wilkes, 'The Paradox of Masculine Agency in Jane Austen's Early Works', *Jane Austen and Masculinity*, ed. Kramp, 61–77.

15 Cheryl A. Wilson, *Jane Austen and the Victorian Heroine* (Houndmills: Palgrave Macmillan, 2017).

Index

For Product Safety Concerns and Information please contact our EU
representative GPSR@taylorandfrancis.com
Taylor & Francis Verlag GmbH, Kaufingerstraße 24, 80331 München, Germany

www.ingramcontent.com/pod-product-compliance
Lightning Source LLC
Chambersburg PA
CBHW070012140726
47908CB00020B/1277